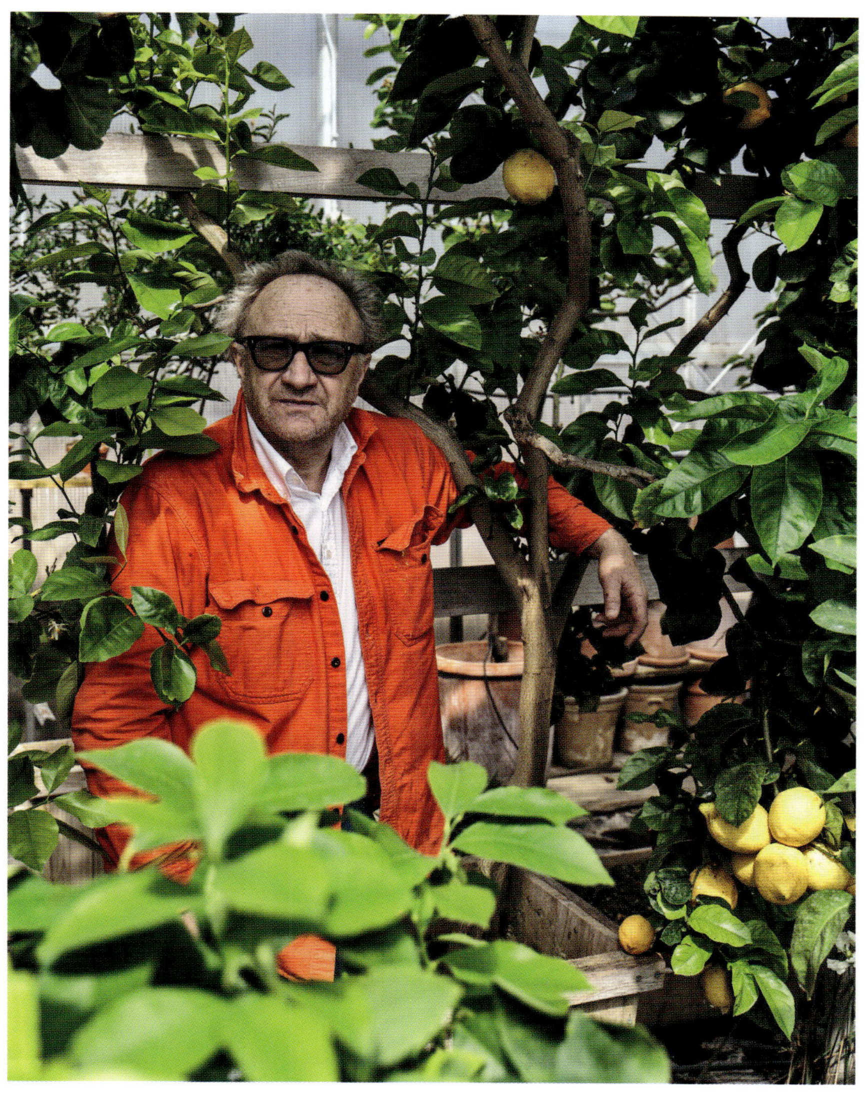

Peter Nadin; Old Field Farm, Cornwallville, NY, 2022

The Invisible World

Off Paradise, New York City, Winter/Spring 2024

Peter Nadin   *The Invisible World*

SilvanaEditoriale

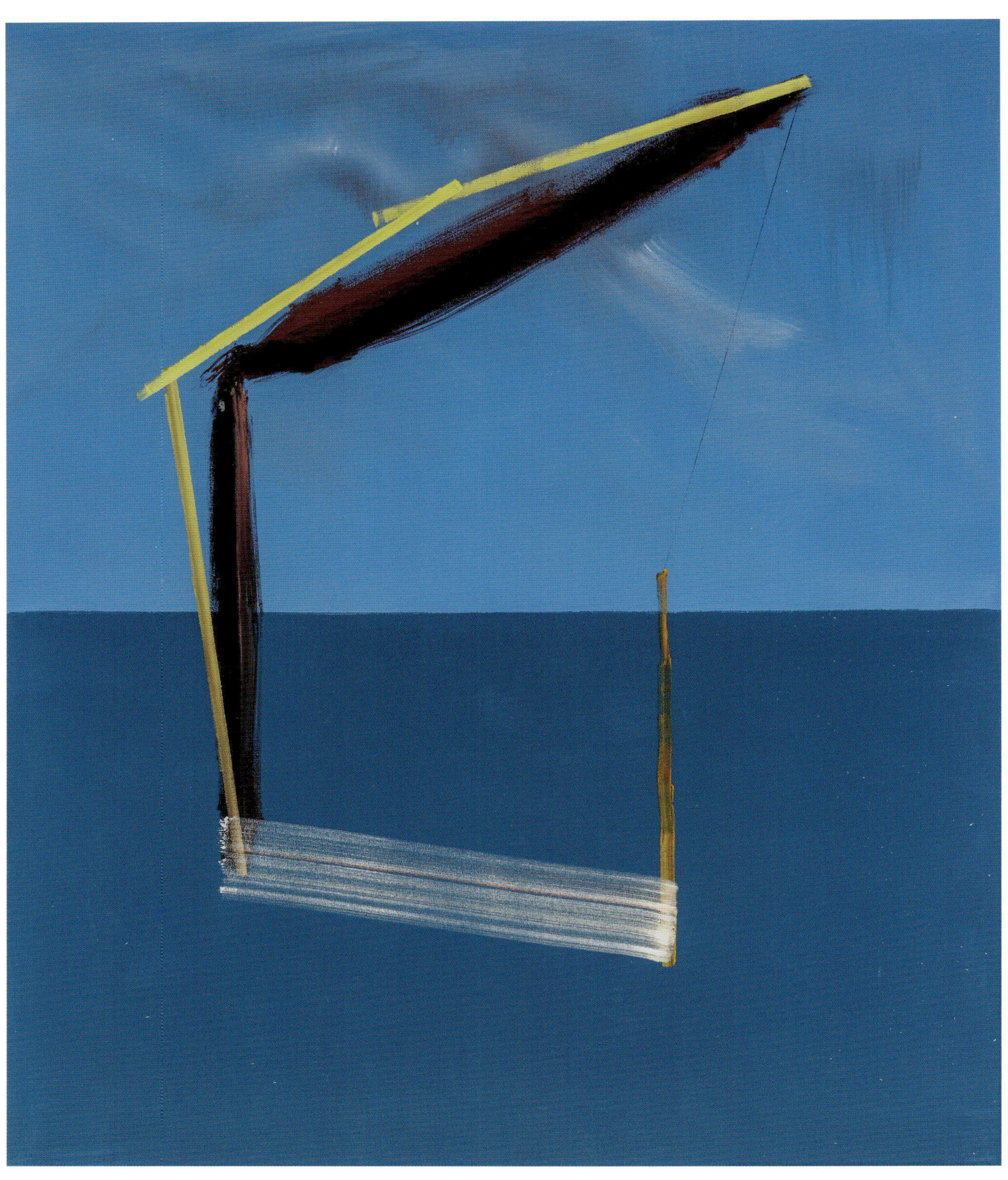

View II / The Artist, 1986
Oil, acrylic, and enamel on canvas
72 x 63 1/2 in

Contents

Green & Pleasant Land

by Randy Kennedy

Before the mountains a broad river delta spreads between inland seas.

Delta rises to plateau. Streams shape valley and hill. The earth cools and the Wisconsin glaciation advances, leaving in its wake tarns, looping moraines, tongues of ice, gorges, kames, defiles.

Ten thousand years ago near present-day Athens in Greene County flint is quarried. The Kanien'kehá:ka and Algonkian speakers hunt the lower reaches of the mountains, living in the valleys and along the shore. In 1609, the eighty-five-foot *De Halve Maen,* captained by Henry Hudson, Englishman in service of the Dutch, sails inland north from New York Harbor and on September 14, Robert Juet, first mate, writes in his journal: "The Land grew very high and Mountainous. The River is full of fish." In his entry of September 30, Juet writes: "The people of the Countrey came aboard us, and brought ... a stone aboard like to Emery ... it would cut Iron or Steele: Yet being bruised small, and water put to it, it made a color like blacke Lead glistening; It is also good for Painters Colours." On the 1st of October Juet records an attempted incursion by a group of natives: "... one of them that swamme got hold of our Boat, thinking to overthrow it. But our Cooke tooke a sword, and cut off one of his hands, and he was drowned."

In 1656, on a map of New Netherland, engraver Nicolaes Visscher, for reasons still unknown, marks the land near what is now the mouth of Catskill Creek *Landt van Kats Kill* [Land of Cat's Stream.]

In 1790 a farmer named Selah Strong purchases property near Durham, New York, west of the Hudson. He clears land and builds a house. In 1800, the New York State Legislature demarcates the territory around him as Greene County, for Continental Army major-general Nathaniel Greene, "the Fighting Quaker." In 1814, Selah Strong falls from his horse, drunk. The following year, his wife and three grandchildren all die within ten days of each other. Strong is seen later walking into the woods with a rope. He is prevented from hanging himself but is excommunicated from his parish for acts against God.

In 1827 Thomas Cole, born in Lancashire, establishes his studio at a farm known as Cedar Grove in the town of Catskill and the same year paints *The Clove, Catskills,* an idealized view of the Katerskill Falls gorge that omits the tanneries proliferating on the land and the ragged, stripped hemlock forests that supply the industry with tannin. In 1897, Thomas Edison's film company makes *Waterfall in the Catskills,* a short, static shot of the waters rushing over nearby Haines Falls; in summer months, the falls are often dammed, requiring a fee from tourists to turn on the spectacle they have traveled to see.

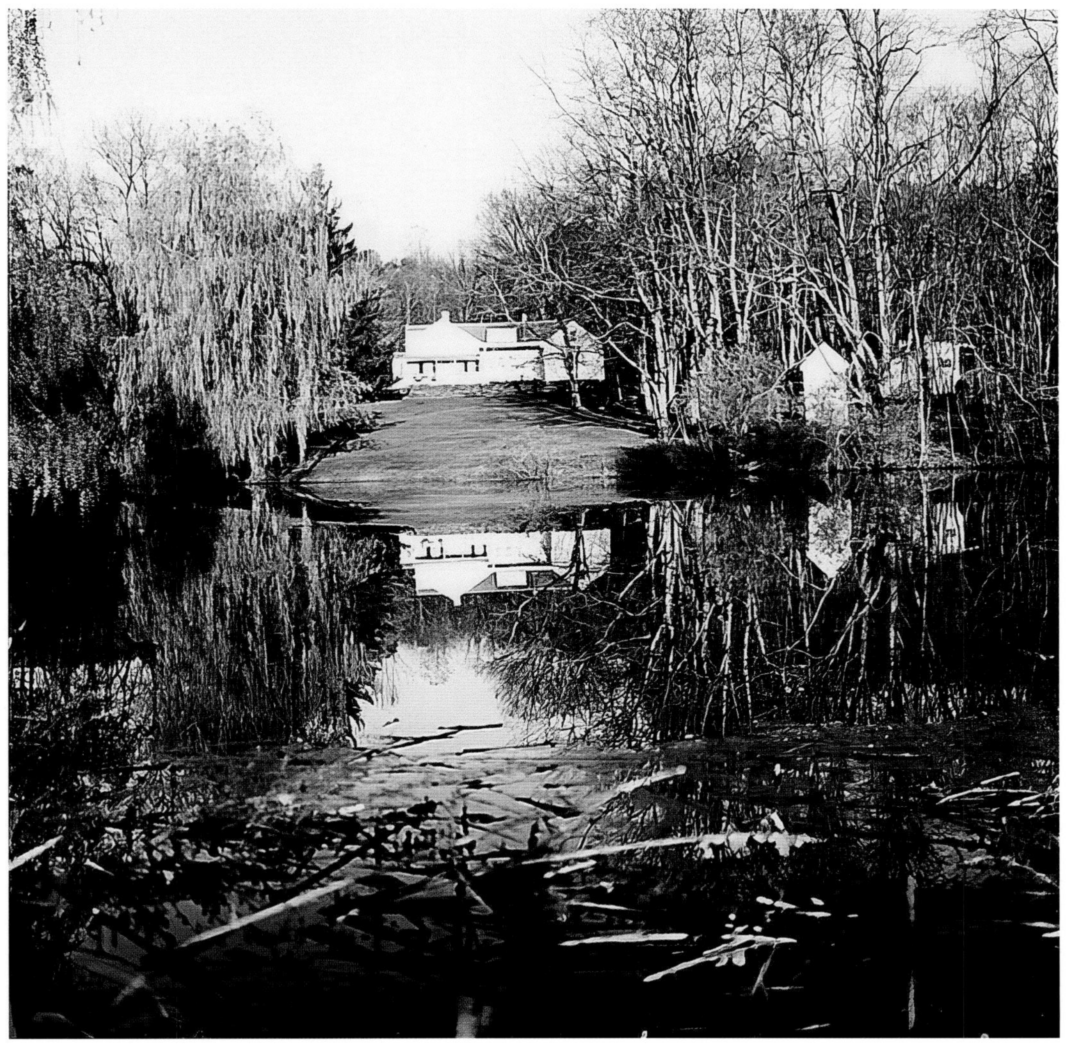

Old Field Farm, 2015

In 1931, outside the Aratoga Inn and Auto Rest in Cairo, Greene County, the bootlegger Legs Diamond is shot three times but survives the attempt on his life, and in 1939 near Phoenicia folklorist Norman Studer founds the utopian leftist Camp Woodland for children; Pete Seeger, a victim of the blacklist, performs at the camp and is introduced by a Cuban counselor to the protest song *Guantanamera,* which becomes a staple of Seeger's repertoire.

In 1954, Peter Nadin, son of a sea captain, is born in Bromborough, near Liverpool, and in 1976, after studying art at Newcastle University, moves to New York City. Painting at night, he works days as a floor sander and handyman and forms a collective art space in his loft on West Broadway. In 1987 Nadin and Anne Kennedy, his wife, buy the farm and house built by Selah Strong near Durham. In the 1990s Nadin withdraws from the commercial art world and begins to paint mostly in the Catskills while cultivating bees and raising pigs and chickens. The marks of Selah Strong's adze remain visible on the beams of the barn adjoining the house.

In 2006, Nadin publishes *The First Mark: Unlearning How to Make Art* and travels to Cuba as a delegate to the South American Beekeepers' Conference. On April 28, 2013, in the journal he keeps at the farm, Nadin writes: "3 days of rain — ponds full, still cold." On May 7 he writes: "D. says that for locals Durham is a black hole — once sucked in they can never escape. He was at party last Sat. Three stabbed, girl attacked. Someone brought three dynamite detonators to the party. DJ stole the money and four of his friends got locked up. Picking stones from field. Beautiful weather." On June 11, he writes: "At 8:30 bear ambles across lawn. 600 lbs. No more than fifty feet from house. I go out to chase him off. He turns and looks — a momentary contact — then slowly moves into the woods. We communicate through marks, symbols and gestures. I know him, know his moods. Not unlike art — but a much greater set of meanings. It's a transaction."

The Mark Series

"The Fish Swim in the Mind": Emanations of an Invisible World
by Chris Murtha

"To achieve accuracy there has to be equilibrium between ocular
representation and emanations from the unseen."
— Peter Nadin, *The Mark Series*

When visiting Peter Nadin at Old Field Farm in upstate New York, the artist will likely take you to the greenhouse before entering his studio. You might also explore his archive, the most recent addition to the complex of buildings uphill from his farmhouse. If they happen by, you will meet some of his neighbors, who have increasingly become collaborators and characters in his paintings. There will always be a meal prepared from the farm's yield, elegant and seemingly effortless. All this grounds Nadin's art practice in the physical reality of the farm: its labor, activities, and products; sights, scents, and sounds; the surrounding community. But the aggregate of his artistic output—stretching from one of his earliest paintings, a small childhood copy of Van Gogh's *Langlois Bridge*, to his tripartite "Mark Series"—is just as palpably present, whether on display in his studio or archive, or as motifs cropping up in recent paintings.

The farm's operations are currently less robust than when Nadin was producing *First Mark*, an interdisciplinary body of work that seemed to emanate from the landscape, like any other product of the farm. Today, there are no more chickens, pigs, or goats. His 800-pound boar Abe is long gone, along with his attendant bounty and burden. After some dormancy, Nadin's beehives are once again humming with life (and work). But his primary focus of late has been on cultivating fruit (the bees help with that) and revitalizing the land, which had been so ravaged by the livestock. Where pigs used to wallow and forage, apple and pear trees now grow. Central to this endeavor is the greenhouse, where Nadin propagates and grows citrus trees, like bergamot orange, Meyer lemon, and kaffir lime, as well as ginger, turmeric, and bananas. As Nadin points out, the farm is on the same latitude as Mediterranean Europe, so cultivating crops more accustomed to that climate is just a matter of harnessing the sun's warmth and light, while keeping the frigid air out. During the brutally cold and dreary winters, the greenhouse also provides the artist with a lush, geothermally-heated studio for easel painting. A climate transposed.

The greenhouse, studio, and archive overlook a pond stocked with golden orfe fish and lined with cattails that, when I last visited, provided a protective thicket for a chatty family of red-winged blackbirds. Each building is situated to admit the farm's light, air, and scenery to varying degrees. Each has its own character, befitting its function. The greenhouse is, by design, the most porous to light, but the corrugated windows and the abundant plant life obscure the view of the surrounding landscape. Connected to the greenhouse by a short path, the

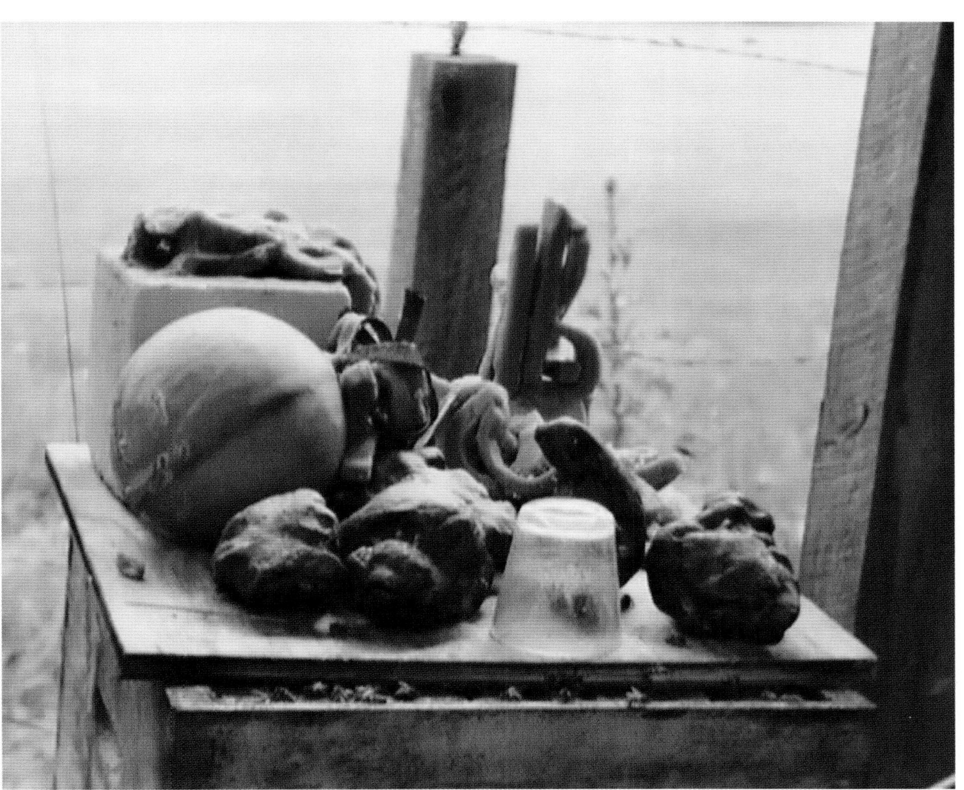

First Mark Film Still, 2011

artist's studio is a cavernous barn crowded with art, old and new, seemingly in conversation with one another and with the artist himself. Two opposing pairs of fourteen-foot-tall sliding French doors draw the outside in, permitting sightlines to the woods in one direction and, in the other, to the pond with the Catskills beyond. The archive, in contrast, is a cinderblock fortress with a single sliver of a window. Most of Nadin's art is stowed away in racks and flat files, but a career-spanning, salon-style hanging frames the window. I have come to think of these three structures as embodying Nadin's interest in ocular, haptic, and psychic perceptions of reality. The haptic is exemplified by the greenhouse, and the farm at large. The archive represents the psychic—Nadin's memory, his mental storage. While not limited to visual experience, the studio becomes the site where the haptic and psychic converge and interact with the ocular, generating the images we see before us.

Nadin and his wife, Anne Kennedy, purchased the farmhouse in Cornwallville, New York, in 1988, and have since acquired the remainder of the original farmland: 172 acres of woods, pastures, and fields, with three connected ponds. After presenting a well-received series of allegorical paintings at Brooke Alexander in fall 1993, Nadin withdrew from the artworld. He did not exhibit his work again until 2007, when he toured *First Mark* (as El Primer Trazo) through Cuba and Ecuador. Quietly produced during those years of retreat, it was the first body of work Nadin created entirely on the farm. And it shows: The paintings and sculptures are of the farm as much as about the farm. For the large-scale paintings on raw linen, Nadin used pigments derived from black walnut, elderberry, cochineal, and indigo; affixed wool from his cashmere goats to the canvas with beeswax and honey from his apiary; and even allowed the bees to "work" the canvas, marking it with their resinous propolis as they reclaimed some of their honey. In a series of floor-bound works, bronze, ceramic, and wood sculptures float like islands in viscous, stagnant pools of honey speckled with crushed eggshells. At the time, Nadin's practice was so entwined with the farm's cycles that he worked during a "painting season," which began in mid-September, when the black walnuts started falling from the trees, and ended about two-months later, when the "heavy frosts" arrived.

The gestural abstractions of *First Mark* embraced the material realities of the farm, privileging the haptic and olfactory over the optic. (Those lucky enough to sample the farm's provisions also enjoyed the flavor of his work.) "The ocular mechanism," Nadin asserts, "does not solely define reality or reveal the full truth." Relying so heavily on our visual perception of reality is not only limiting because we have allowed it to supersede the other senses, but also because it ignores other perspectives. "The visual world of the farm does not exist as I see it," he wrote in *The Mark Series*. "The perceptual and conceptual world I create is but one of many, many possible constructions of reality…. One is no more truthful than the other." What Nadin calls the "paradox and contradiction" of our own condition is that the reality we perceive and desire to be singularly true does not actually exist as such. As humans, we are limited to the parameters of our minds and bodies, the visual and mental processes we are equipped with, just as pigs are limited to their own pig mentality. But the two coexist. Nadin's non-anthropocentric approach to art making gives equal consideration to the perspectives and consciousness of each plant and creature that contributes to the farm's equilibrium, including his own.

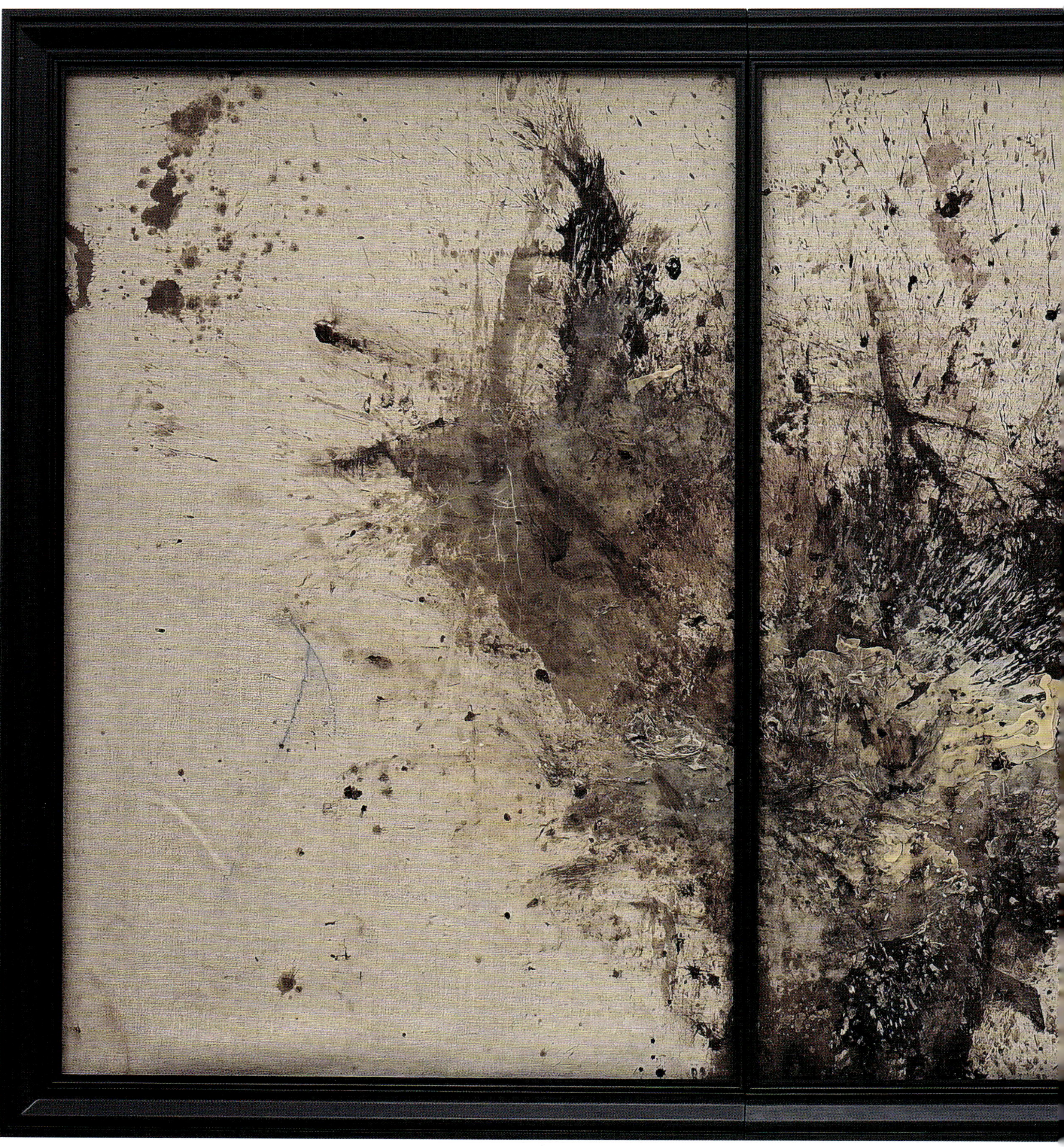

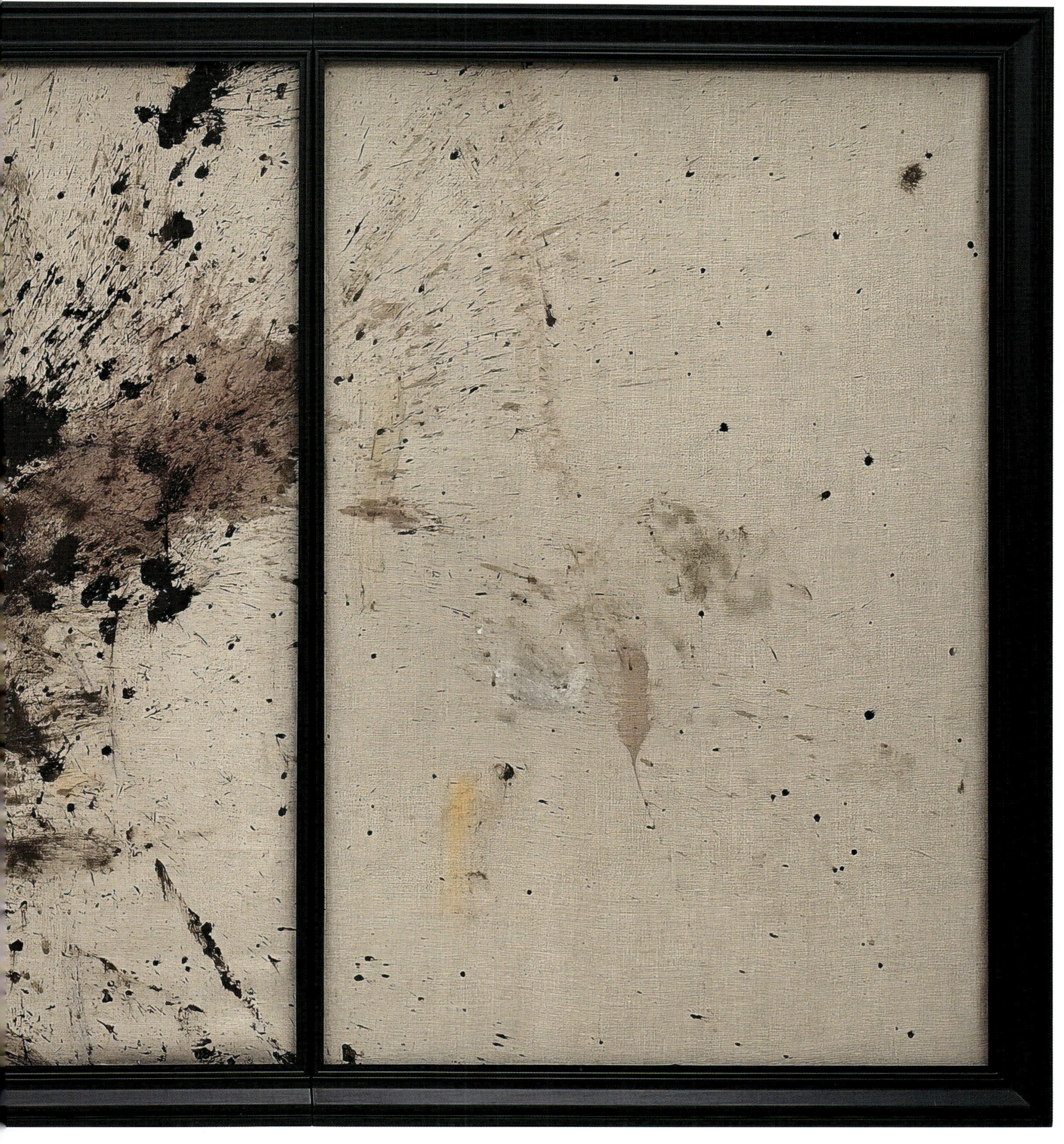

Landscape and Instinct, 2011
Wax, honey, black walnut and
cashmere wool on linen
82 x 165 in

House and Dream

Stars pull dreams through sleeping eyes
To return the world that entered as light—
As tithe to worlds where dreams prefigure the play—
And we already are known by our gifts
Offered freely in the service of dreams

Nightly, the dream rises—like a weightless string of pearls
Each dream-pearl formed from a single speck of mind-sand—
That when encrusted by a star's borrowed light
Become the iridescent grains of experience—
And strung together compose our lives—
And entwined the single human dream

Rising—these dream-strings—spin, twist to make a celestial nest—
A roost for other worlds to hatch then fly
For blood threads stars to eyes to snow
And dreams are the harvest sown from seeds of light

— Peter Nadin, 1993

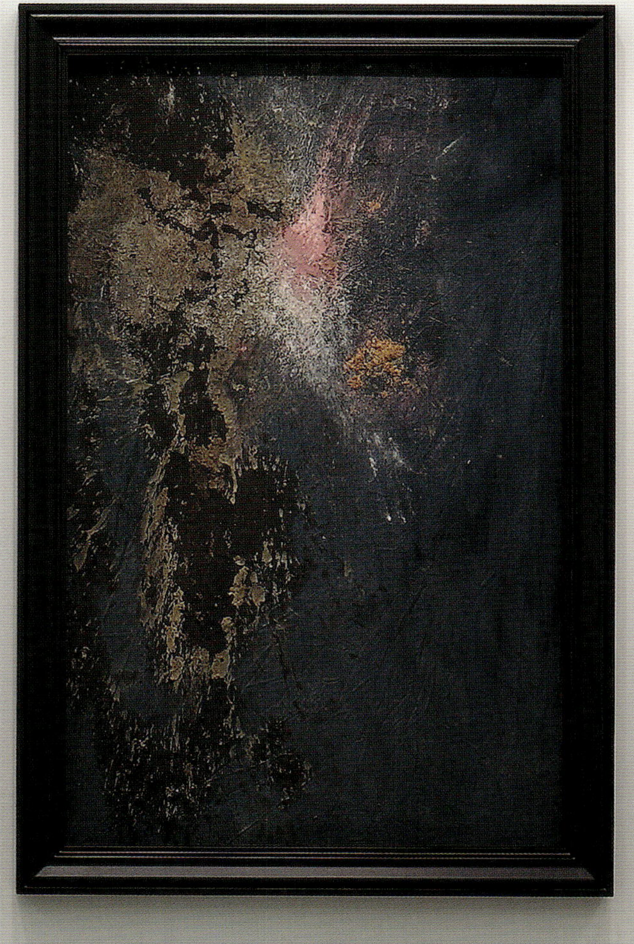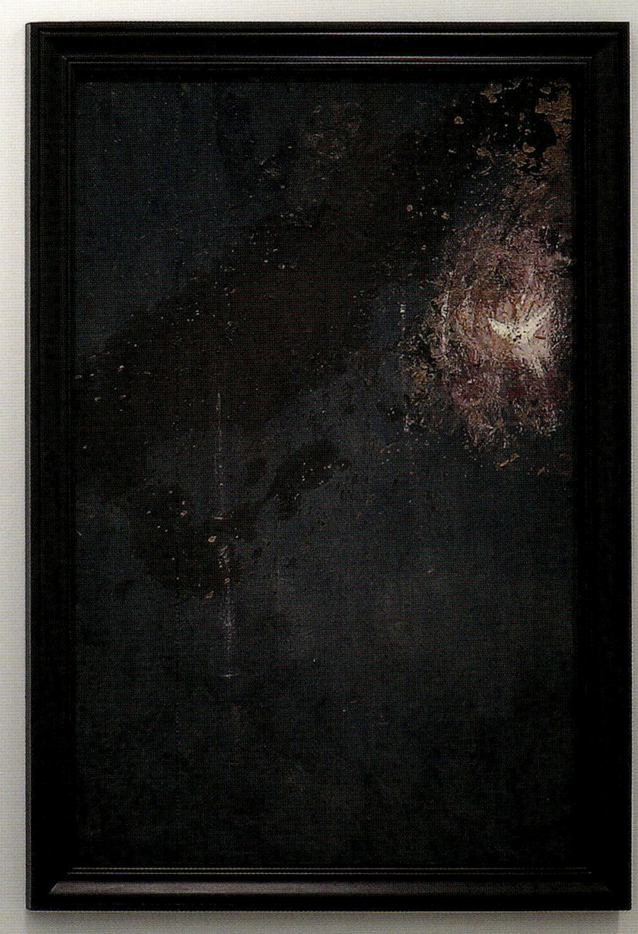

House and Dream (III & IV), 2010
Gavin Brown's Enterprise,
New York City, 2011
Wax, honey, black walnut, indigo
flake white on linen
82 x 55 in

If *First Mark* epitomized "an ocular reality that is held in balance with the haptic," Nadin's two most recent cycles of paintings, *The Distance from a Lemon* to *Murder and The Invisible World*, attempt to reconcile the optically perceived world with the hidden realm of the mind. Reality, in Nadin's work, is not restricted to perceived phenomena, but inclusive of memories, associations, ideas, and dreams. What one sees is shaped by what one has seen before. Too often though, this palimpsest of thoughts and perceptions—an "aggregate of previous selves, species, and cultural traces"—is repressed in favor of a "banal orthodoxy." For his part, Nadin has long sought to represent, in all its murkiness and incongruity, the cognitive interaction between the inner self and the external world. He has described his paintings from the decade prior to his withdrawal as "representing consciousness." Since then, he has focused on "embodying" consciousness, by painting "the experience, not the objects, of the underlying process of consciousness itself." The canvas or panel is a blank slate on which he can freely explore the constant churning of consciousness. After all, paradoxical and contradictory images can coexist in art, as they do in our thoughts and imaginations. Fish, for instance, can leap out of the pond and fly through the air. Lemons can tear up and leave the hothouse.

Inspired by his experience growing fruit trees, Nadin relates the moment of convergence between "the ocular, perceived world" and "the interior world of experience" to the graft, the "point of connection" between a branch and the rootstock of a different species. Since fruit seeds produce wild, inedible offspring, farmers use grafting to reproduce the desired fruit. In the greenhouse, Nadin splices the branch of a fruit tree (the scion) with the hardy rootstock of another cultivar, so that their vascular tissues fuse together and duplicate the genes of the scion. But he cannot fully control the grafting process, especially within such a contained environment; unexpected hybrids can result. (The bees, as pollinators, also have a say in the matter.) In the studio, he "grafts" ideas and images onto the canvas, but they are not always so faithfully recorded. The narrative can veer off course.

When Nadin returned to figurative and narrative painting in early 2020, the grafting process provided a metaphorical framework for the merging of ideational and representational approaches. He began with studies of lemon trees, painted from life inside the greenhouse. One painting is explicitly diagrammatic, with labels identifying the Marrakesh lemon sapling, the sour orange rootstock, and the grafting site. But the still life re-

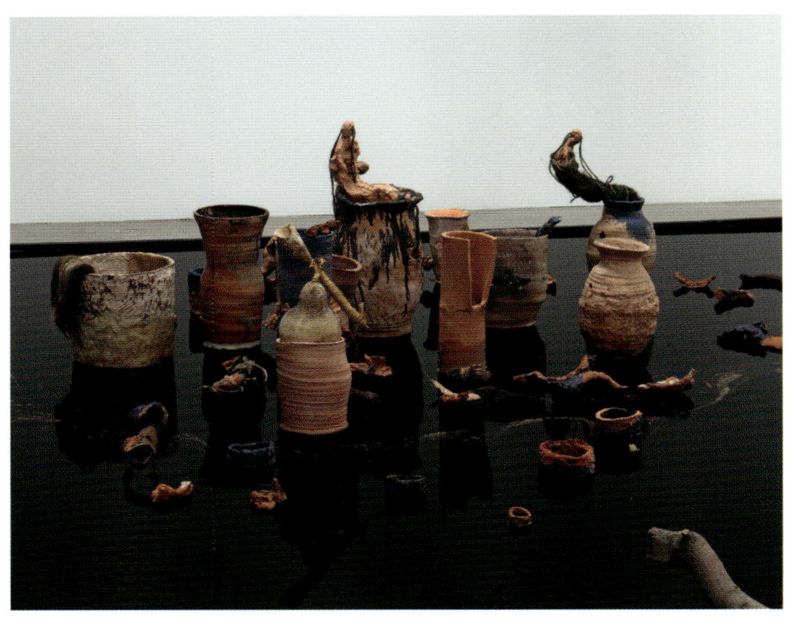

The Bo'sun's Chair, 2010 (top)
Gavin Brown's Enterprise,
New York City, 2011
Hemlock trees, terracotta, wood,
string, nutria fur, wax, fabric,
indigo pigment, bronze,
galvanized nails
5 ft - 10 ft 2 in

Raft, 2010 (bottom)
Gavin Brown's Enterprise,
New York City, 2011
Honey, terracotta, wood, twine,
bank run, wax, ham
24 x 24 ft

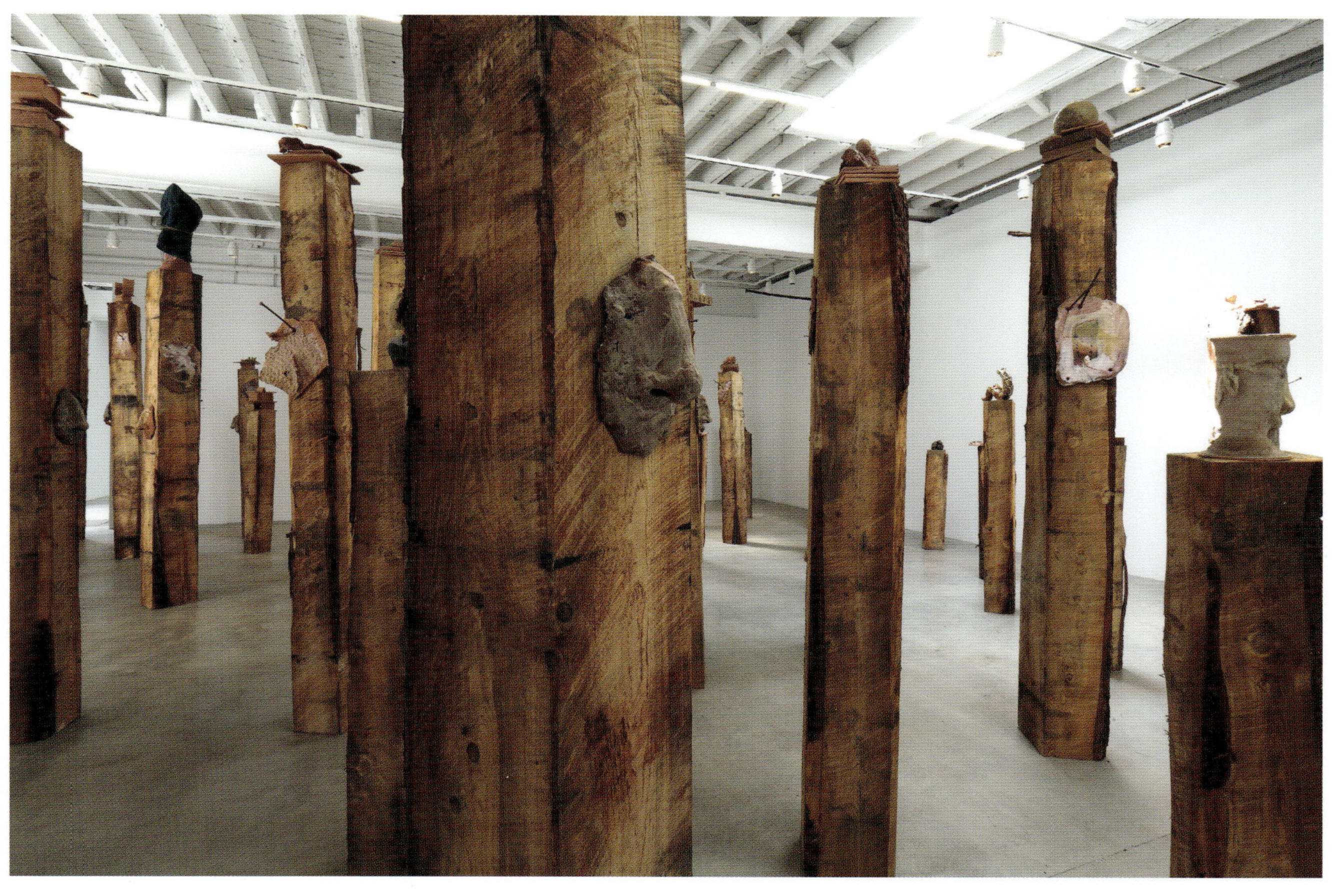

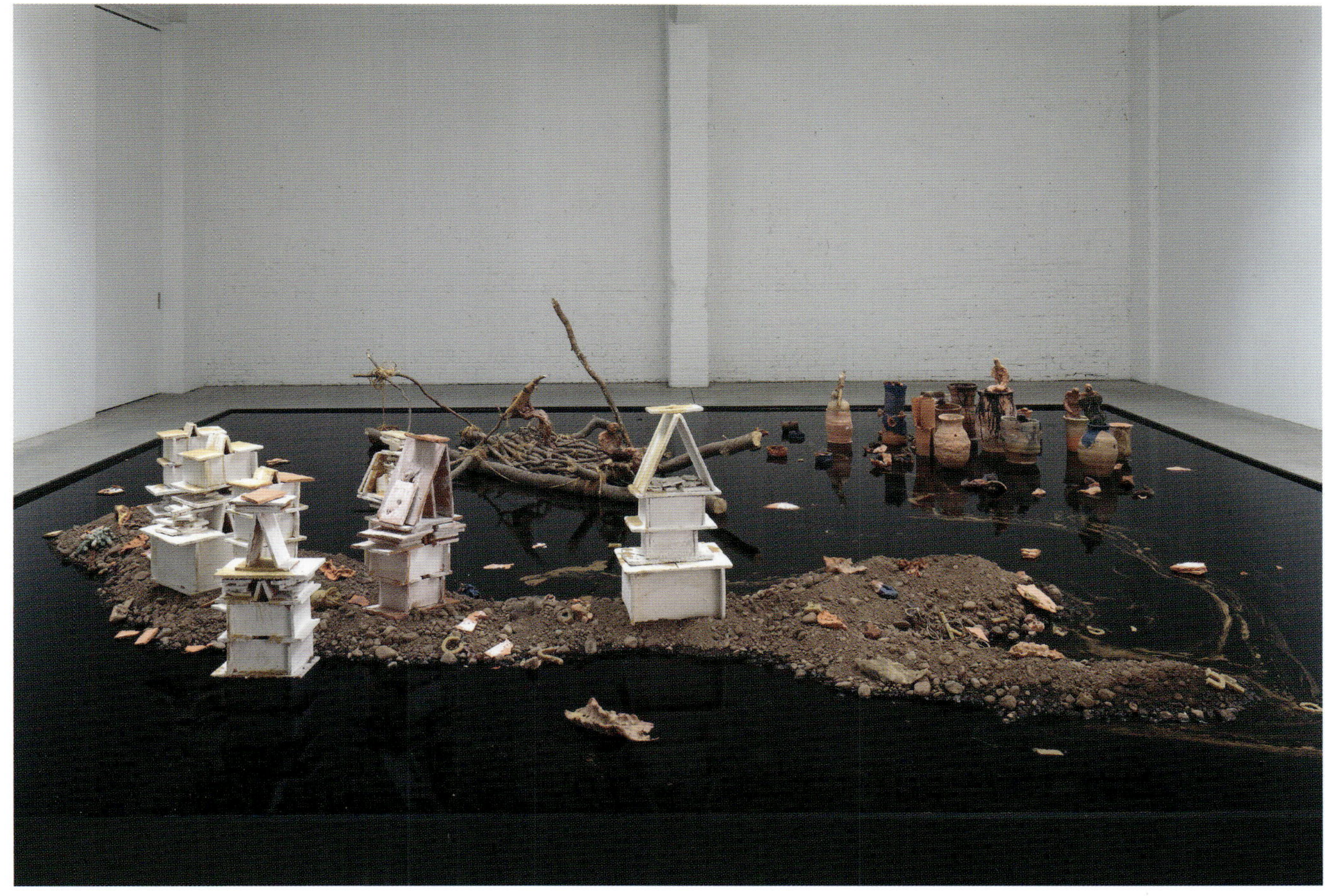

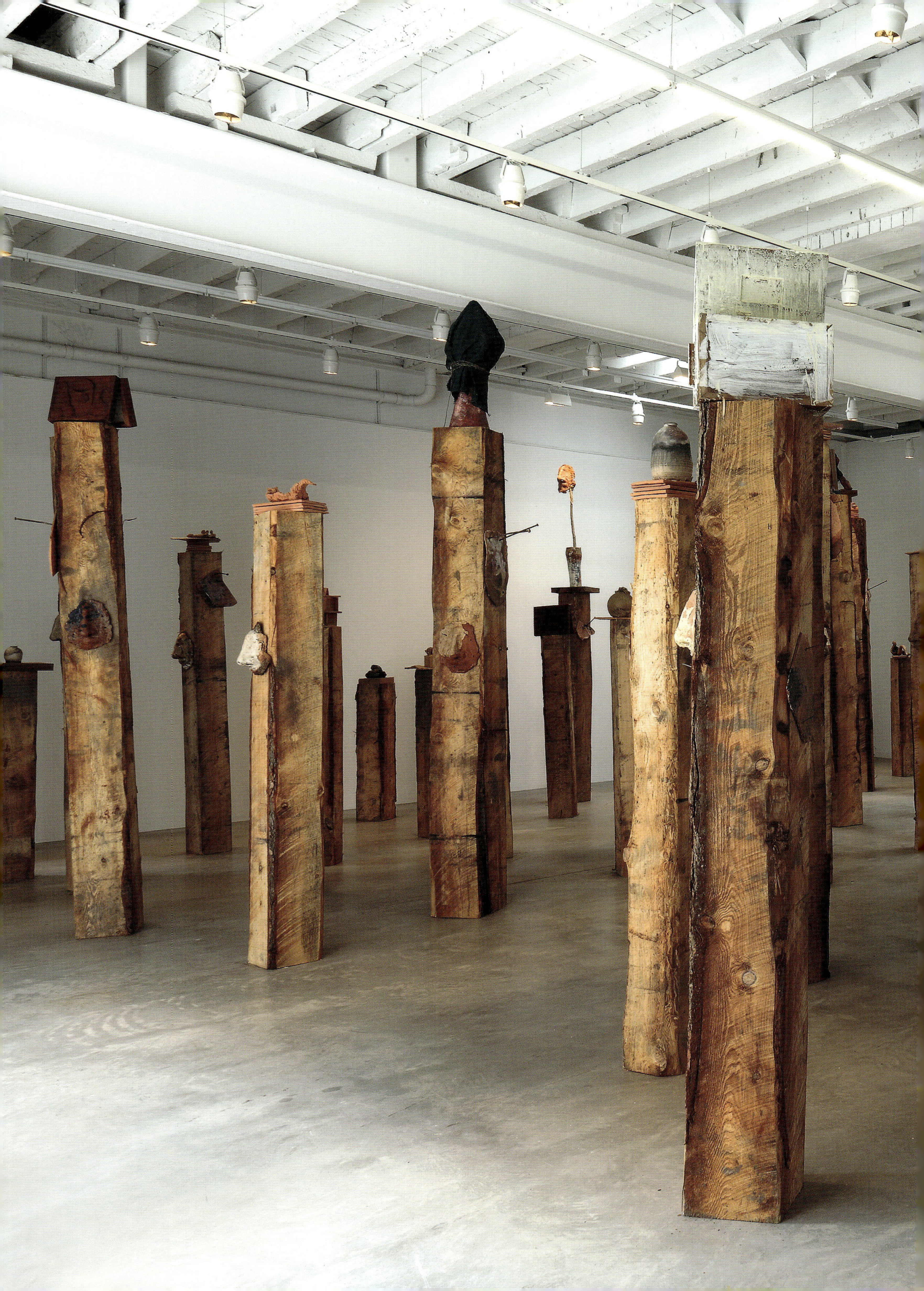

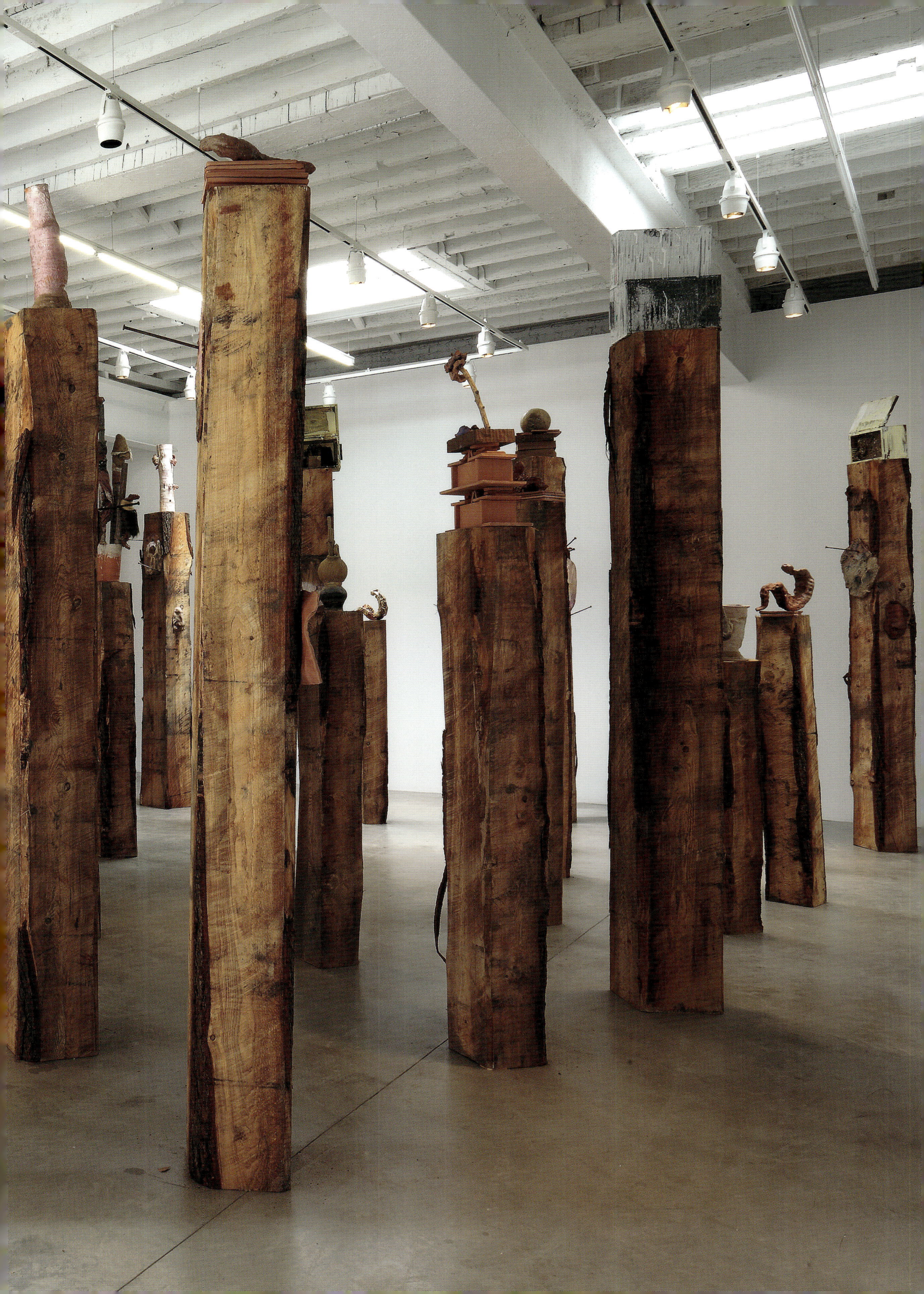

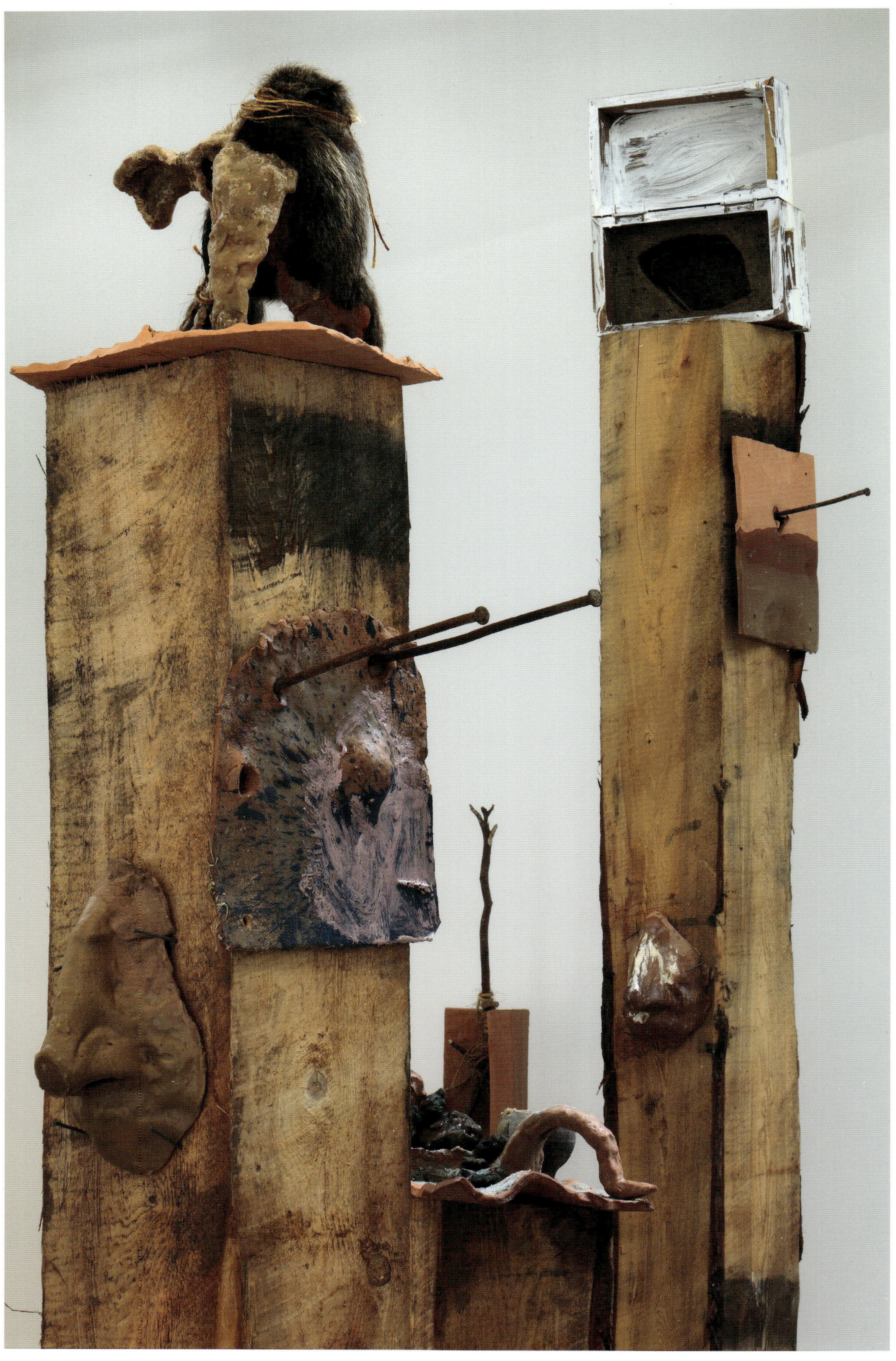

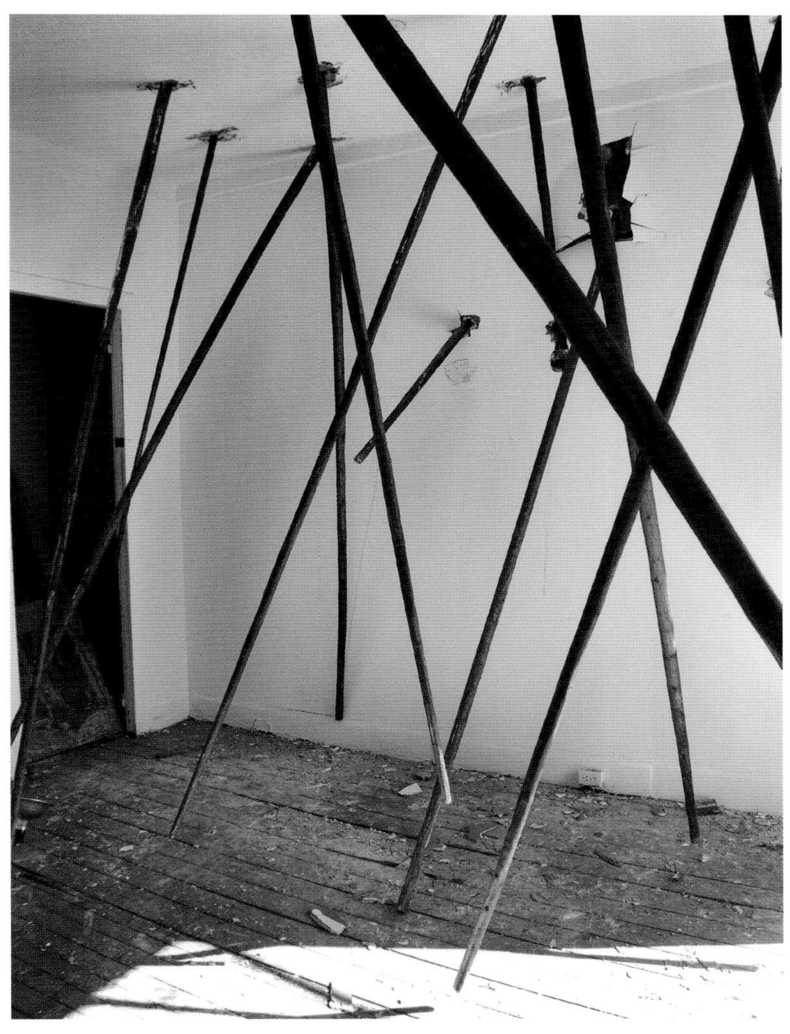

First Mark installation (detail)
KKProjects, New Orleans, 2010

fused to sit still. When the artist left the greenhouse for the studio, the lemons followed, lingering in his mind. In a resulting work, *Anne and Lemons Leaving the Greenhouse*, 2020, Nadin depicts his wife's image multiplying and trailing away as she exits the greenhouse. Meanwhile, the captive lemons take the opportunity to escape through the open door. Since Nadin frequently incorporates elements from past works, these same lemons may wander into future paintings. Maybe they even found their way onto this canvas from some of his earliest still lifes—a long and meandering path.

When Nadin "unlearned how to make art" with *First Mark*, he sought to shed the painterly habits and associations he had accrued over the years. But some things cannot be shed—they remain within and re-emerge. His mark making is more exploratory now, even liberated, but his recent paintings retain references to themes and motifs that have long infused his work. There are the rudimentary houses with lollipop trees, the Tower of Babel, and a preponderance of cliffside vistas. The hovering fruits, so menacing in his early still life paintings, now feel more buoyant, benign. Repeated often, an early self-portrait has become iconographic, a relic

Second Mark

of another age. With their mélange of styles, disparate imagery, and probing narratives, the paintings especially evoke those Nadin completed just before his artworld hiatus. Elongated letters stretch across pictures, assembling (or not) into words. The numerous divers and swimmers recall the main figure of *The Diver*, 1993, a topless woman teetering on a burning precipice. The three cops milling about, out of place, in , 1993, reincarnate thirty years later as a trio of Cuban soldiers in a beachside scene. The vaguely familiar mountains and landscapes are a constant, but not quite unchanged, presence.

Populated with family members and neighbors, Nadin's recent paintings also find him returning to human narratives for the first time since the early 1990s. On trips to the Milk Run, a local diner and truck stop, he catches up with neighbors, many of whom makes appearances in the paintings. Nadin's seasonal diary, which has been excerpted in previous books, primarily chronicles the pleasures and trials of small-scale farming. But stories of his neighbors, some quite tragic, punctuate the reports of crops and livestock, homecooked meals, changes in the weather (meteorological and emotional), and battles with ever-encroaching predators. There is Gary, the farmhand, and his son Rick; Sharkey, a South Bronx detective turned dairy farmer; the local historian, Doug; Dimitrios, dubbed "The Greek"; and many others, identified only by initials, who come and go. There are weddings, divorces, and deaths; a house burns down; Balashek, "the bee man," tragically freezes to death while caring for a pregnant cow. There is also the lingering presence of Selah Strong, the initial farmer of this land, who "lies underground, a few feet from the house." The stories accumulate, whether real or imagined, like marks on a painting.

Off the Rack (detail), 2019
James Fuentes, New York City, 2019

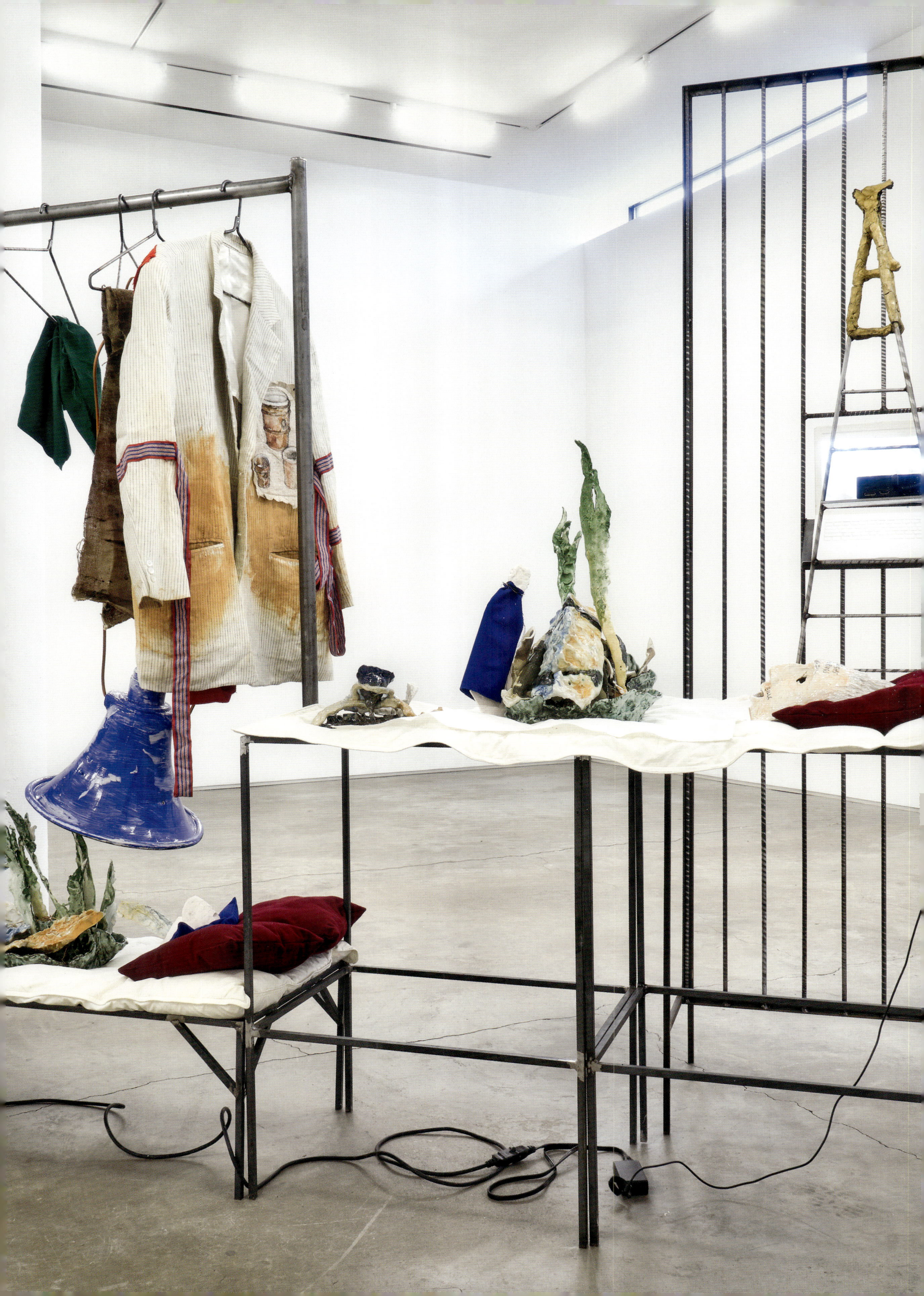

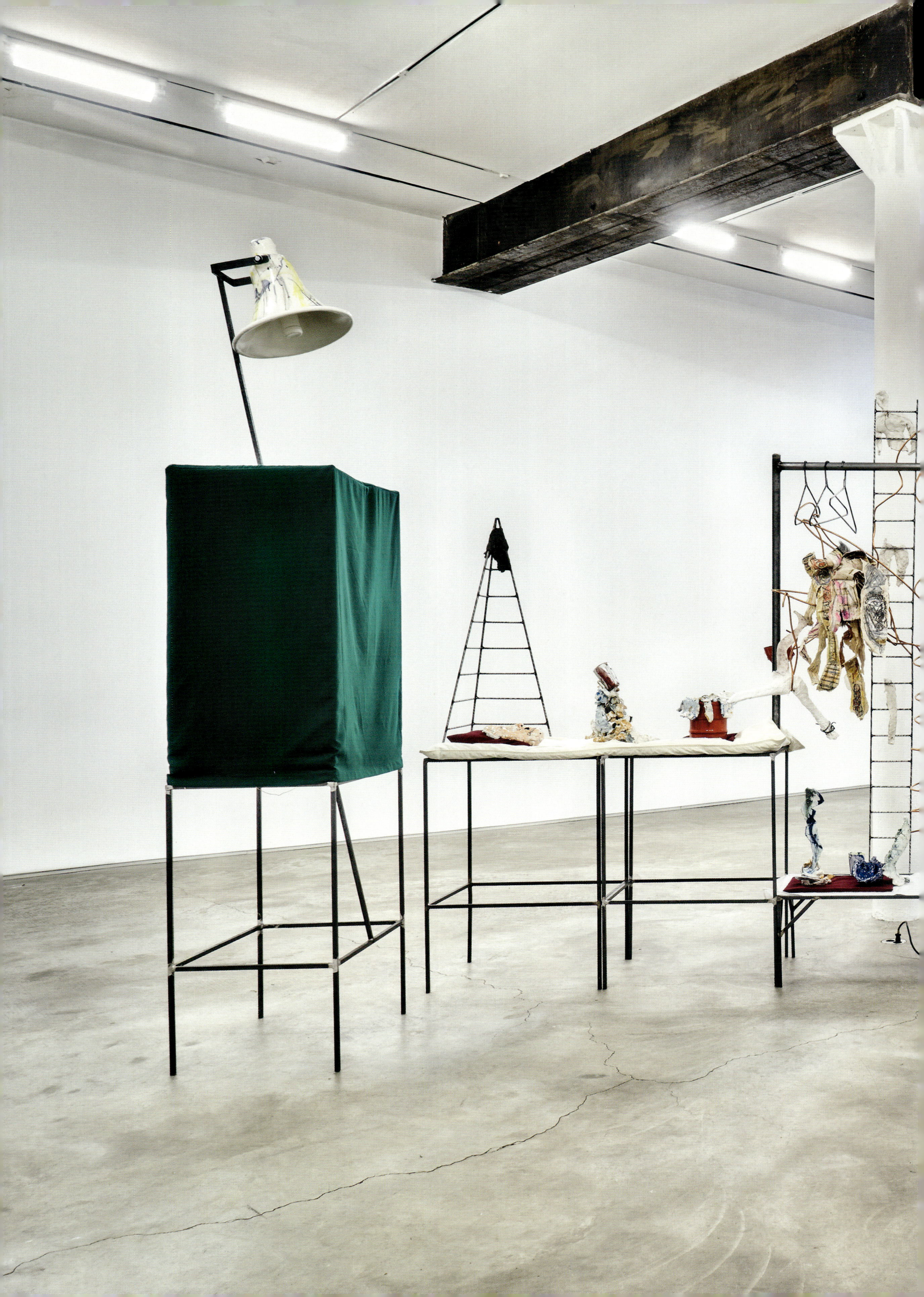

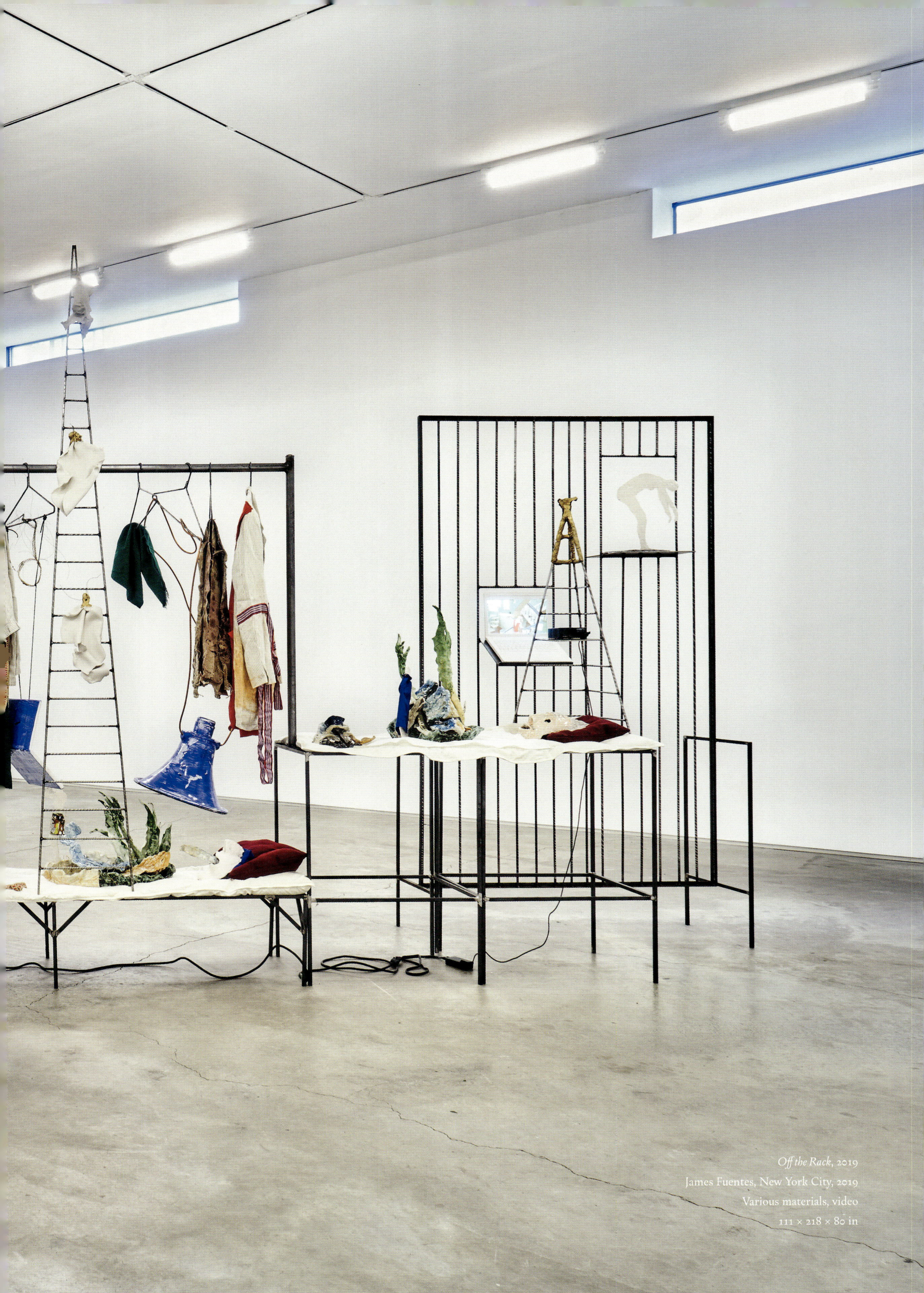

Off the Rack, 2019
James Fuentes, New York City, 2019
Various materials, video
111 × 218 × 80 in

10,000 crows

Glide above

10,000 histories

Hidden beneath

Beneath the blanket of fresh snow

Black crow, white snow

Flesh produces productions of flesh

I've got teeth

You've got meat—let's eat

My nose sniffs black oil

On Houston Street

Oily water

Smoothes the cratered road. The spray of taxi wheels

Soaks the weatherman. I read the weather

I read the news,

But stare at my sodden shoes

Wet soles compact melting snow and

Skate the white tile floor. I wait

To sit silent, in the damp, in the dark

Strangerful room

I star in movies,

On screens

Fake I Calls Real Me You

I

You

Know

I know

I know

You know...what?

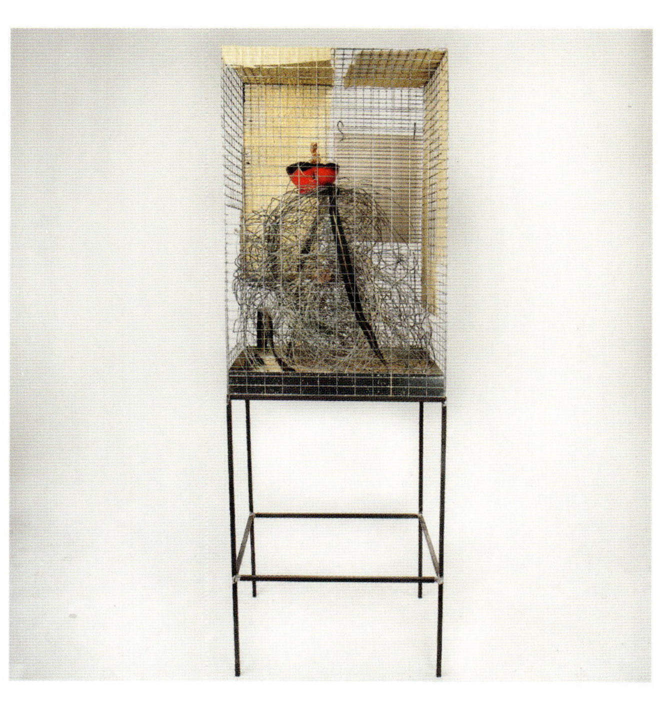

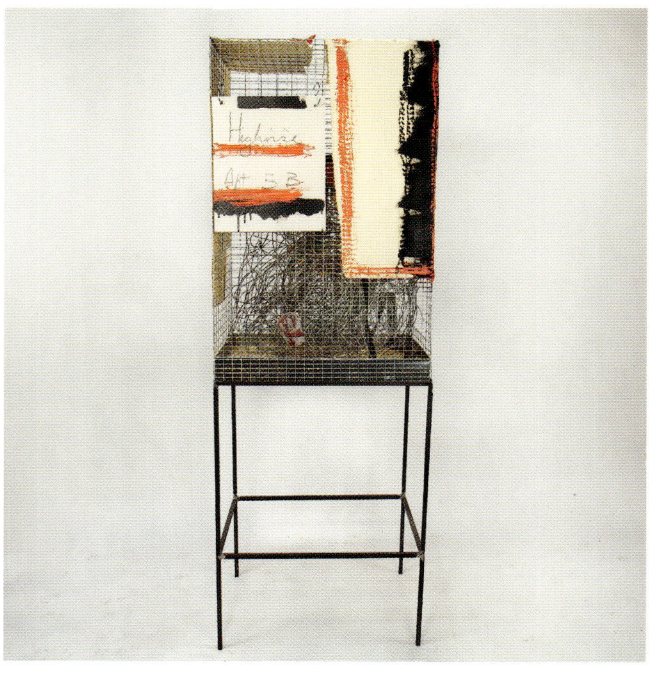

Movie screens, computer screens, TV screens

Always colored

A pastel palette, both soft and hard

I mix the paint to create the form

But off screen, I rehearse

Now for you, I'll read the news and weather

Sometimes sun, sometimes rain, sometimes snow, sometimes sinew

It wasn't, it was, now isn't

I create Gods and sausages

For you to salivate...anticipate

I'll look where light enters your body...hidden place

Nostrils, ears, eyes, mouth and anus

Genitals see have eyes too...recognize, look

See, you already know me

Chewed meat moves

Peristalsis, squeeze, chew. Squeeze...teeth

Tongue to esophagus; stomach, small, large intestine, rectum

I know, you know, the soft red illumination of the

Skin wrap. Dawn light discovers bodies and their parts

Displayed in the market for intimacy...eyes, lips, and asshole

A gold mine for the pornographer, lawyer, and psychiatrist.

— Peter Nadin, 2018

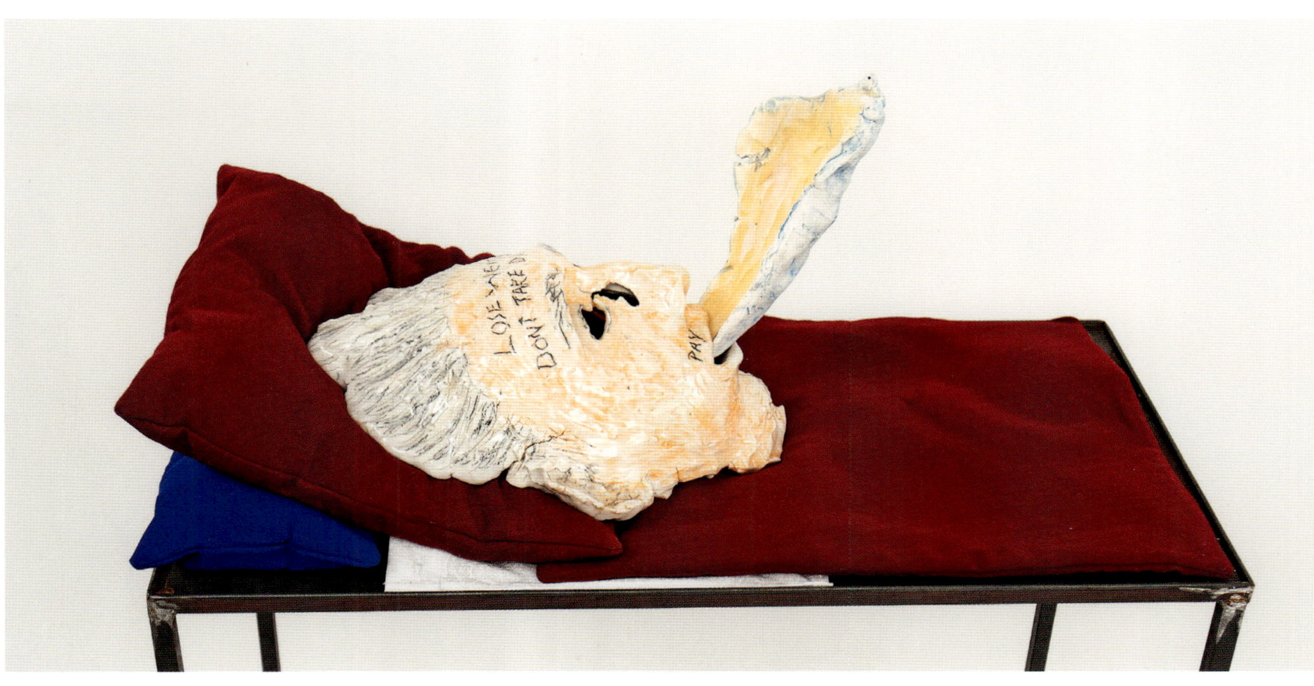

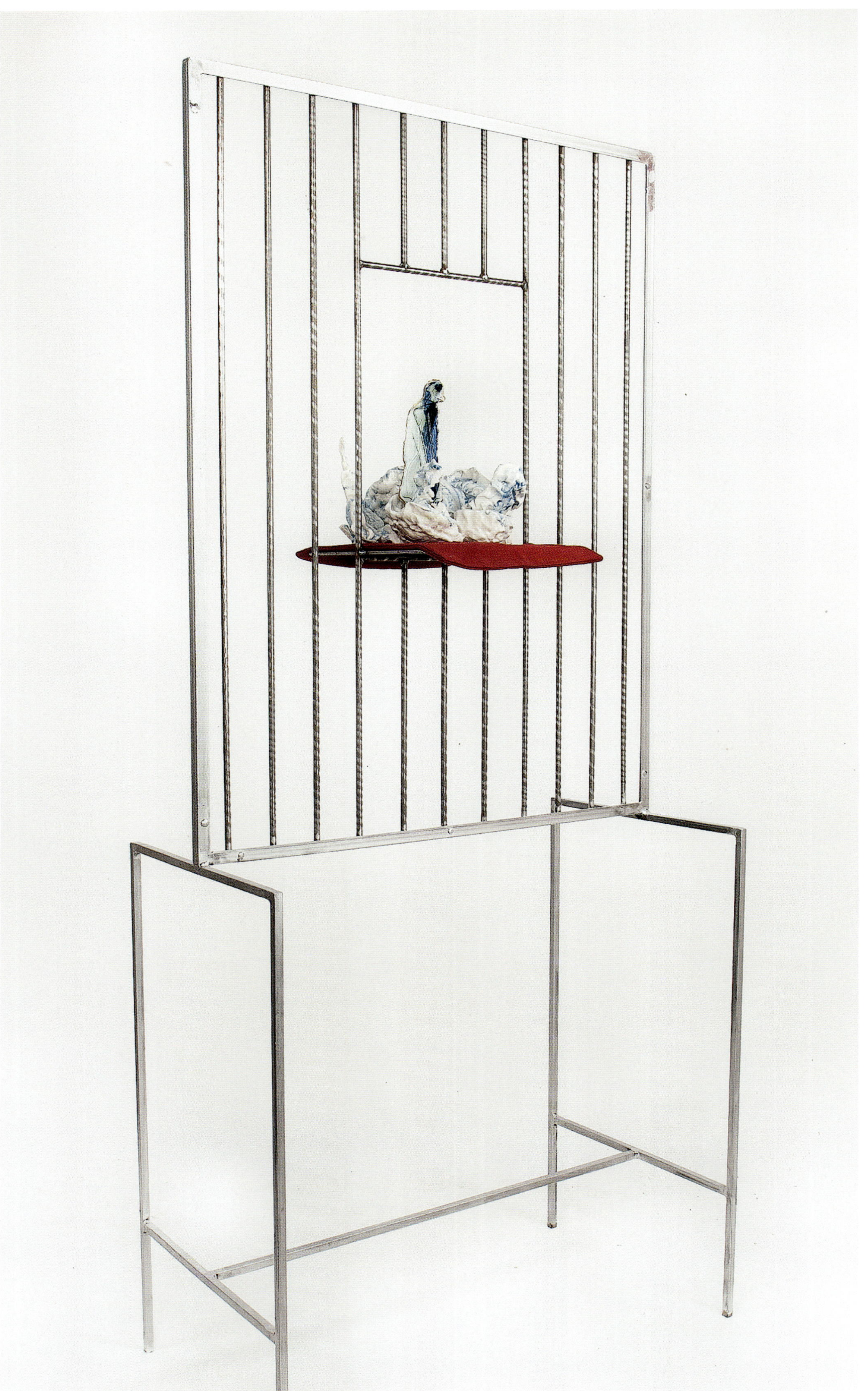

Just as he liberated his farm's products from their natural and market cycles by repurposing them as materials for paintings, Nadin has reassembled the characters and scenery of his upstate environs to produce oneiric visions in which nothing is restricted to its own individually perceived reality. His realistically portrayed figures roam landscapes of the mind, abstract but uncannily familiar vistas rendered turbulently with swirling and scribbled brushstrokes. Skies, mountains, and trees overflow with agency. Everyone and everything seem untethered. Nothing is, for instance, as successfully bound as the motorboat is to a dock in *The Blue Rope*, 2023. In *The Crow Catches a Golden Orfe (Sharkey and Amanda See It)*, 2023, a man has been inexplicably flung into the air, destined to leave the picture frame. But the entire scene—the coiling trees, the swelling cliffs—appears in the process of being swept up, sucked into the atmosphere.

The migrating flock of golden orfe depicted in several paintings and sculptures are, in actuality, confined to the water. They will not leap out to navigate the dewy morning air or relocate to the next pond over. But once Nadin observes the fish in the pond, they are, as he says, "free to swim in the mind." And anything can happen in the mind or, by extension, within a painting. In Sharkey's *Donkey Watching a Fish (A Migration of Golden Orfe)*, 2023, the fish take to the air. Below a picturesque cliffside village, two donkeys graze in a patch of land jutting out into the water. While one ass eyes a bright orange fish swimming in the water, others have taken flight behind its back. The scene is a reminder that we can never know with certainty what happens when we are not looking. In another painting, Nadin visualizes what it's like in Baracoa, Cuba, when he's not there. He'll never know, but he can envision it (and that is a type of reality).

Nadin conceives of painting as a dialogue with the paint itself. What, he wonders, do the oils and brushes bring to the painting? How do they guide him? How does one brushstroke lead to another, or suggest unintended forms? Within the space of a single painting, he utilizes the full range of marks, from precisely rendered figures and houses to more gestural landscapes. Scratched and curled lines resemble distorted letters approaching language. Unruly brushstrokes trespass onto the hand-painted frames, as the pictures push beyond their proscribed borders. A series of small nocturnal landscapes are rendered swiftly with a minimum of animated, fluid brushstrokes, as if the view threatened to disappear before his eyes.

Off the Rack: The Programmer (detail), 2019
Metal, ceramics
74 3/4 x 33 1/2 x 18 in

Third Mark

While the narrative paintings attempt to describe a self and its multifaceted reality, Nadin's scenic studies suggest a self seeing. Titles such as *Looking North, Seeing Mount Pisgah* and *Looking East, Seeing West*, both 2023, invoke an active, embodied observer. Yet, the "looking" and "seeing" are in conflict, disoriented. The viewer looks in one direction but sees in another. For instance, the wave-like peak of Mount Pisgah, a recurring form in these studies, is actually southwest of the studio, not north. The mountain's name hints at further significance. When, in the Old Testament, God brings Moses to the summit ("pisgah") of Mount Nebo to show him the Promised Land, he adds a caveat: "I have let you see it with your eyes, but you will not cross over into it." The Promised Land is thus a place to behold, or imagine, but it remains physically inaccessible. Unless through paint.

Anchored by the painting *Adam Installing Utilities in the Garden of Eden Under the Devil's Fire*, 2023, the myth of Eden serves as an archetypal subtheme of *The Invisible World*. As with the *Promised Land*, or any religious tale, the origin story is a shared vision that many have come to accept as reality, despite its absurdity—an imaginary world that only becomes visibly manifest through artistic interpretation. In Nadin's rendition, Adam and Eve appear twice, before and after the fall. The pair walking away in shame clearly references Masaccio's *Expulsion from the Garden of Eden*, ca. 1424–27, one of countless depictions. Adam appears again, alone in the immediate foreground, as a utility worker in orange coveralls. The serpent takes the form of a fire-breathing culvert, spitting flames down onto the fledgling mortals. Amid this fiery purgatory, Adam digs a trench, laying the groundwork for civilization's infrastructure. Nadin's vision of Paradise may be haywire, but like *The Invisible World* at large, it is no less real for it.

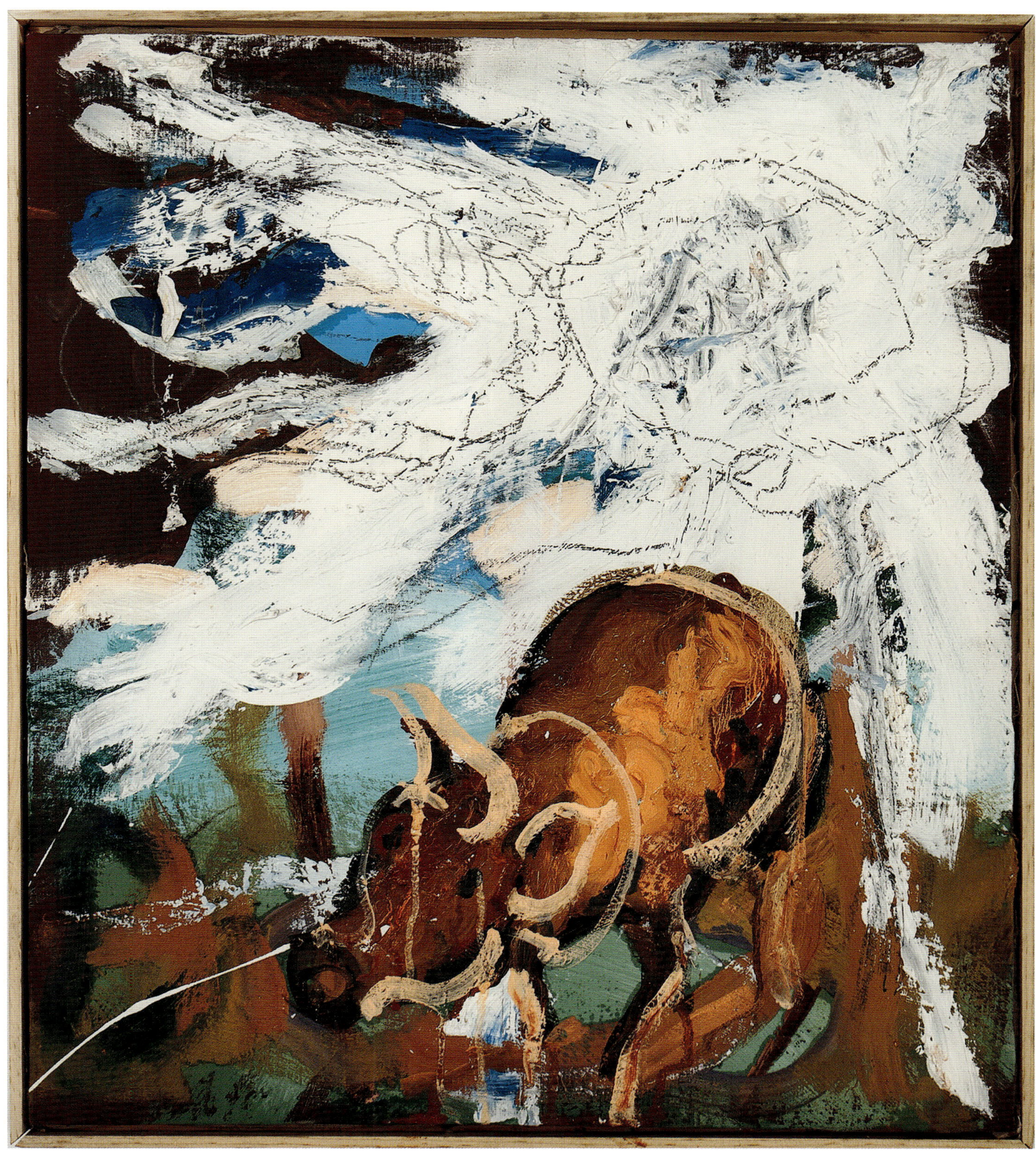

Abe in Landscape Rooting, 2015
Oil on panel
21 x 19 in

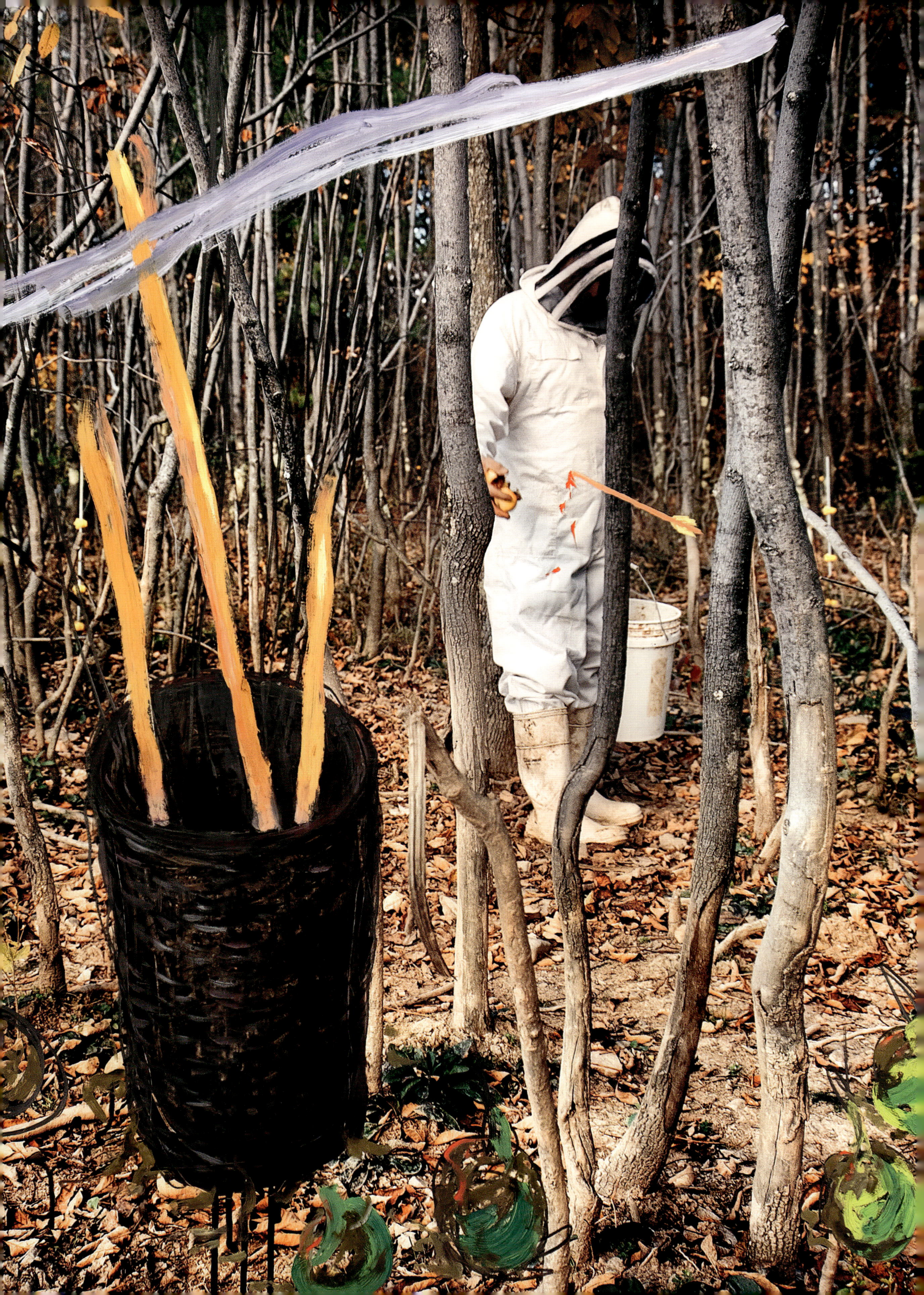

Heracles/Saint Sebastian, 2015 (left)
Oil on photograph
36 1/2 x 36 1/2 in

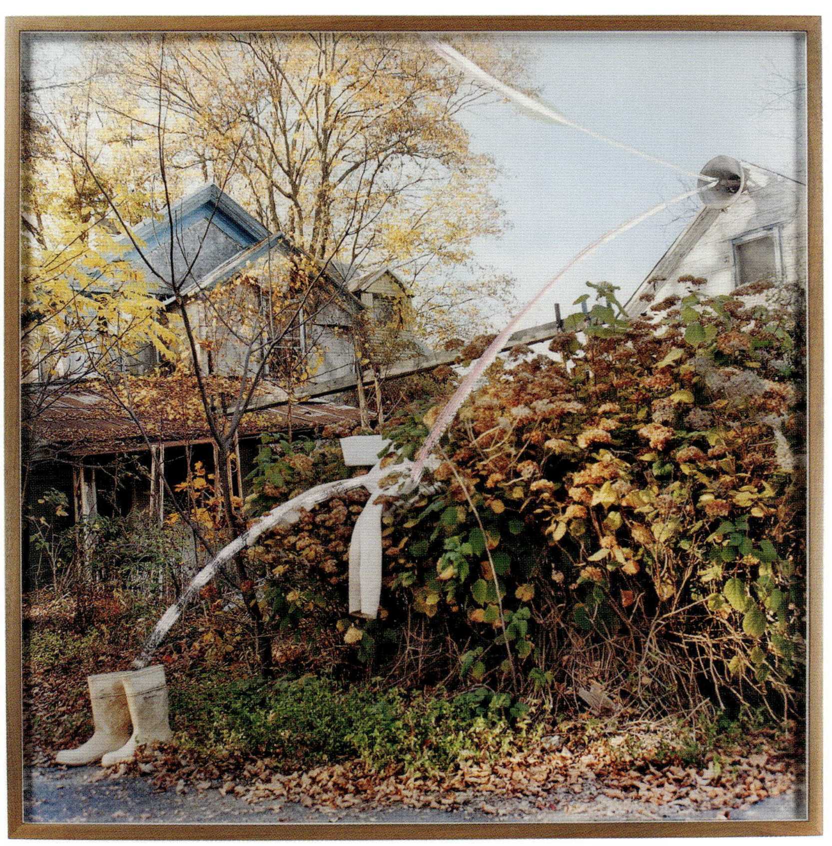

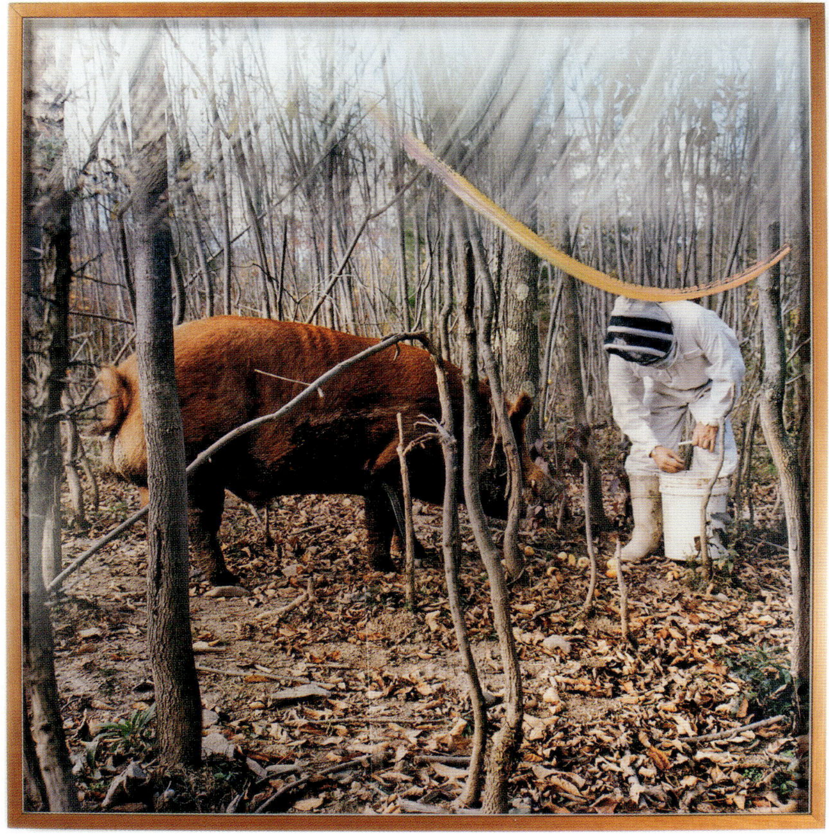

Cedrini's Lodge with Mark, 2015 (top)
Oil on photograph
36 1/2 x 36 1/2 in

Feeding Abe, 2015
(bottom)
Oil on photograph
36 1/2 x 36 1/2 in

Abe and Me, 2015
(right)
Oil on panel
43 x 33 in

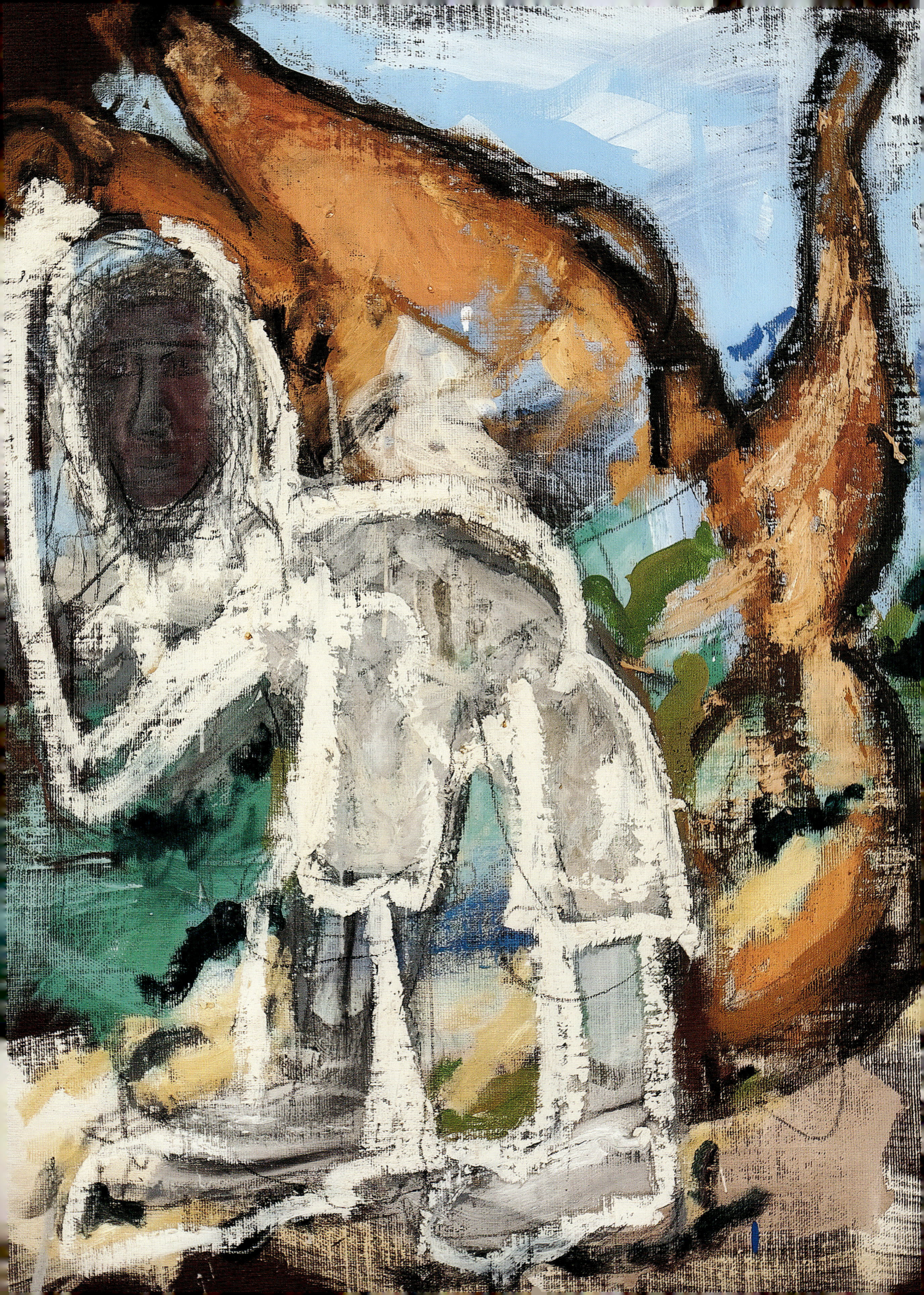

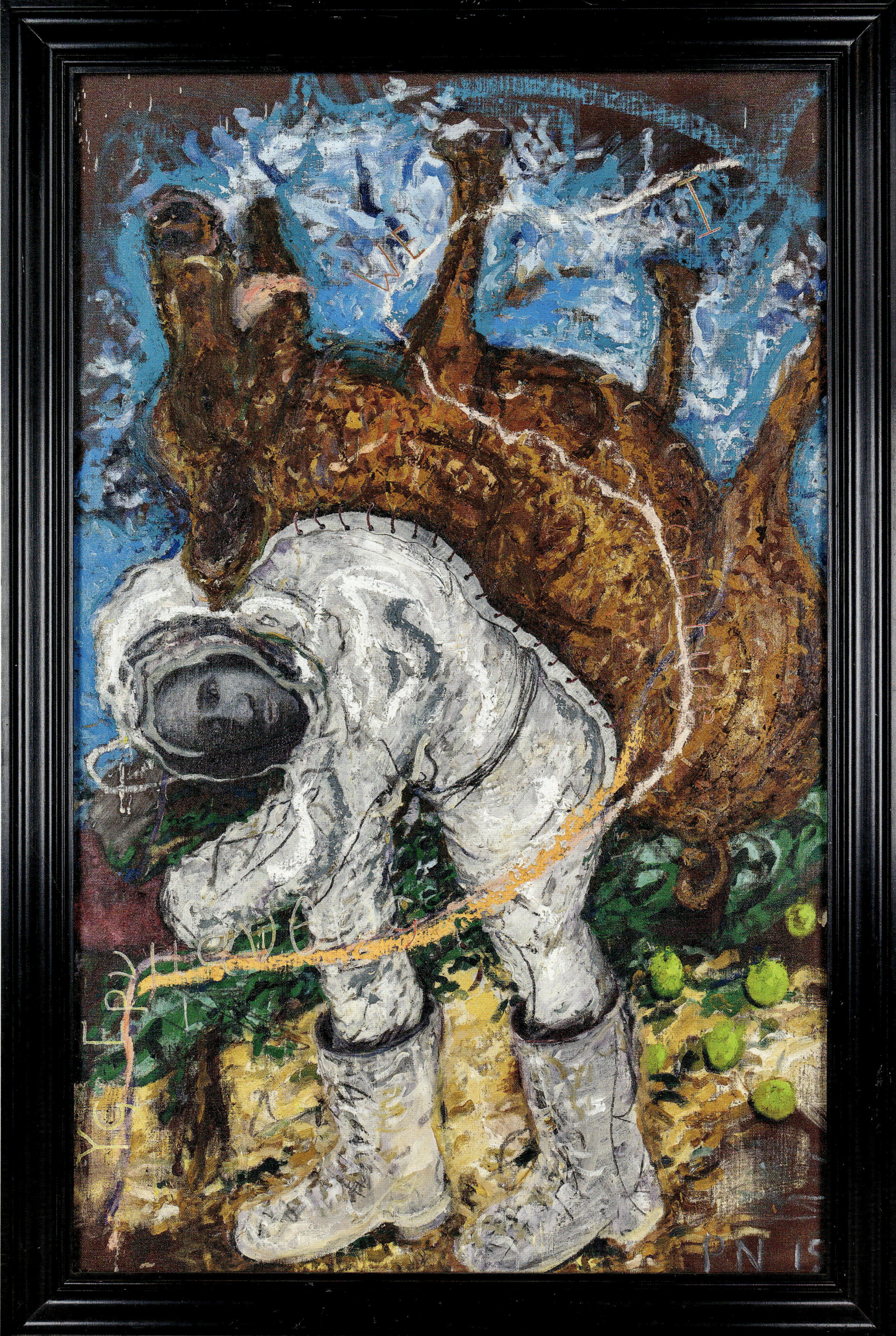

A series of realistically modeled and painted cast bronze sculptures support the Edenic theme and ground us, almost literally, in the real world—the fallen fruit underfoot. *Apple After Eve (Bite, Peel, Slice)*, 2023, depicts three apples on rocky earth, each bearing different evidence of human intervention: one is neatly peeled, another quartered, and the third has a large bite taken from its midsection. There is more than one way to eat an apple, or to tell a story. The tattered, brown leather loafer in *Three Self-Portraits with a Ripening Lemon*, 2023, is poised to crush the forbidden fruit, here a lemon. Painted on the inner sole is a self-portrait as a mask, the same visage that conjures the Baracoan scene. A second face, a reference to that early self-portrait, appears on the heel. Throughout his recent works, Nadin defines the self—in its presence and absence—as an accumulation of thoughts, perceptions, and experiences. As a record of experience, which is also knowledge (that forbidden fruit again), the well-worn shoe is as much a portrait of the self as any visage or likeness.

Reflecting on faith and religious parables in a mid-summer diary entry, Nadin wrote: "Our stories are so beautiful in their evocation and complete misconception. We need a story in which to dwell no less than we need a house for shelter." An entry from a few days earlier compared the human need for narrative structure to the pig's intrinsic drive to make a wallow: "Our world is of paradox and contradiction, because even though the world does not exist as we perceive it, we have to act as if it does. This is because our biological need for narrative, our need for the story to place ourselves in. Maybe this is our wallow." Imbued with a sense of myth and allegory, Nadin's paintings and sculptures demonstrate a concern with the stories we tell ourselves, and how those stories, in turn, mold our perception and conception of reality. In this way, his art interweaves the physical and metaphysical worlds, giving form and meaning to the wallow.

On a recent visit, Nadin took me to the archive via the back route, up the hill through rocky woods—hardly any kind of path. Noticing the sporadic lines of stacked stones, some more structured than others, I asked him if they marked any kind of boundary, perhaps old property lines. He told me they were cleared from the soil in the nineteenth century by penny-a-day laborers, and that the positioning of the stacks is more or less incidental. Later, I found Nadin's musings on the stones and the laborers who, passing through, cleared the soil of what is now, in one reality, his land. "There is something beautiful about a stone that has been plucked from a field and placed on the edge and still there," he wrote. "Never moved or touched again. It houses the ghost of the laborer. The simple human activity still hovers around the stone." It's this kind of presence and record that forms and informs the landscape, infusing it with stories that still resonate.

*Abe and Me / Heracles and the
Erymanthian Boar*, 2015
Oil on panel
82 x 55 in

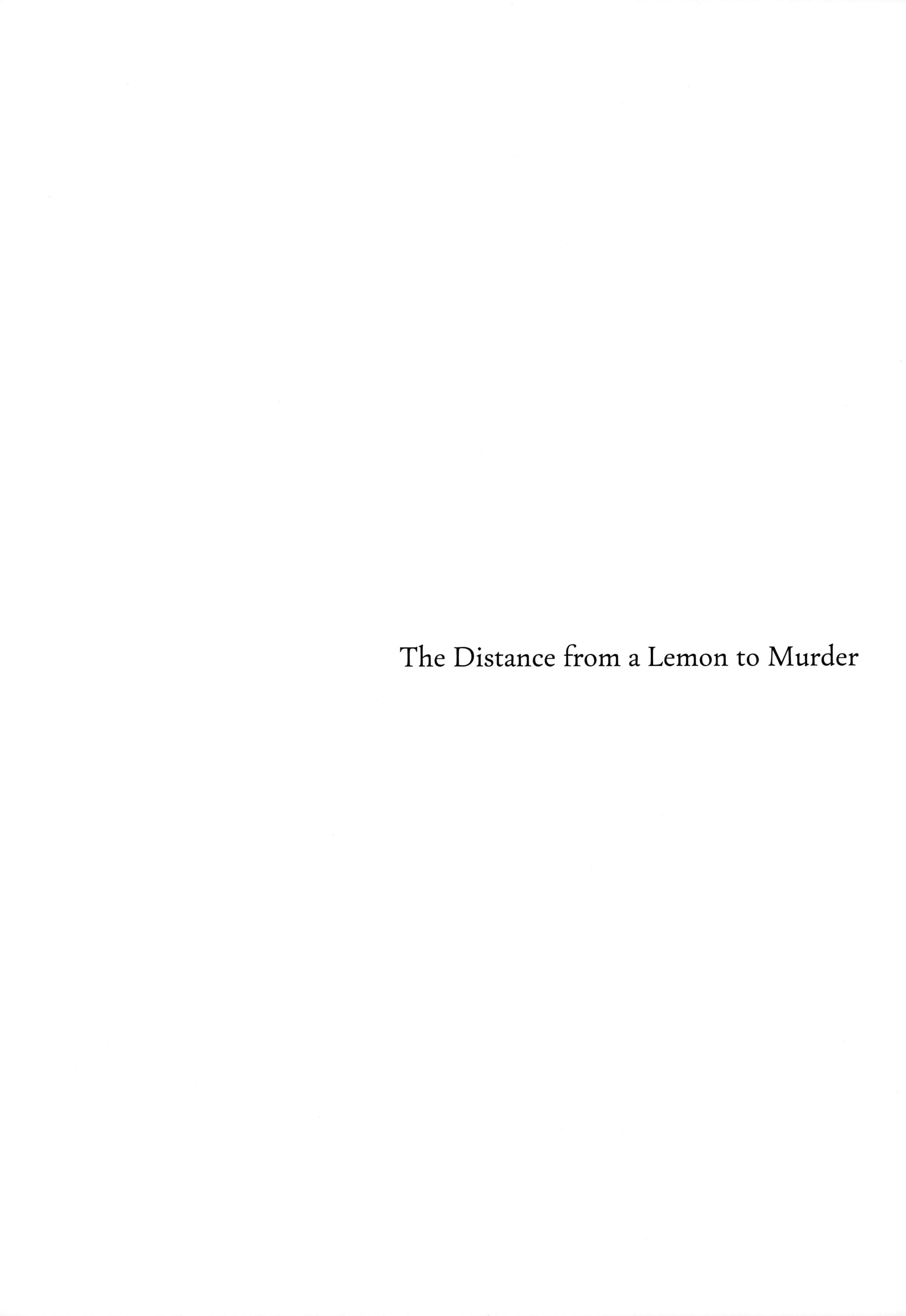

The Distance from a Lemon to Murder

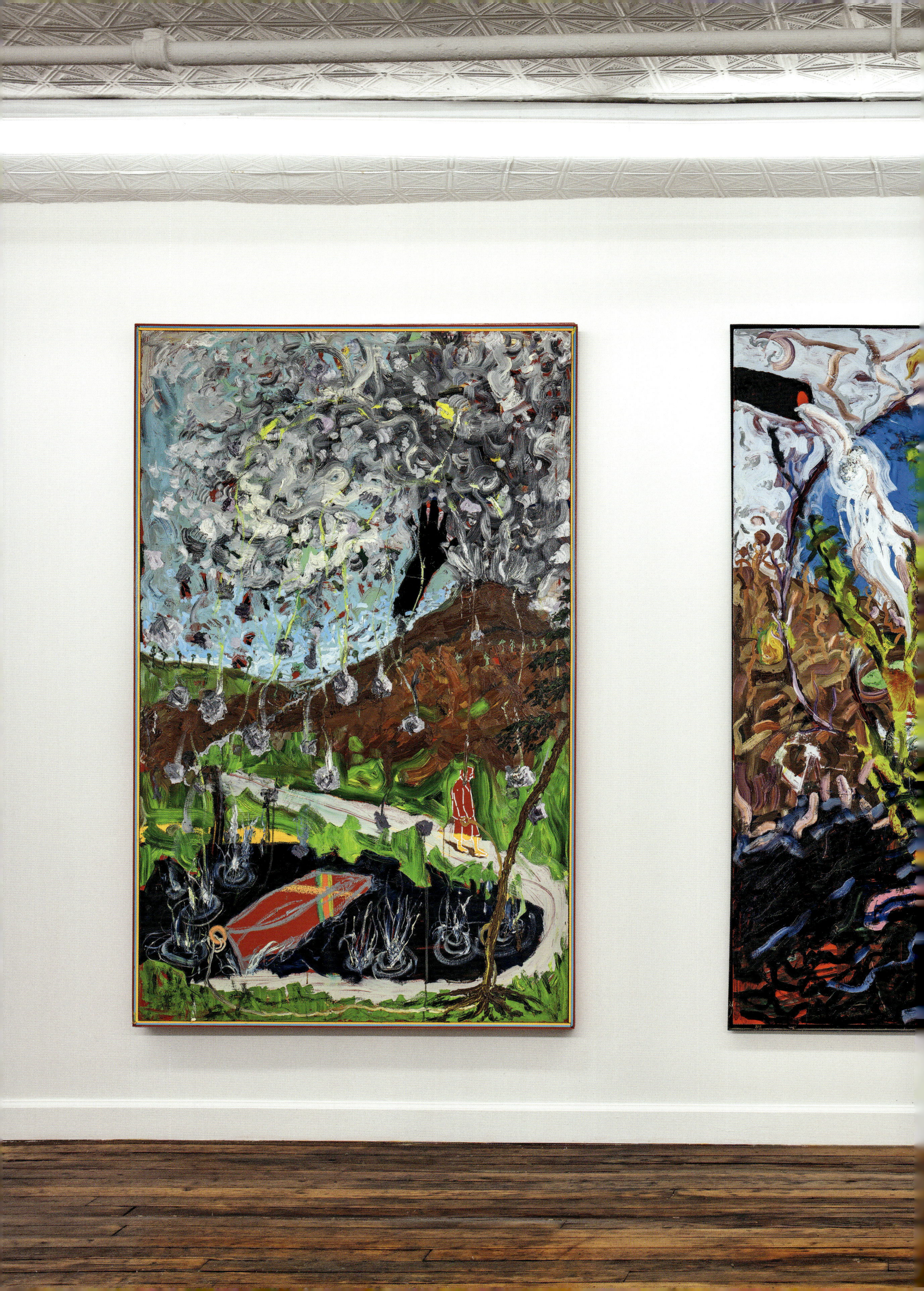

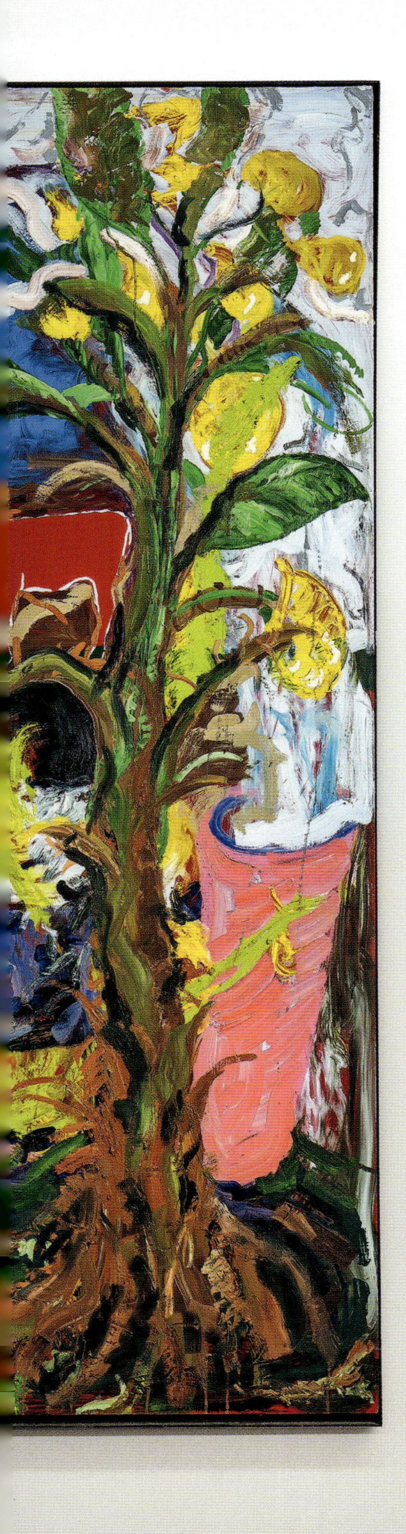

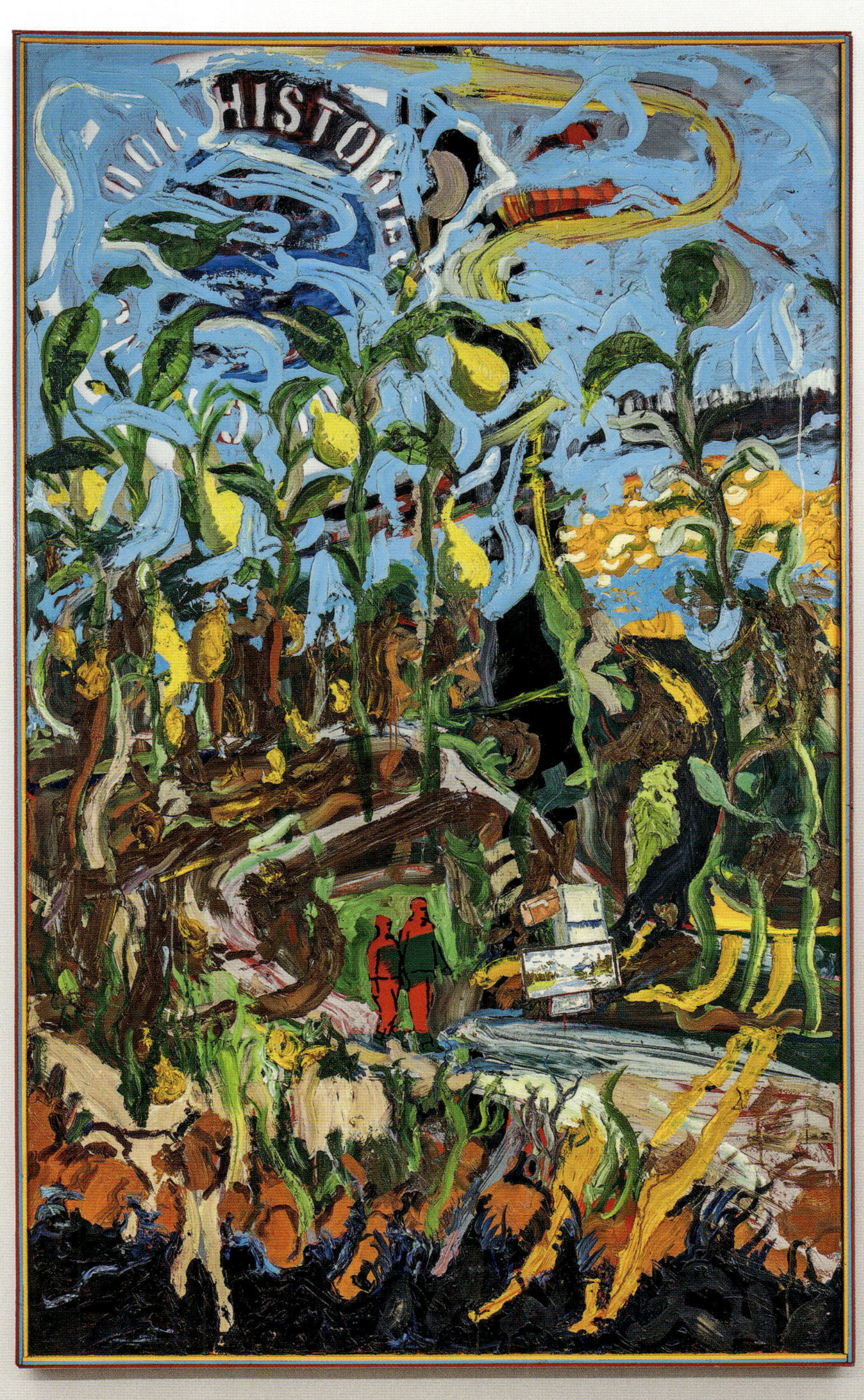

The Distance from a Lemon to Murder
Off Paradise, New York City, 2020

A conversation with Peter Nadin

conducted by Randy Kennedy

The Paris Review, 2022

Kennedy: More than any other artist I've ever met, you seem to look at the very big picture of the art-making, the long story, about how we are animals and have, like other animals, evolved to do certain things. Plants do certain things, and animals do certain things, and among the things that Homo sapiens have always done—in fact, we now know it predates Homo sapiens and goes much further back—is make art. Your work is deeply knit up with the history of painting but seems even more knit up with that thinking, about how our species creates culture as a function of what we are, the same way bees make honey.

Nadin: I certainly think the biological process is central to our art-making. That comes both from the experience of the body and the visual process. I've always been fascinated by how one constructs reality from principally visual experience. It's really curious that it's not the eyes that do the seeing but the brain. But in the brain, there is no space. There is no image. There is no word. So there is a point of interaction between the perceived visual world and the stored knowledge of experience in the brain, where those two meet. I've always tried to figure out where reality lies, because purely ocular reality is a construction. The boar that we used to have up on the farm for years in the Catskills, old Abe, he'd construct his reality as a pig. We'd construct our reality as humans. Our experience of the world is really contradictory and paradoxical. Because even though we know that the world doesn't exist as we see it, and there are no colors, for example, we still create them in the visual cortex in the same way Abe would create his own sense of the world.

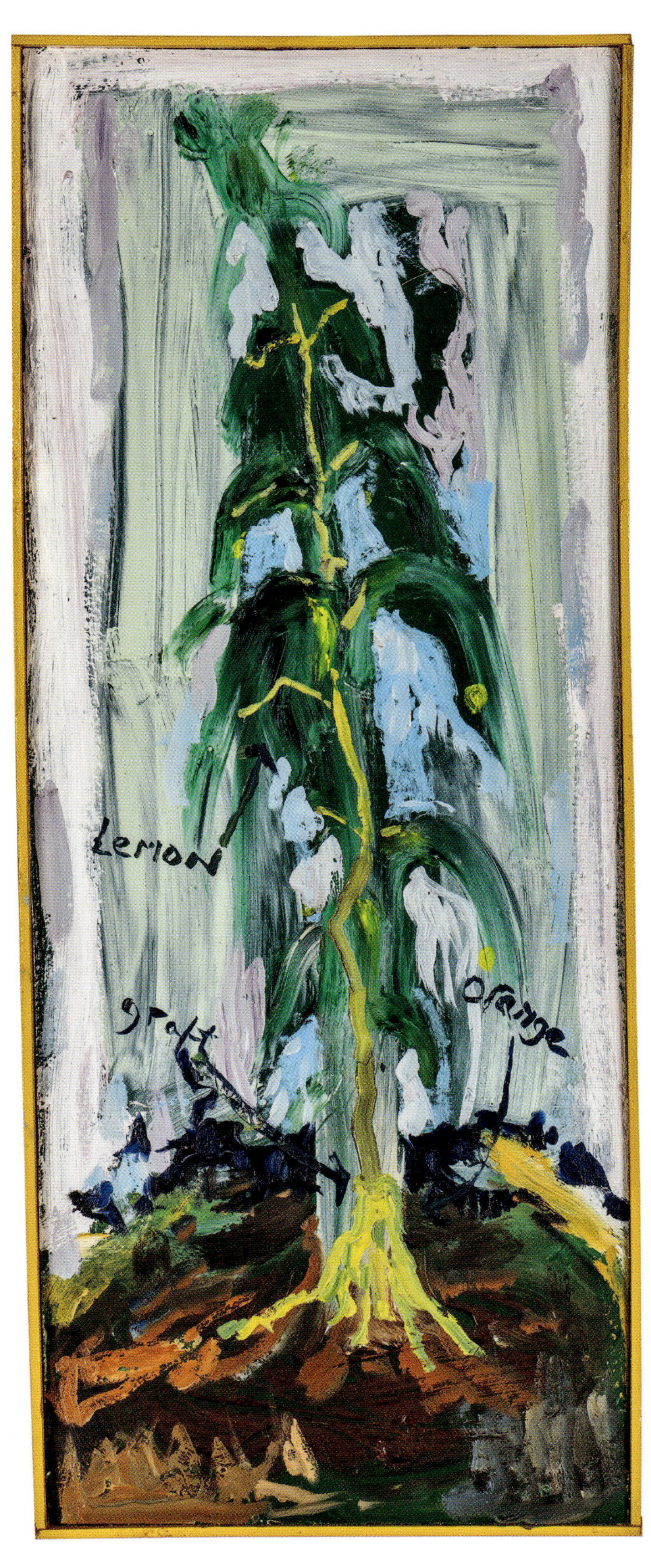

A Graft of Marrakesh Lemon onto Sour
Orange Rootstock, 2020
Oil on panel
18 1/2 x 7 11/16 in

47

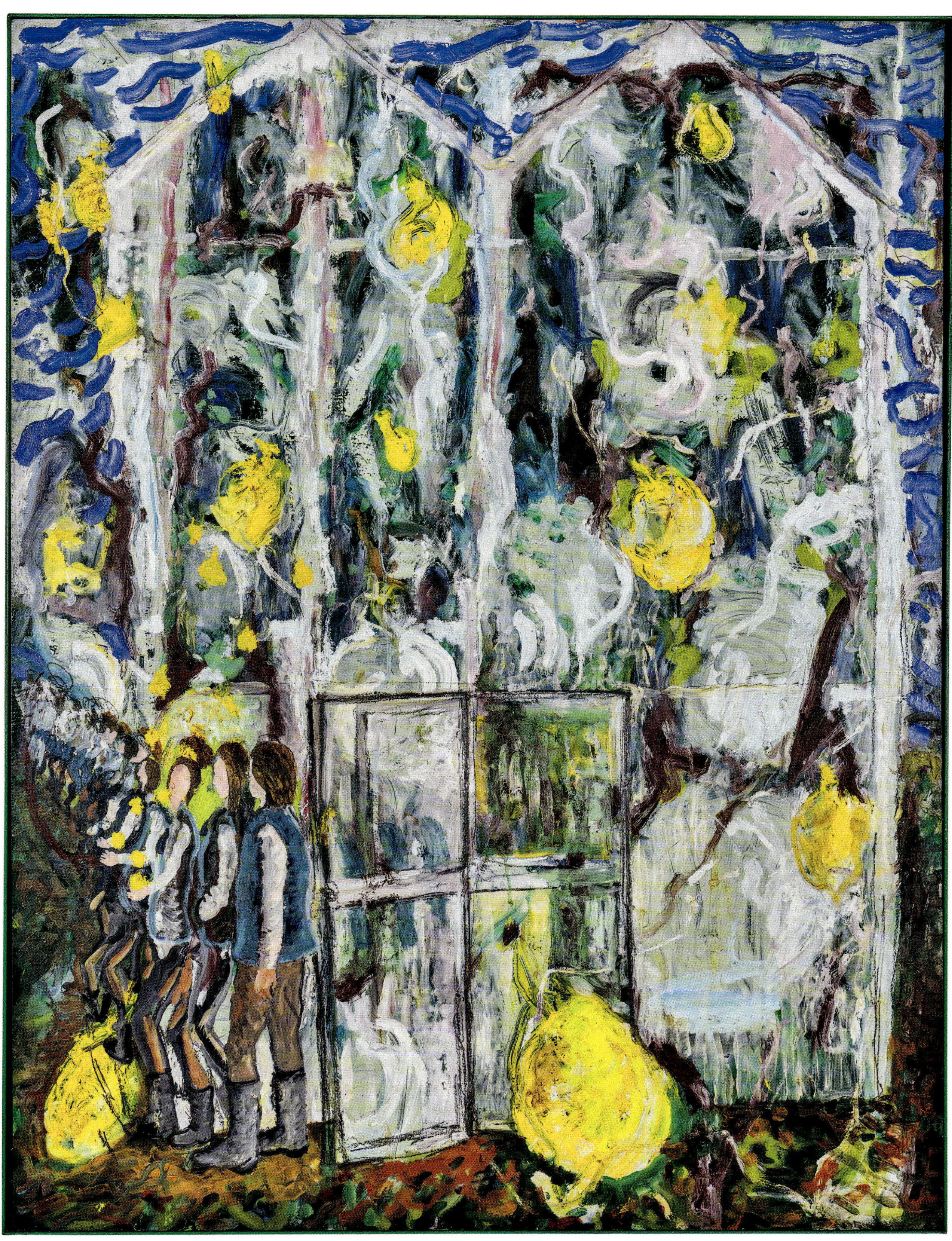

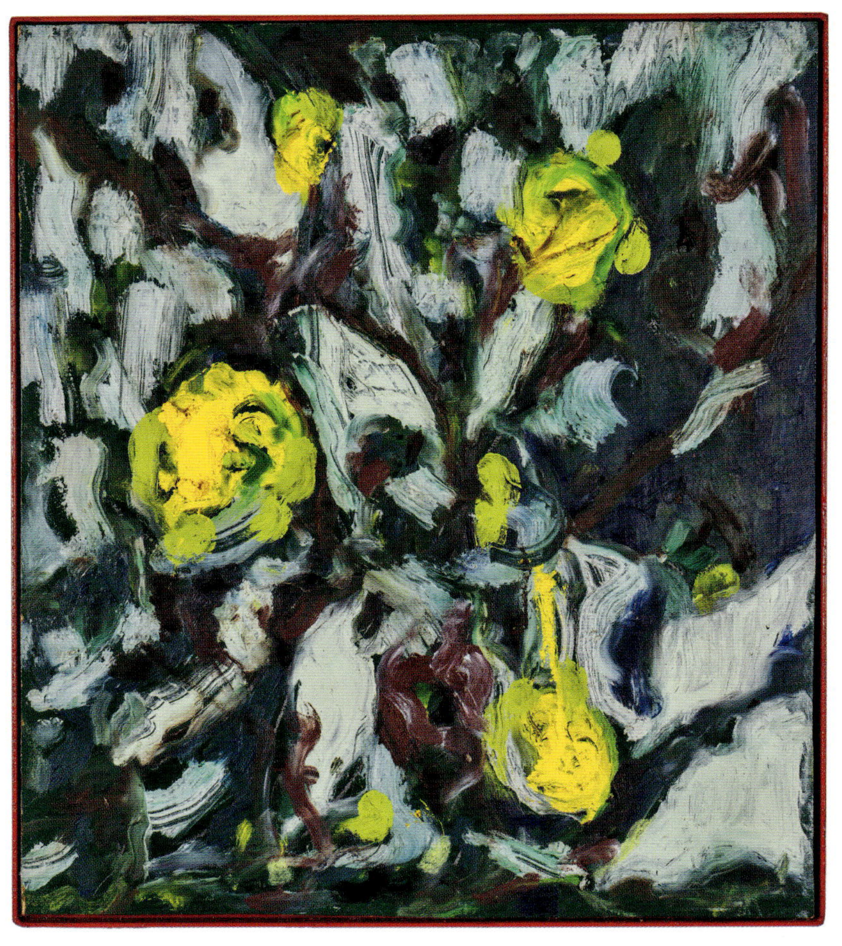

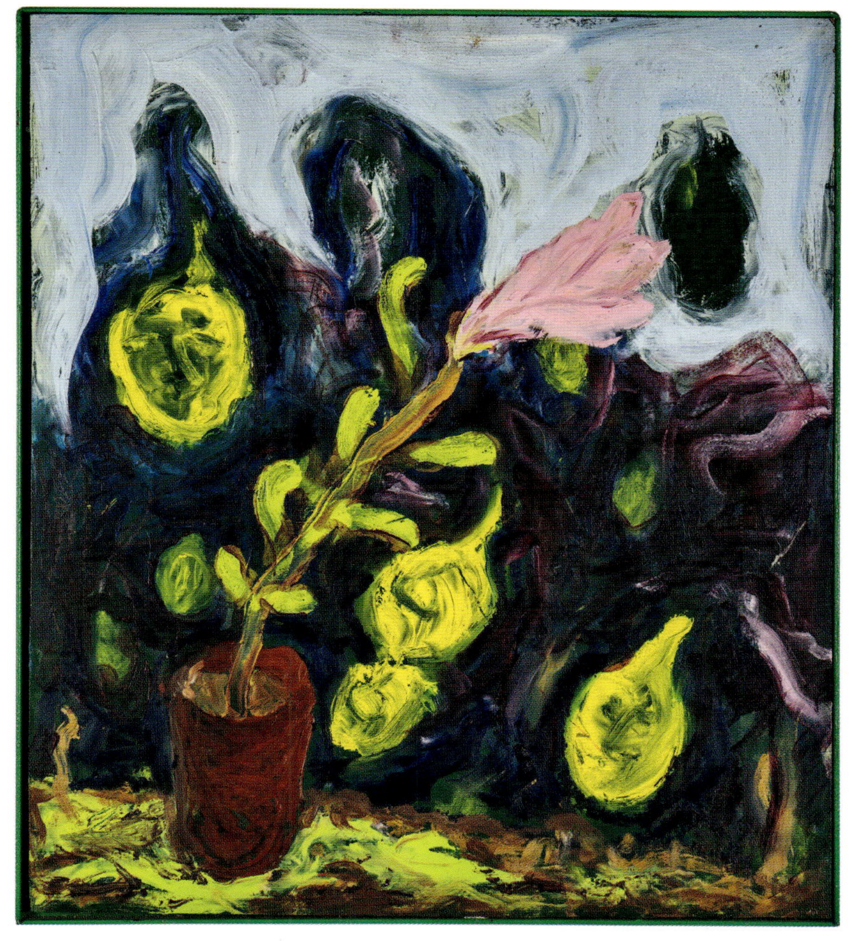

Lemon or Yellow, 2020 (left)
Oil on panel
20 3/4 x 18 3/4 in

Lemons and Mountains, 2020 (right)
Oil on panel
20 3/4 x 18 3/4 in

K: You withdrew from the commercial art world, and yet there's never been a time when you've stopped making work. You've also run a working farm in the Catskills for more than twenty years now, and I've seen how parts of the farm form parts of the work, obliquely and sometimes in a very straightforward way—as when your boar, Abe, all seven hundred pounds of him, became a subject in a series of paintings. Over the last six or seven years, whenever you've taken me up to your studio on the hill, we never go into the studio first. We always go into the greenhouse, which seems lately to be the focus of your work and as important to you as the studio.

N: Well, no, it's not as important because I would be making my art whether I had a studio or not. Whereas if I didn't have the greenhouse, I couldn't be grafting citrus trees. But they are completely integrated, and one thing leads to the other. My daily routine is to go up to the greenhouse, see what's what, and then go to the studio, do some work, then maybe go to the greenhouse later. And during the summer months, to be in the garden, and then to go to the studio later in the day.

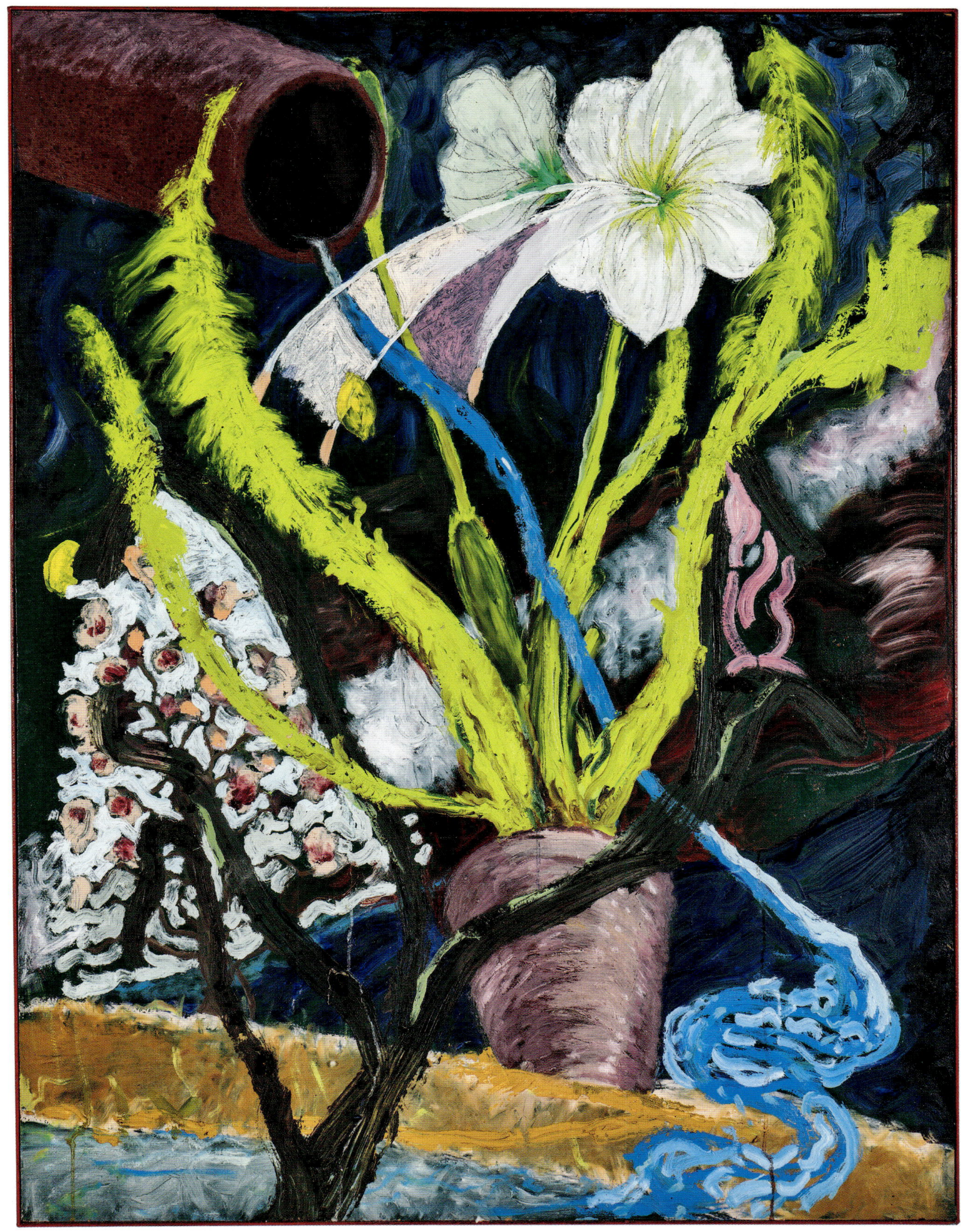

*The Culvert Drains into the Pond While
the Lilies Blossom in a Pot,* 2020
Oil on panel
43 3/8 x 34 in

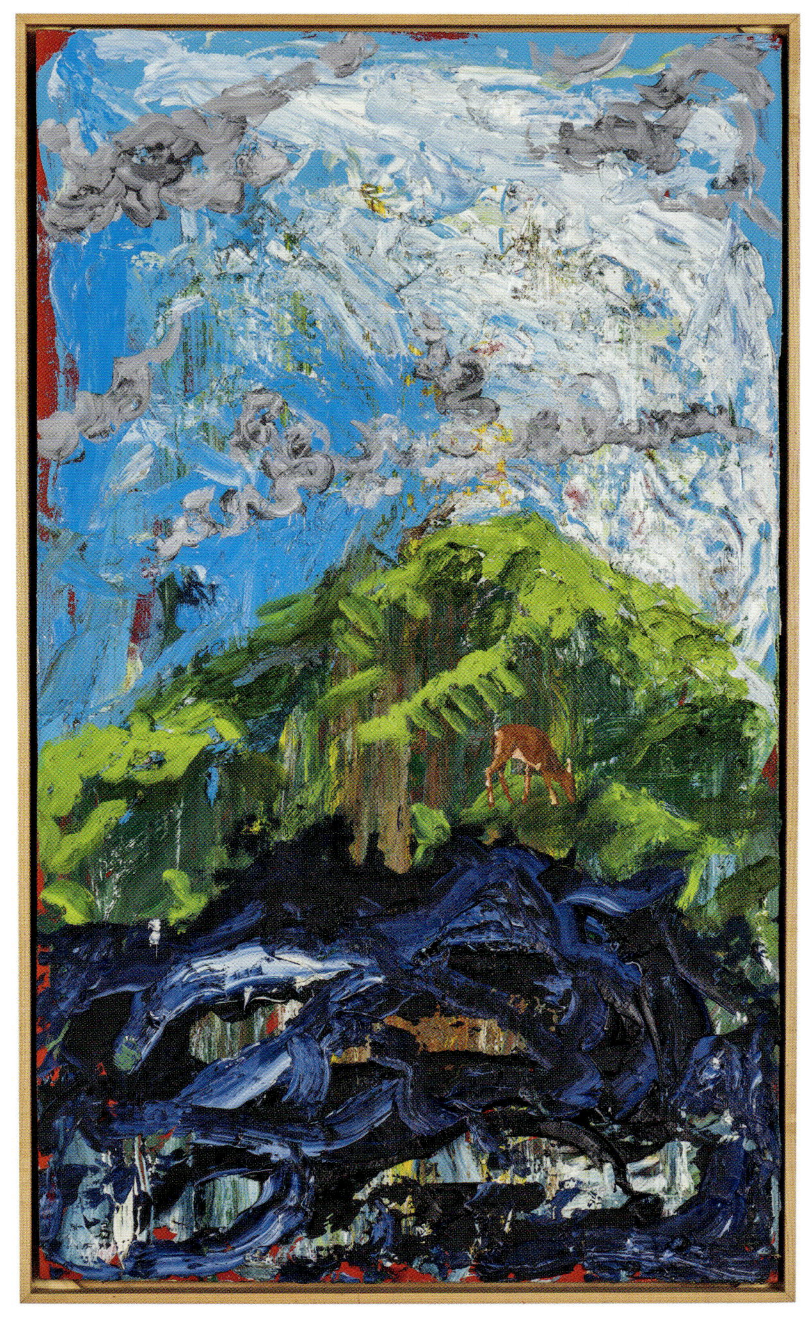

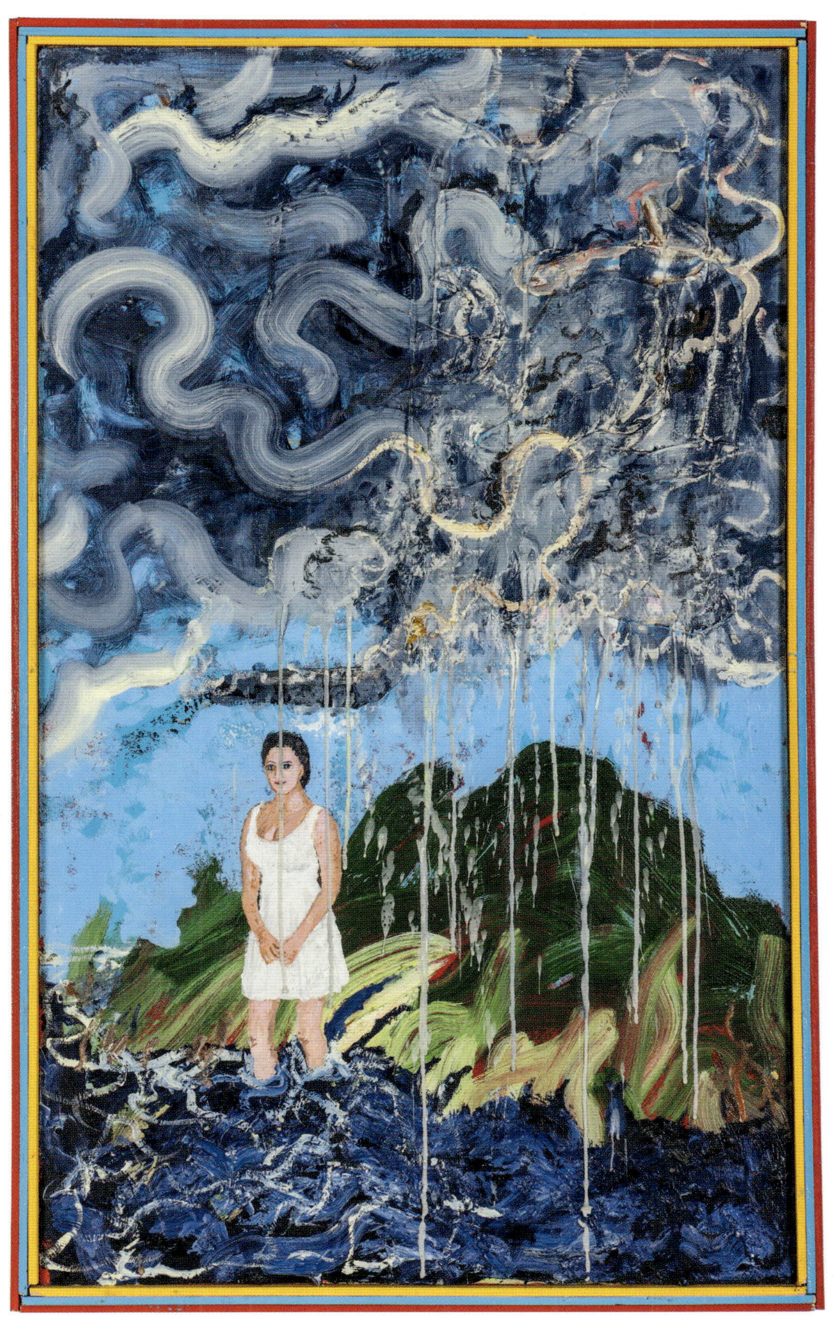

Young Deer by the Pond, 2020
(left)
Oil on panel
30 15/16 x 18 7/8 in

*Annaliet Quero Standing in
the Water*, 2020 (right)
Oil on panel
32 1/2 x 20 11/16 in

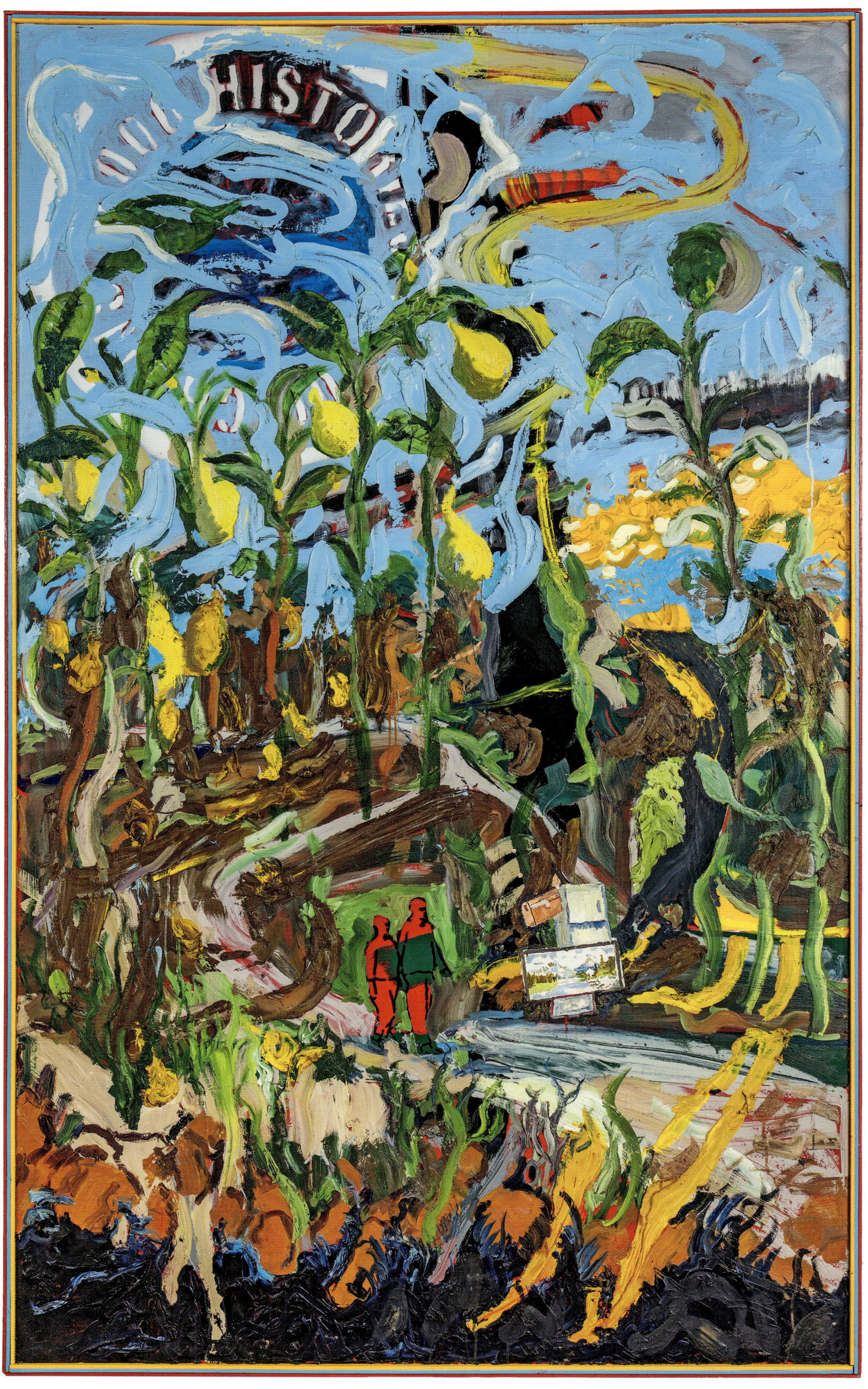
HISTO

K: The paintings that you've been making recently are a lot about citrus and the art of grafting. When did you start learning grafting?

N: Five or ten years ago I became curious about the differentiation between the grafted scion and the rootstock. You can't take a lemon seed and grow an edible lemon. There are many different varieties of mutations, and there are mutations that we as a species have found to be desirable to eat. Yet other species may not like them at all. It's just to our taste. So create the kind we like. Once you have the mutation, be it a Villafranca lemon or a Marrakech Limonetta or a Yuzu, you maintain the mutation through the process of grafting a small part of a tree onto a lower portion of another tree.

K: What drew you to grafting?

N: My interest initially was purely practical. I wanted to be able to grow my own citrus like we grow our own lettuce and we, for a while, had our own pigs. Then I became fascinated by the process and the delicacy of it. There are several different methods, but if you do a bud graft or a cleft graft, what you're trying to do is to line up a very small microscopic layer underneath the bark called the cambium layer with the rootstock. You try and put those two things together, and wrap it with a little bit of tape, and then it takes a month, maybe two months, to see if the graft has taken. And then maybe another two months to see if a bud will form. So it requires a great deal of discipline and provokes a great deal of anxiety. You don't know if it's going to work or not. I found that process to be fascinating, but also I found the metaphoric aspects of it interesting. You have this point of connection where the life of the rootstock meets the genetics of what's been taken from another tree. It's like where the ocular, perceived world, meets the interior world of experience. And this produces a very different fruit, if you like. That's where these recent paintings began. I was painting the graft, painting the process.

K: I remember there was a young Argentine artist, Eduardo Navarro, who once did a piece in which he asked a performer to try to experience time in the way a tortoise experiences time. This might sound comical, but he was deadly serious. He was trying to conceive of the ways in which the world would be different if we experienced time the way a tortoise does. Cultivating the patience to wait to see whether a graft will take seems, to a degree, to be you getting on plant time. And some of what I've experienced in these newer paintings of yours is a different sense of time.

N: As we were talking about earlier, we construct the reality that we're obliged to construct as humans, and Abe is obliged to construct his own reality as a pig, and the citrus is obliged to create its own sense of itself as a plant. But there isn't really a hierarchy. One of the things I find questionable is the idea of a hierarchy. When you spend time with those different species' constructions, I think it's inevitable that you realize that it's just one of millions of constructions species are obliged to make that process to be fascinating, but also I found the metaphoric aspects of it interesting. You have this point of connection where the life of the rootstock meets the genetics of what's been taken from another tree. It's like where the ocular, perceived world meets the interior world of experience. And this produces a very different fruit, if you like. That's where these recent paintings began. I was painting the graft, painting the process.

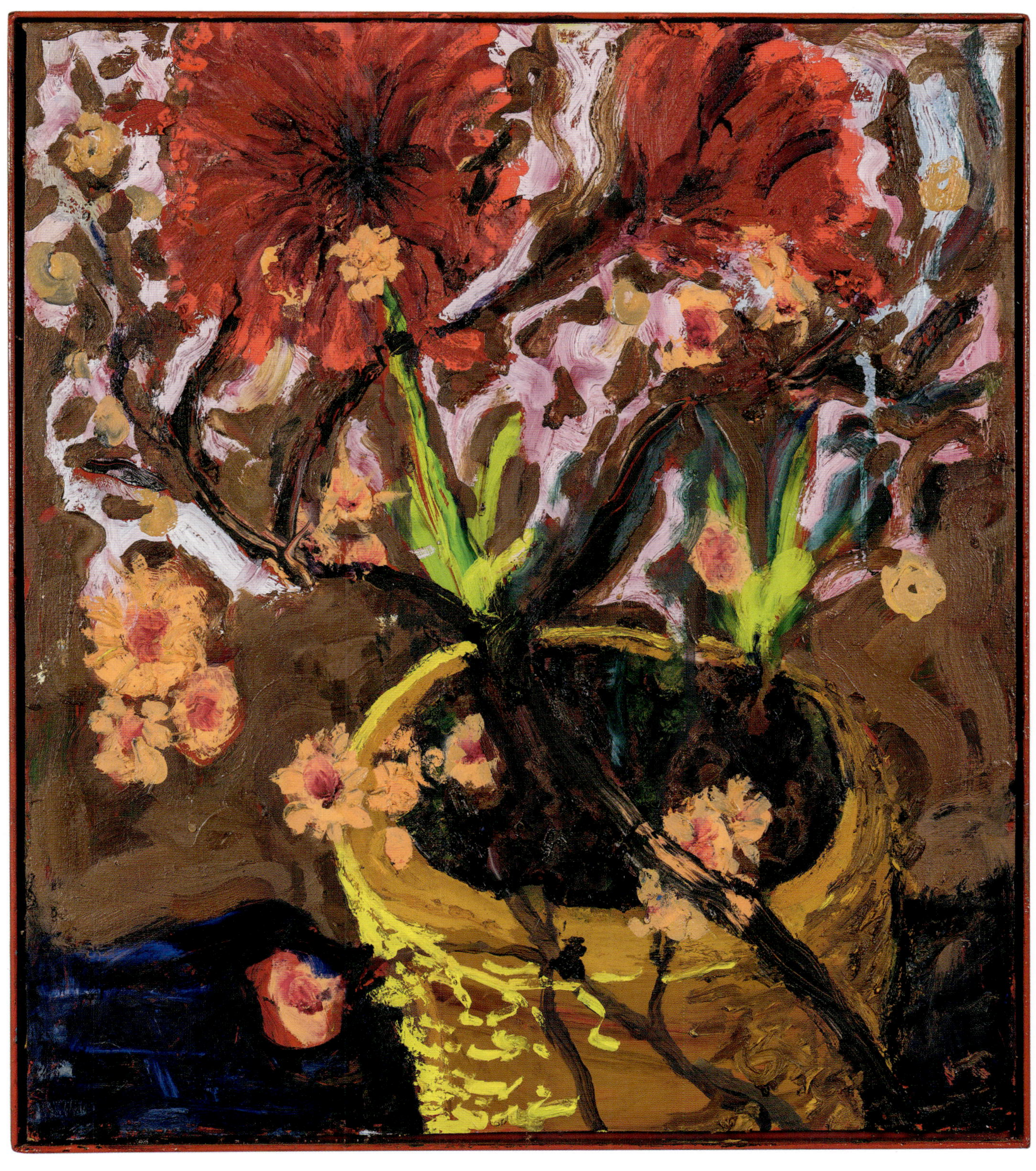

Amaryllis in a Pot, 2020
Oil on panel
20 3/4 x 18 3/4 in

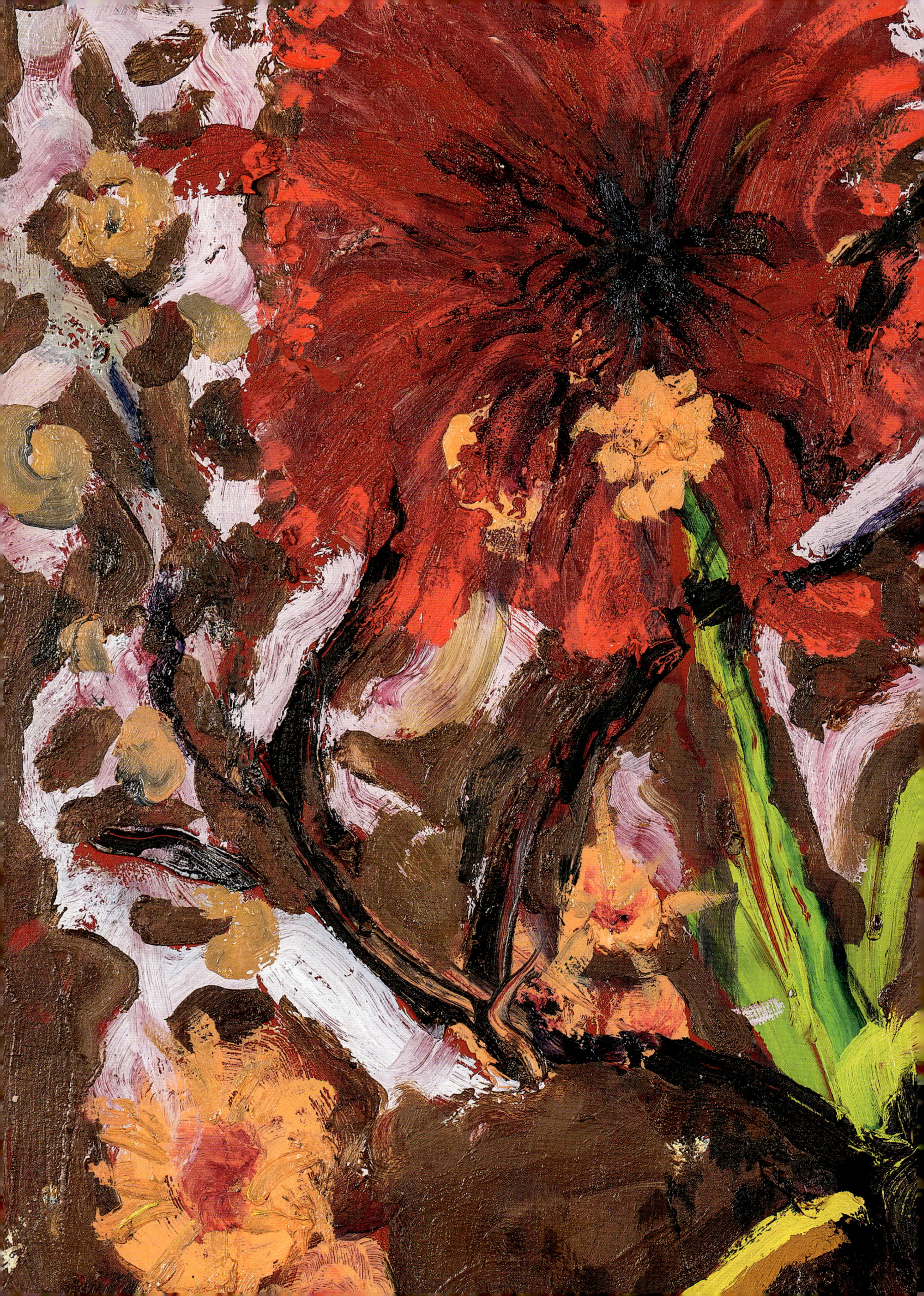

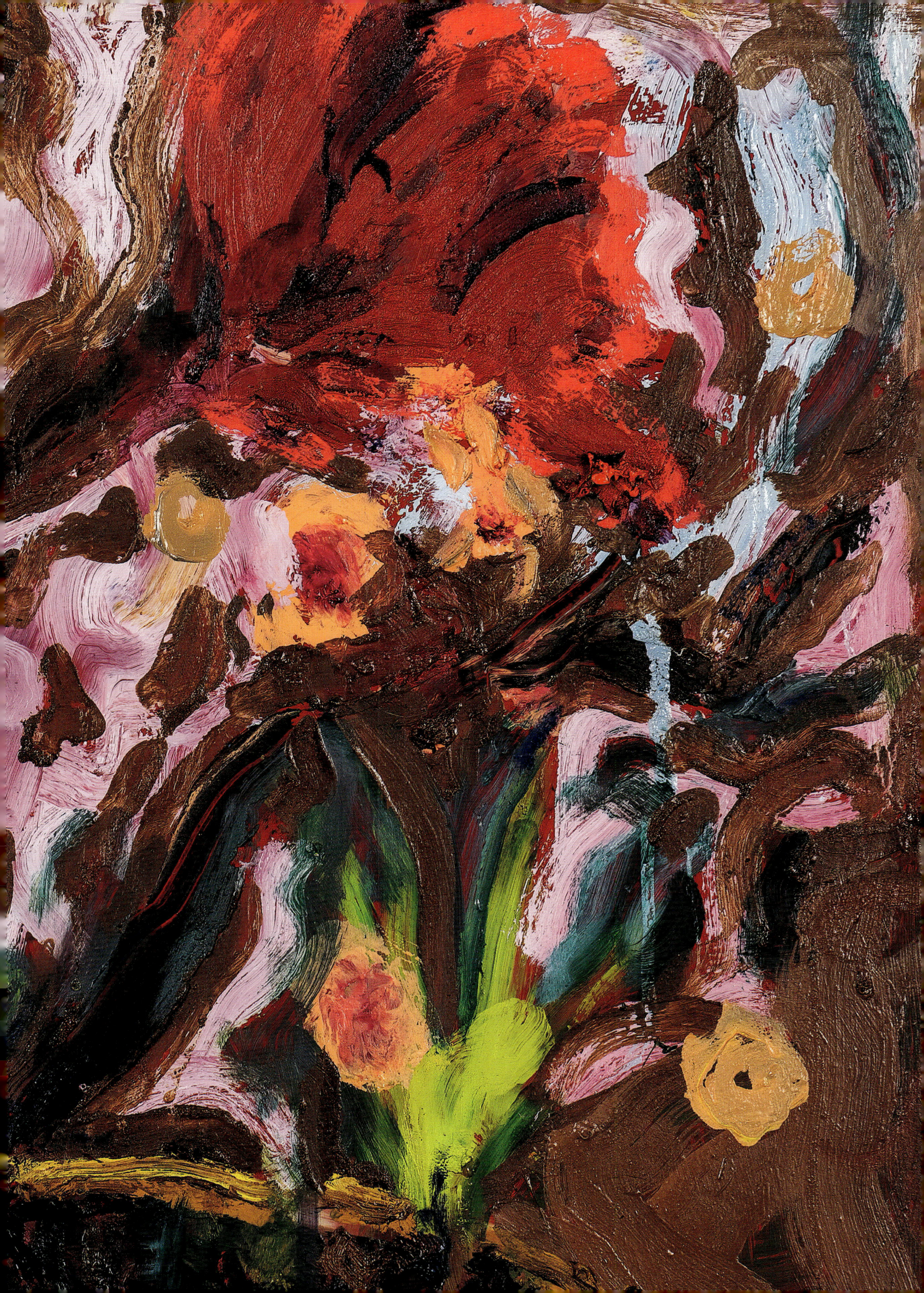

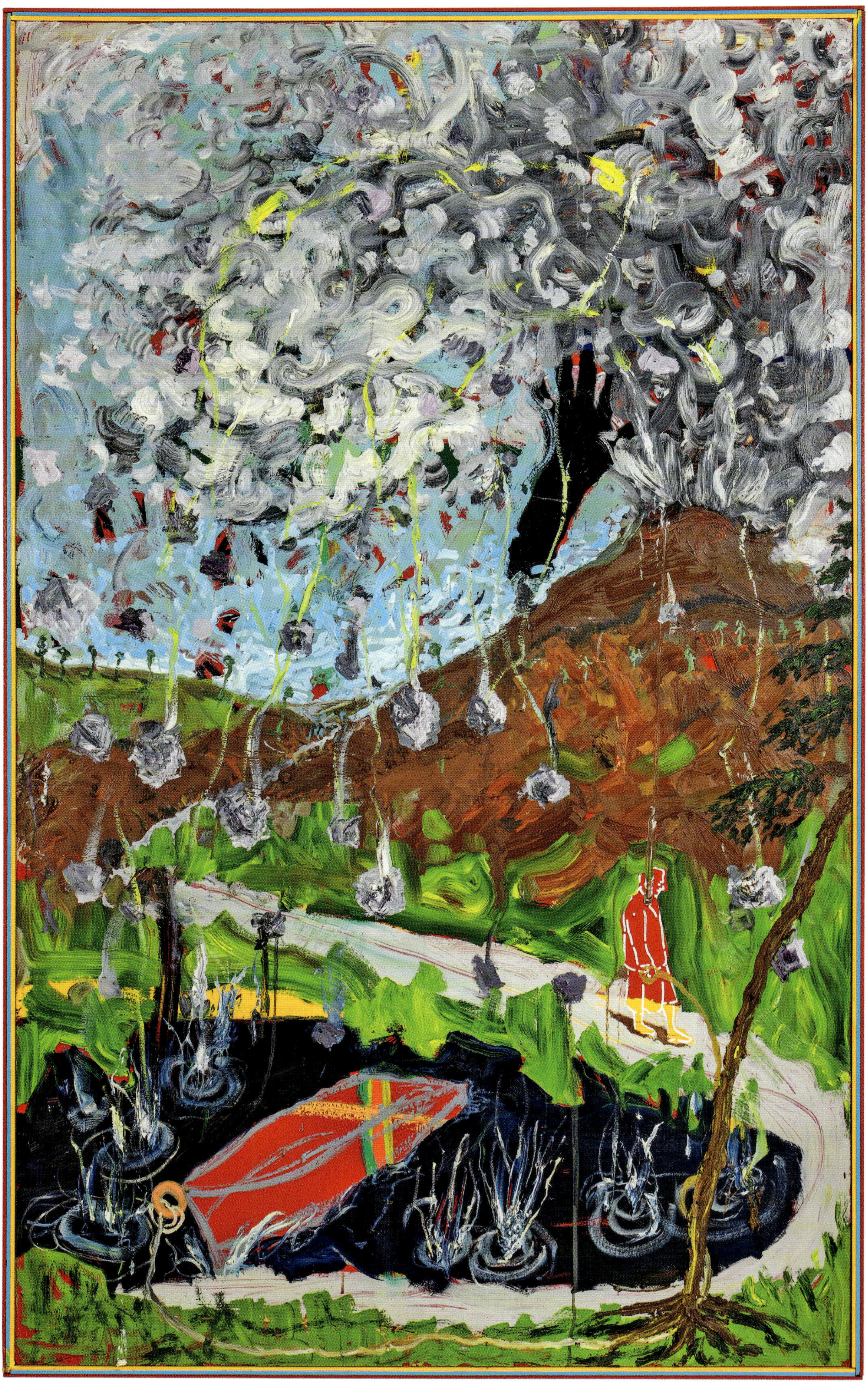

Red Figure Walking to Red Boat
(Volcano Erupting), 2020
Oil on panel
77 7/8 x 49 1/2 in

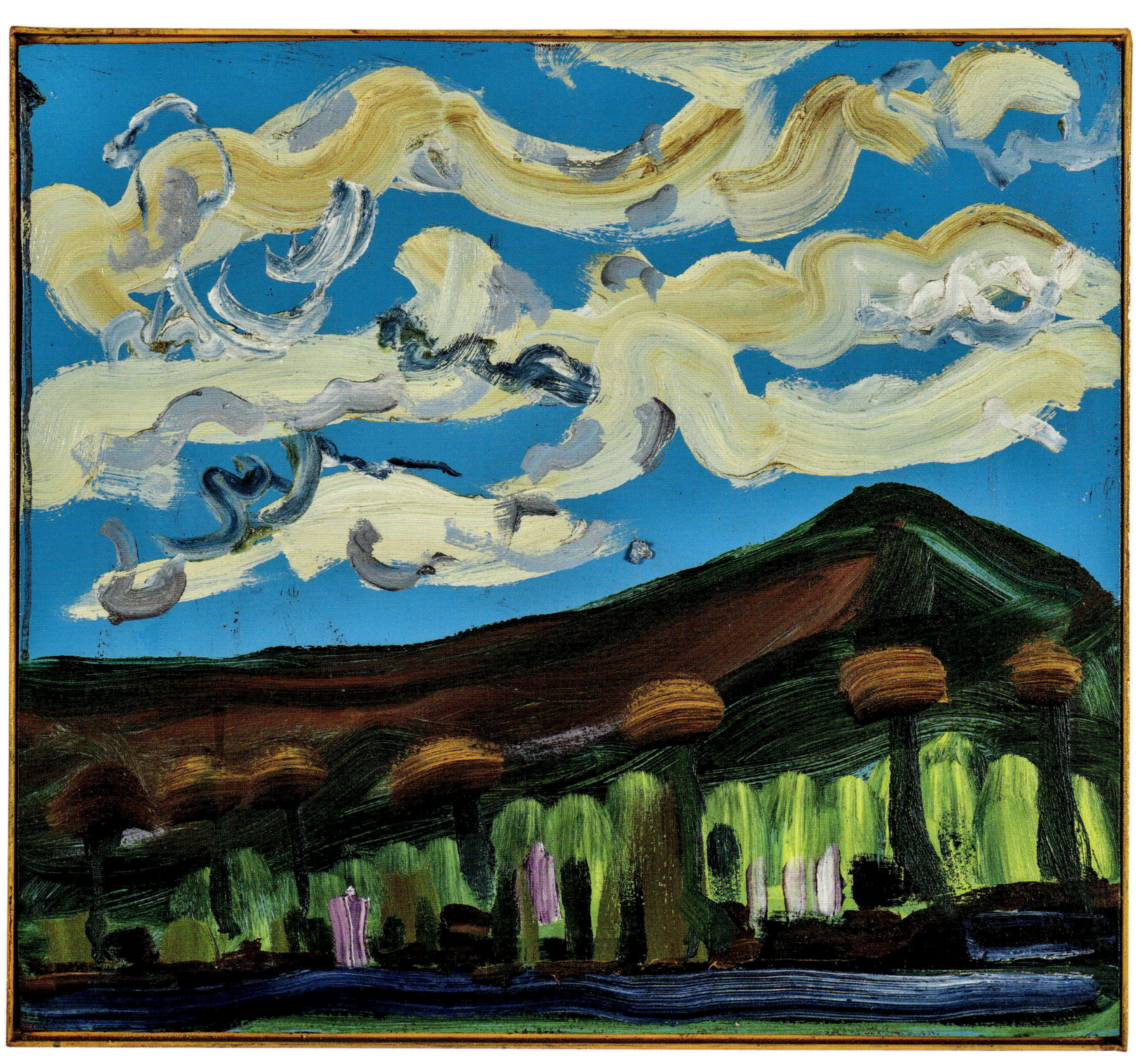

The Water Flows From the Culvert to the Pond, to
Catskill Creek, to the Hudson River, 2020
Oil on panel
18 13/16 x 20 3/4 in

K: Why do you think we as a species began to make objects and put lines and shapes and colors on walls?

N: Young children from anywhere, from a very young age, begin to make marks and to represent their experience. That's how they create their worlds. We create our worlds ideationally and we also create them through representation. Drawing helps set up the cognitive processes that make us human. This idea that kids play through making work–of course they do, but in doing so they're also forming a sense of spatial relationships. So that in later life, for example, when they hold up their hand in front of the landscape and it appears huge, they realize that the hand is actually very small, even though it takes up an enormous amount of the visual field, and the landscape is very large even though it appears to be the same size. We learn from making representations of our spatial experience.

K: There was a psychologist and educator in the Bay Area named Rhoda Kellogg who became obsessed with the art that children made. She traveled and eventually collected millions of examples of art made by young children from around the world. And she found commonalities in the ways children started to understand how to visualize a human body or a structure or what a house looked like across very disparate cultures and economic levels.

N: In a sense, we come to the same conclusions. By repetition, children figure out that the most efficient way of putting the water from the jug into the glass is by moving the hand in a certain way. There's an analogy to the beehive as well, because within a beehive, bees have many different roles, and there's no central controlling force. The queen does not control the hive, except by her pheromone. If the pheromone is strong, the bees will, for whatever reason, be able to adapt to the different roles. So if there are dead bees, the undertaker bees will take them out. Or the undertaker bees will change roles to become nest bees if that's needed, or guards or, if the hive gets too hot, air conditioner bees who cool it off with their wings. But if the pheromone of the queen becomes weak, then the social structure of the hive begins to collapse. It's fascinating because the bees don't know it's the pheromone of the queen that creates social cohesion. It does make you wonder if we really understand what creates or fails to create our social cohesion.

Curt and Mert Landscaping, 2020
Oil on panel
77 3/8 x 48 1/2 in

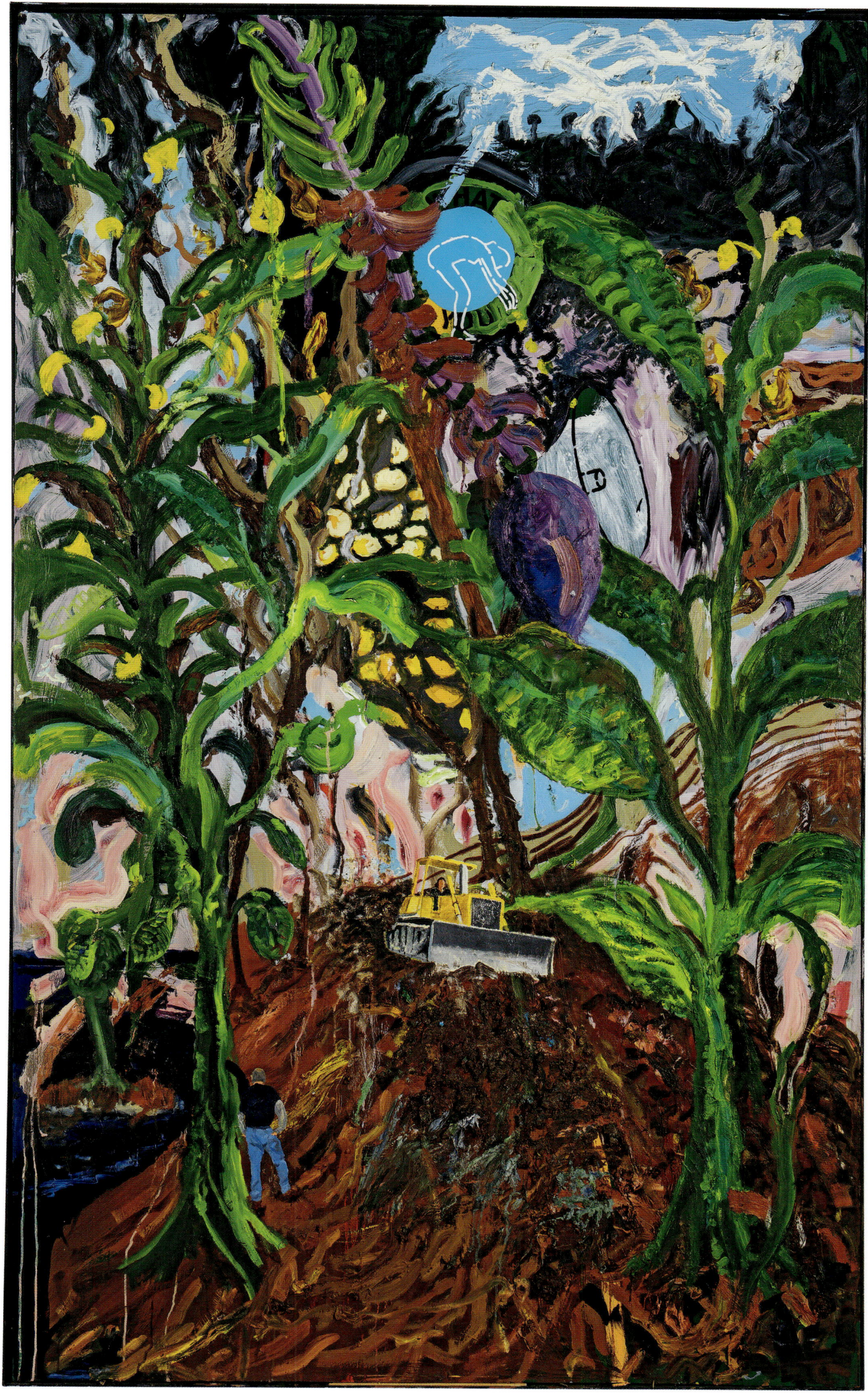

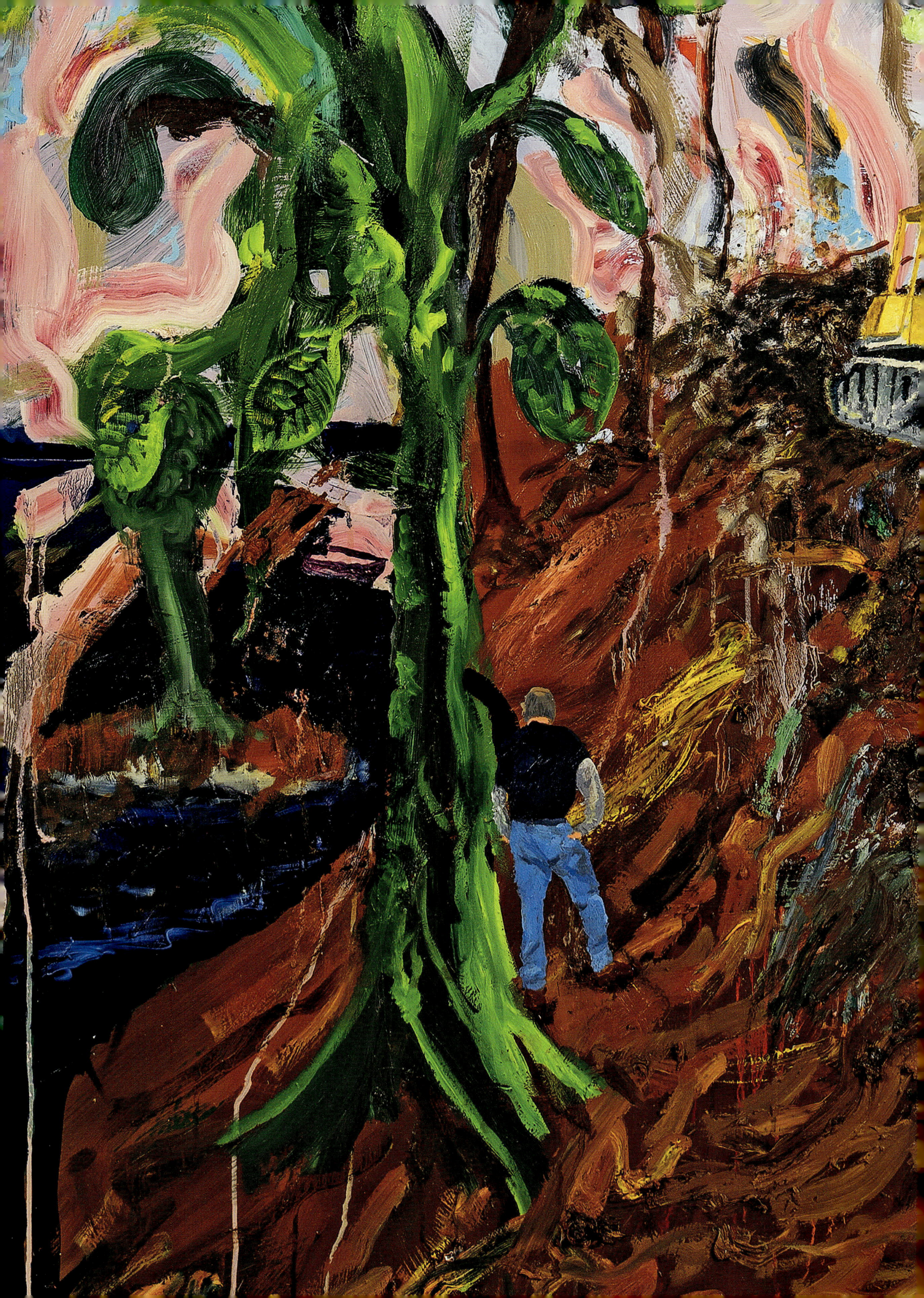

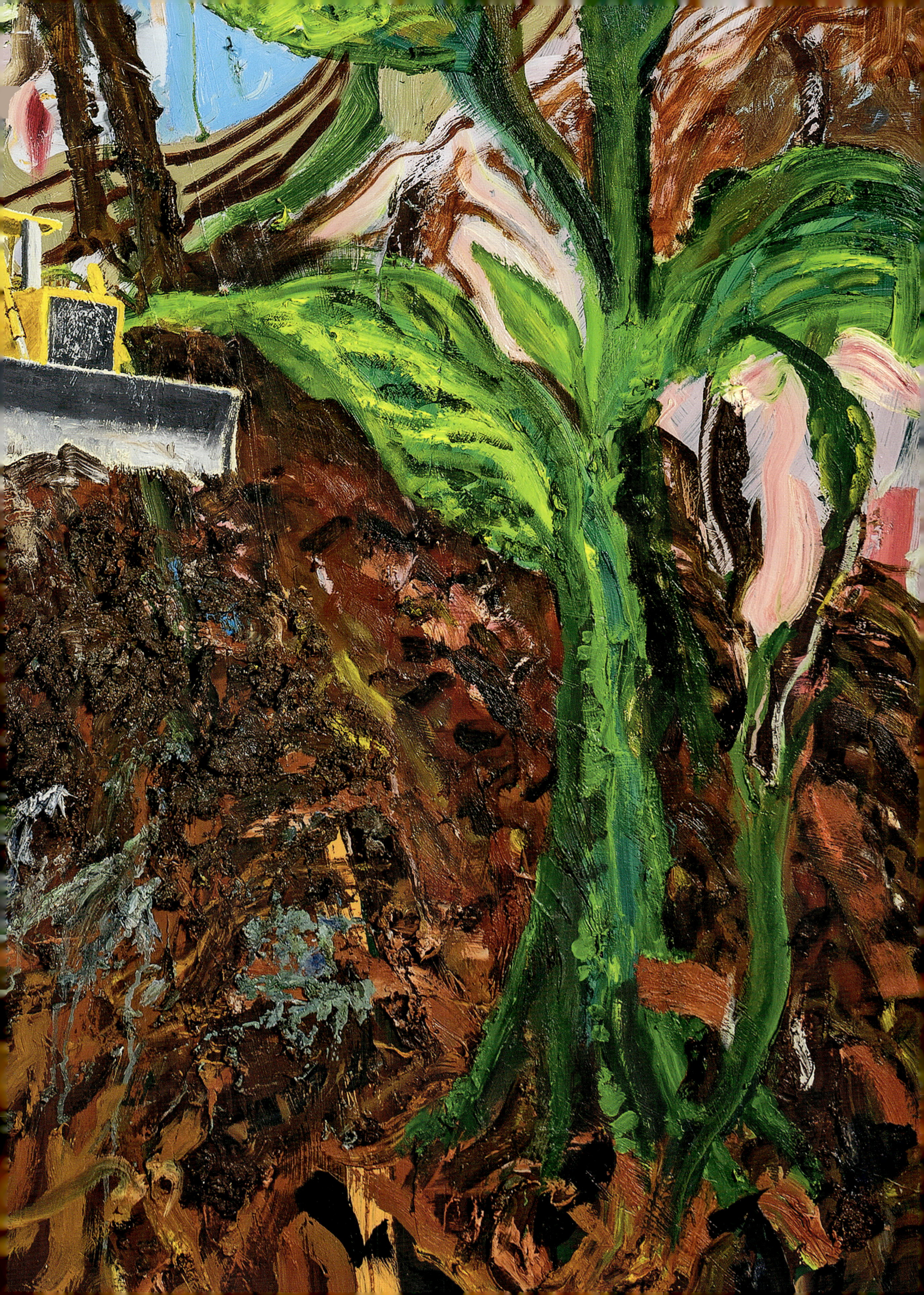

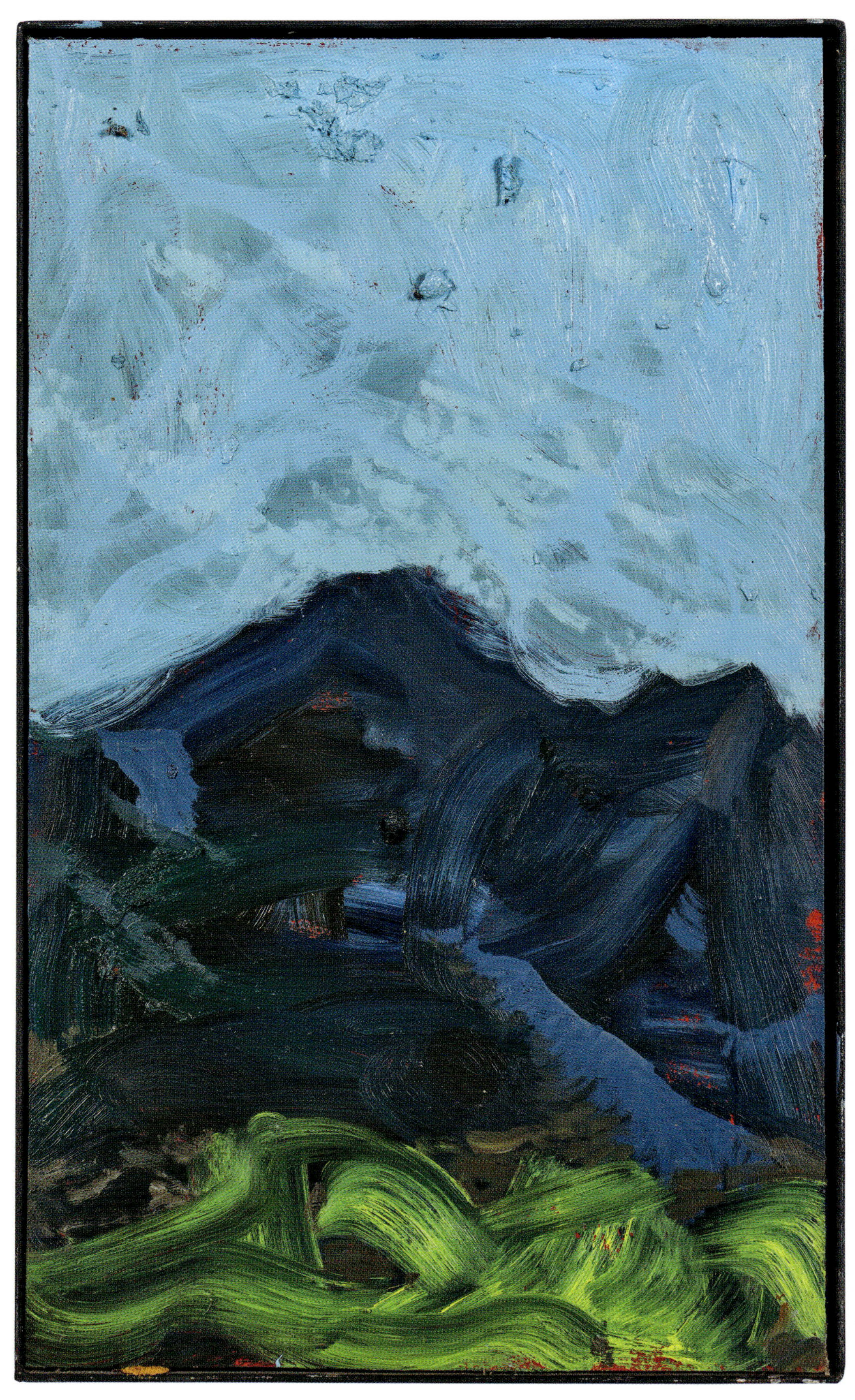

Mount Pisgah at Dusk, 2020
Oil on panel
20 3/4 x 12 3/4 in

K: All of this makes me think about when we use terms like good or bad or quality when we talk about art. I was just on vacation with my family in Rome and Venice and London, looking at Greek bronzes and Renaissance art and medieval art and prehistoric art. And it strikes me that when you go to a museum and look at a broad enough historical swath of art and you think about the term quality, it seems to be a strange word to use. What you see instead is that there were various needs met by what the artists were doing during the time in which they were living, and some artists, of course, met those needs in more highly-skilled and accomplished and interesting ways, ways that other artists couldn't or didn't meet. But those judgments were deeply bound up with the needs that people had, or that the church had, or patrons had, or a religion or creed had. And such judgments are still bound up with our needs, even though the needs— what we want from art and what it can do for us—have become a lot broader and more complex.

N: I agree with you, and it comes back to paradox and contradiction. Because the kind of theologies being expressed by most of those artists are ones most of us now don't believe in. And yet paradoxically, the expression given to the misconception can be extremely beautiful. We don't know where Raphael stood on the question of belief. Maybe he was a true believer. Who knows? I've also wondered, if you were in the workshop of Phidias working on the Acropolis all day, for years and years, then what kind of art did you have in your house? What did you want to look at? Were those guys making little pieces that looked like what they made in their day job? Or did they think, "I've been working all day, and I'm sick of this shit, and I'm going to get a couple of pieces from the market that just make me happy to look at," something that might have been considered the kitsch of its day, but really who knows? Maybe it would look marvelous to us now.

Sharkey's Cow Beneath a Culvert, 2020
Oil on panel
77 3/8 x 48 3/8 in

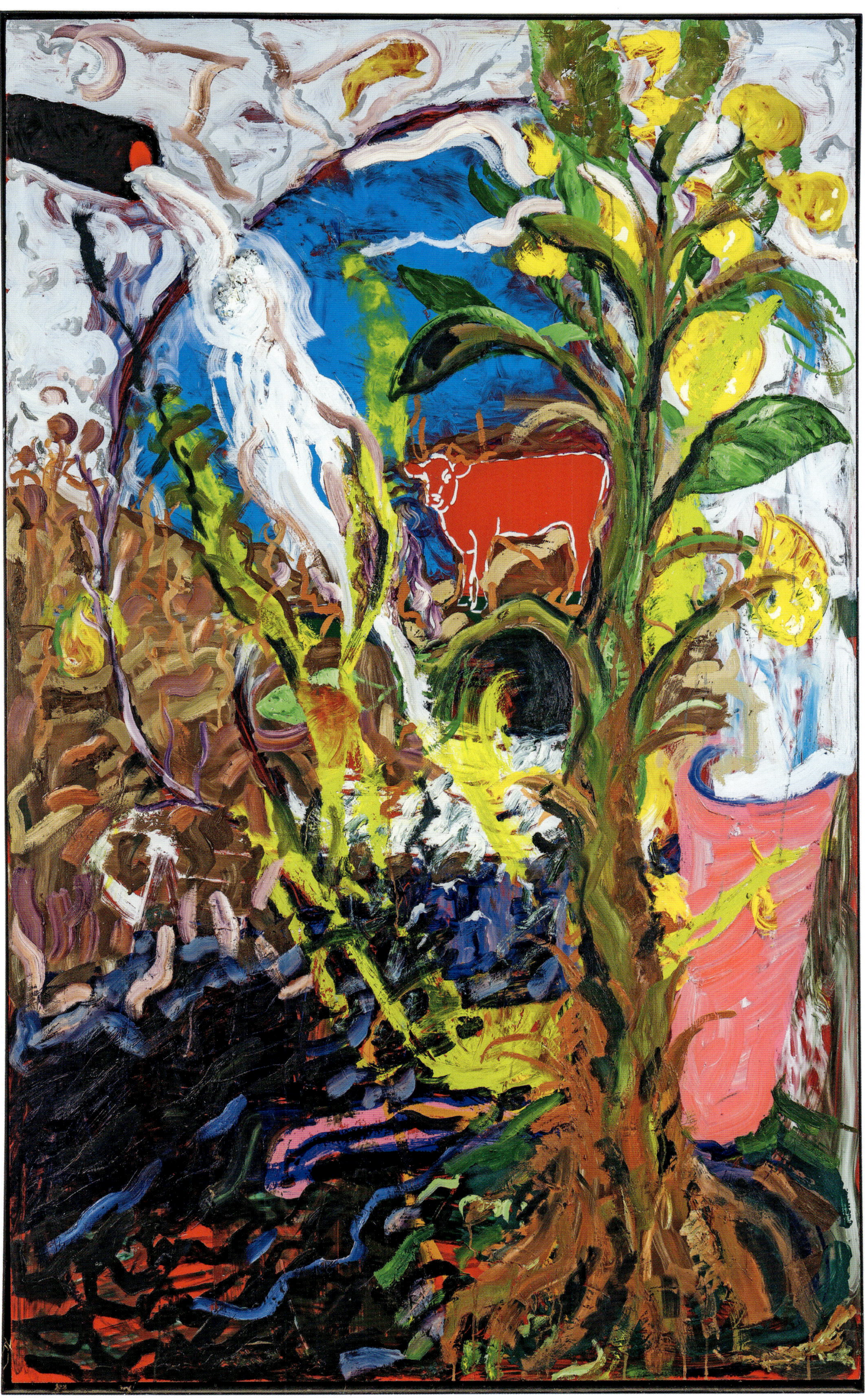

K: I've been reading Leo Steinberg's *The Sexuality of Christ in Renaissance Art.* And he argues that one of the reasons that the early Renaissance, from Giotto on, began to move toward what would conventionally be called verisimilitude was, in part, to stress Christ's existence as a flesh-and-blood man, a fact essential to the mechanics of the salvation theology. It was one way to counter heretical beliefs that Christ had a spectral divine body, not a corporeal one. So all of that beauty and technique and accomplishment and visual poetry, which continues to awe us, might not have come into being in the way it did if it didn't do so in service of specific needs, in service of a particular theology.

N: I think you're right. And the irony is that as it seemed to be more real, it became more ocular. But actually, ocularity isn't anything like the full reality of our visual experience. So a lot of the art that was made by cultures that were once considered—that terrible word—primitive, actually expressed a much more sophisticated and grounded understanding of how we experience the world. But of course, if you moved away from ocularity or the ocular in Catholicism, it could smack of heresy.

K: You've talked about this next question with me before: Do you have any desire to think about portraiture again?

N: I've been working on portraits for many, many years. It's a real challenge because, again, you come up against visual representation but also how that representation actually exists within the mind. So if I'm looking at you, I have ocular input, but then if I turn the other way, how do you exist? You don't exist in an ocular fashion, but you're still there. I can hear you, but I also assume that I can see you. The thing that I'm working on now is how to access and represent, if you will, that invisible world, which is as real as the ocular.

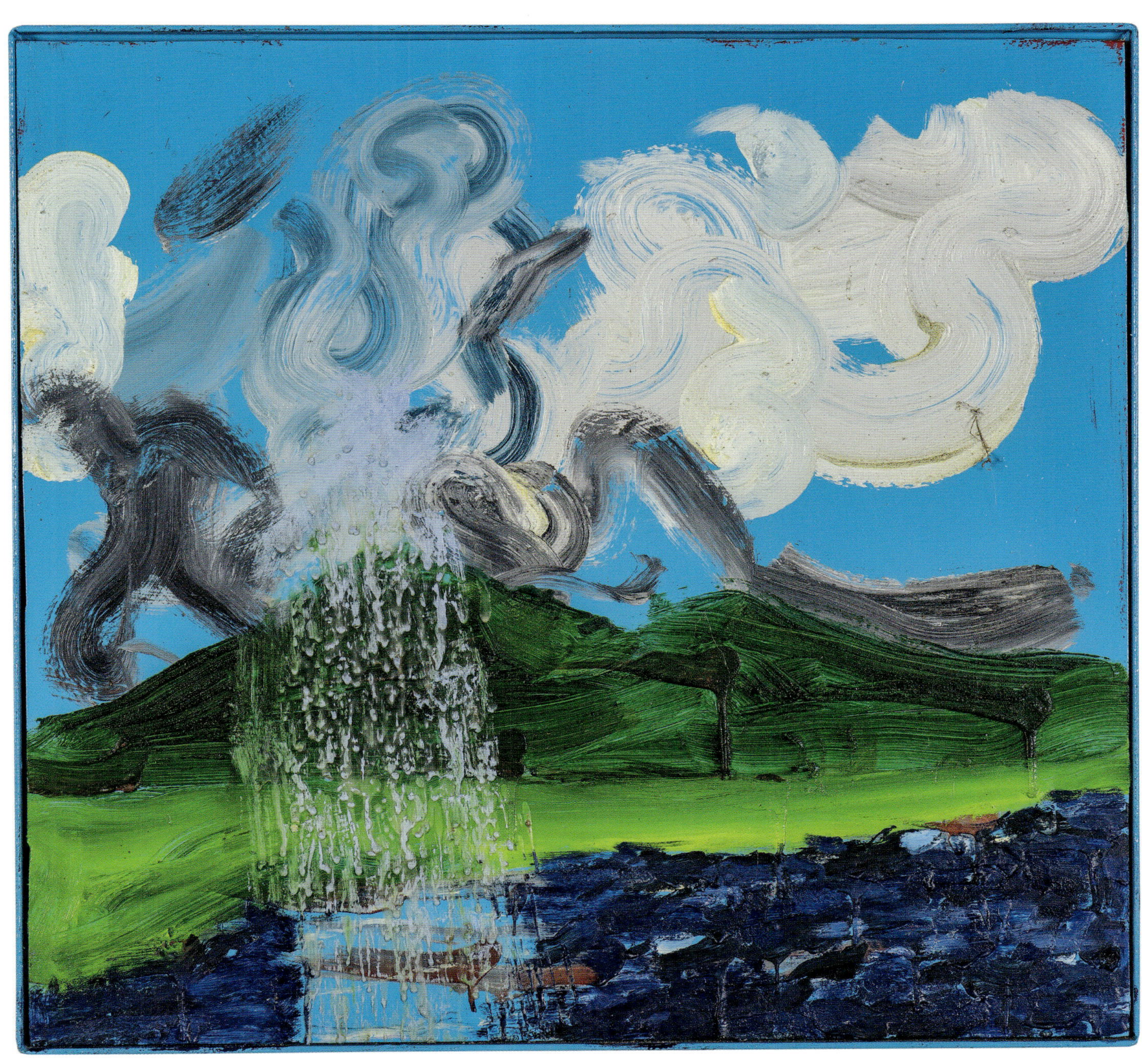

*Cloud Burst of Wax Rain Falls
onto the Pond*, 2020
Oil on panel
18 13/16 x 20 3/4 in

Stu Sugar Standing in the Water, 2020
Oil on panel
34 3/4 x 32 in

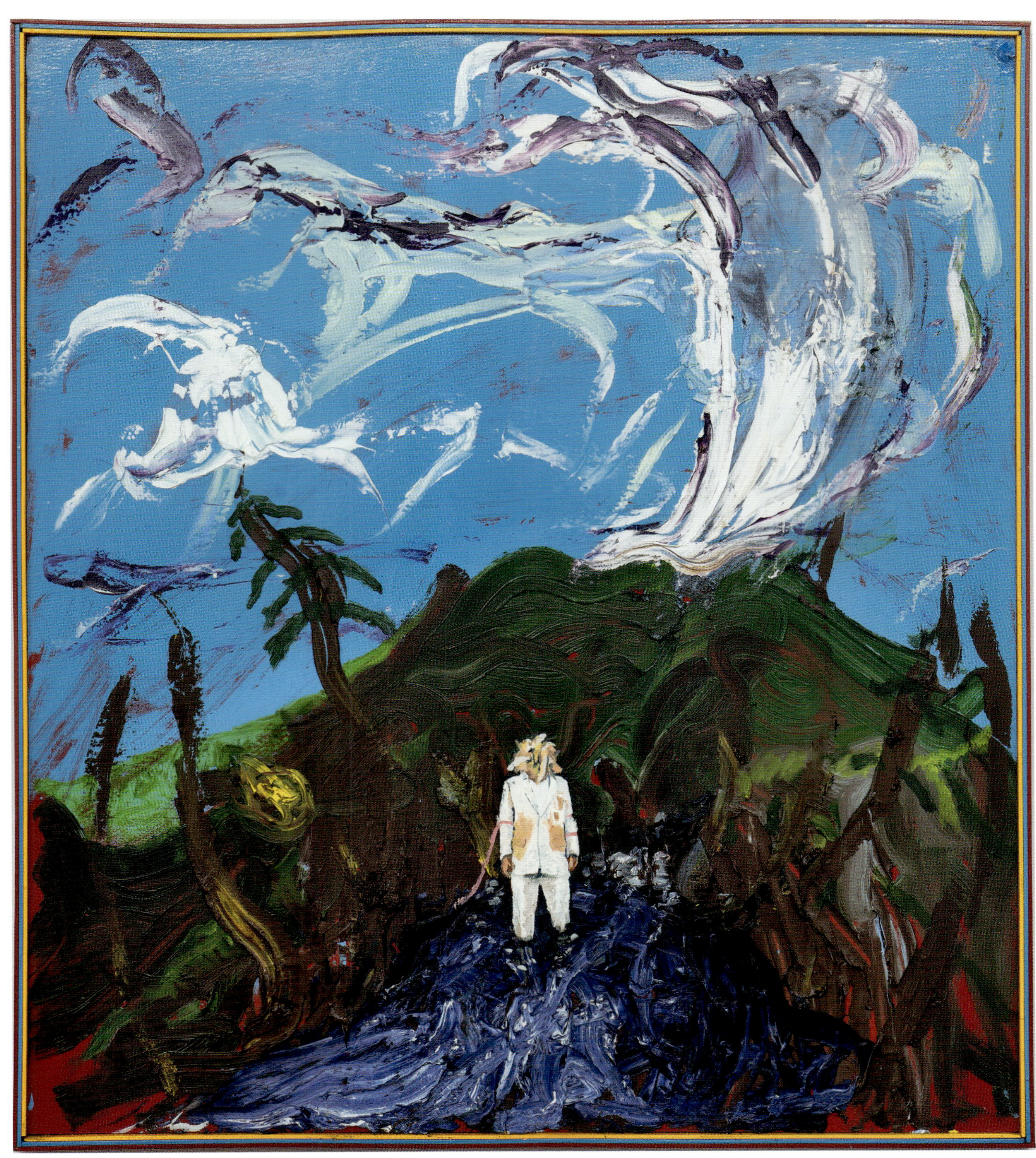

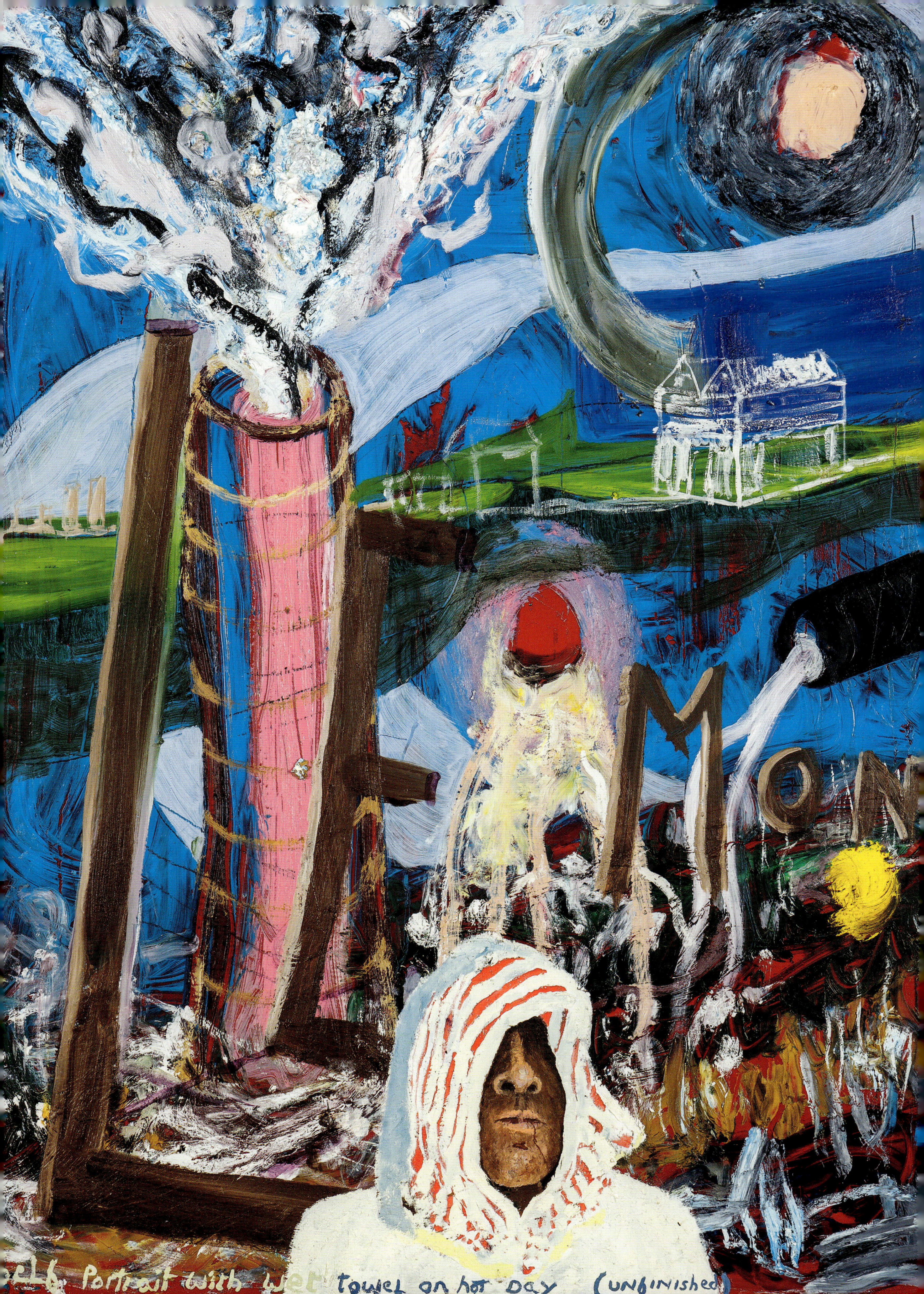

MON
Self Portrait with wet towel on hot Day   (unfinished)

K: The show at Off Paradise is called "The Distance from a Lemon to Murder," which, you've told me, derives from that kind of thinking, about what a lemon "looks like" and how you think about what it looks like and how the idea of a lemon relates to other things in the mind, even things as disparate as murder. It's such a great, weird title. Where did it come from?

N: One thing I'd forgotten that must have been in the back of my mind is that I read a biography of Stalin maybe ten years ago. And it turns out that Stalin was a real devotee of citrus grafting. I don't know why I didn't remember this for practically a decade. But there is an extraordinary scene in the biography, describing how Stalin would spend a lot of his time in Sochi, where he had a citrus grove and he'd be working on the citrus, grafting the trees, taking gentle care of them as you have to do. And then he'd be given lists of all the people who were to be shot. He worked on his citrus. He signed the lists, pages long, and everyone on the list would soon be dead, as Stalin kept working on his trees. That difference between the actions, the careful grafting and the mass horror, I realize now, must have been in my mind without knowing it.

K: And do you sense any totalitarian aspects in yourself as you're sitting there grafting away, grafting your lemons? [Laughs]

N: Well, there is that part of being an artist in which you have the power to construct a world just as you want it, without contradiction, without paradox, without having to understand the basic nature of things. So there's a kind of doctrinaire aspect, a godlike aspect to it, that probably relates deeply to things that were in the mind of Stalin and others of his ilk. I haven't been handed the list thus far. And if they give it to me, I hope I'll say, "You know something? I think that we should tear the list up."

K: Let's let them all live?

N: Let them live. And let them all loose.

*Self Portrait with Wet Towel on a
Hot Day (unfinished)*, 2020
Oil on panel
42 3/4 x 33 3/4 in

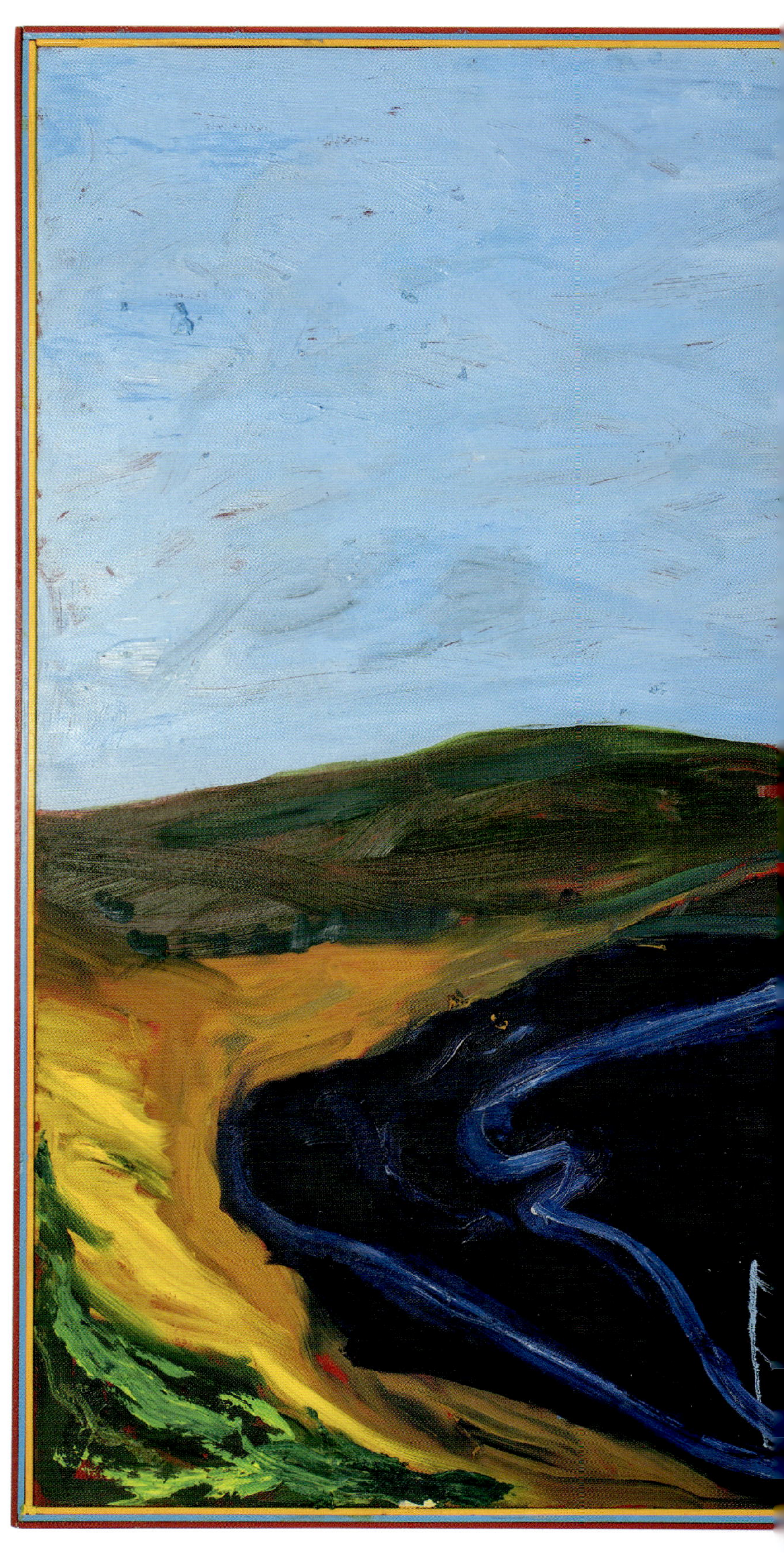

*Johan Jumps from a Tree into
the Pond*, 2020
Oil on panel
49 7/16 x 77 5/8 in

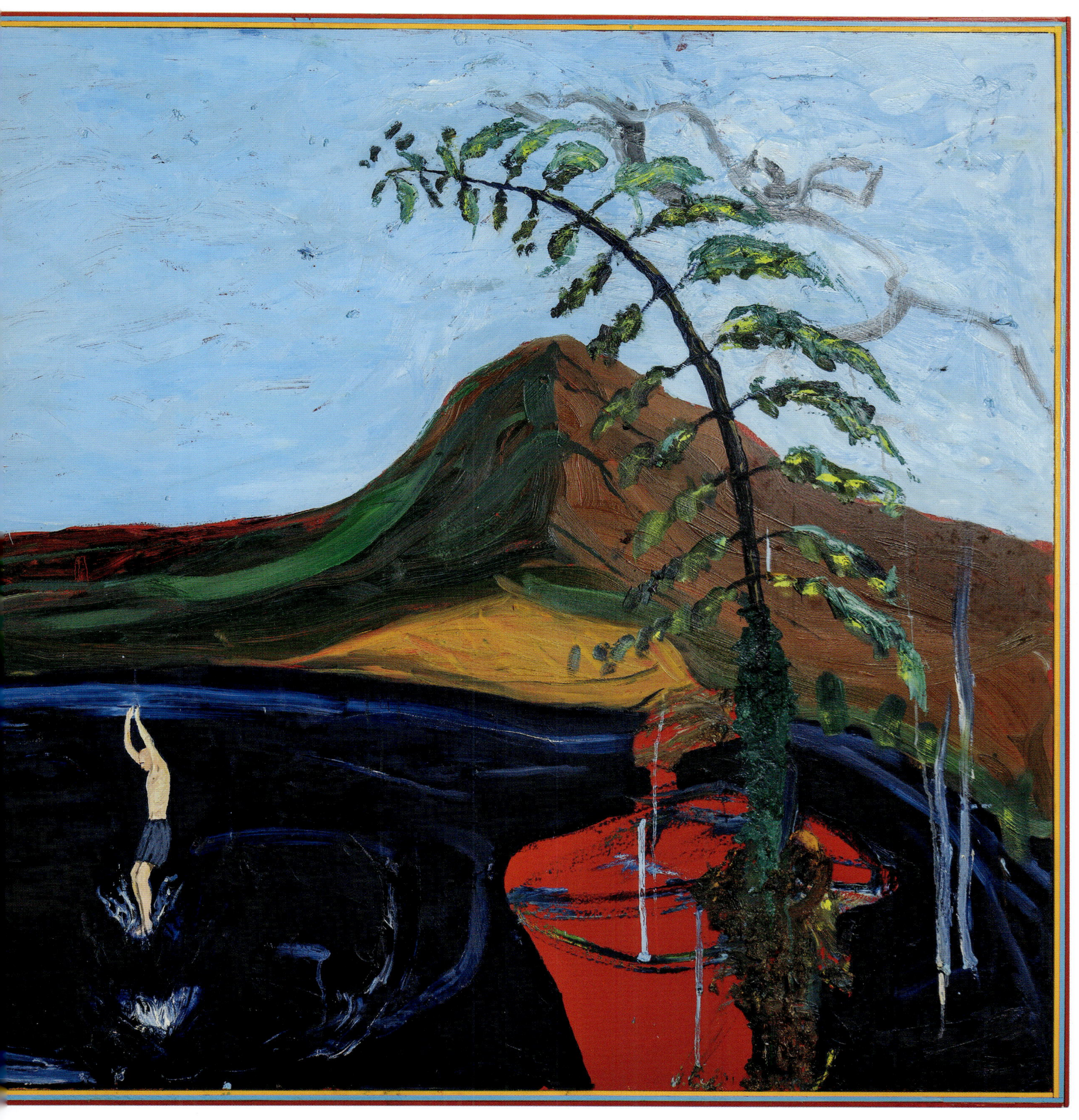

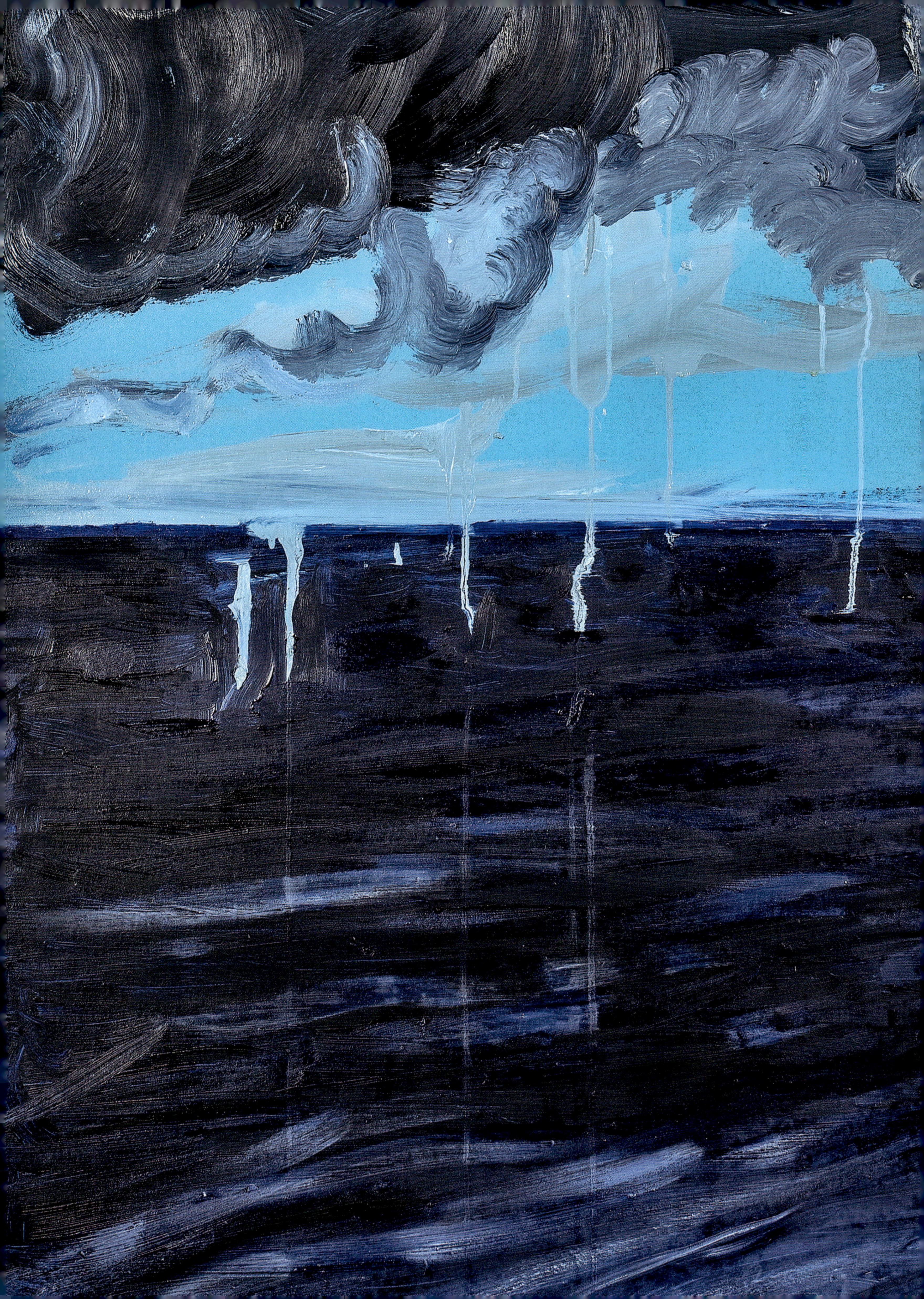

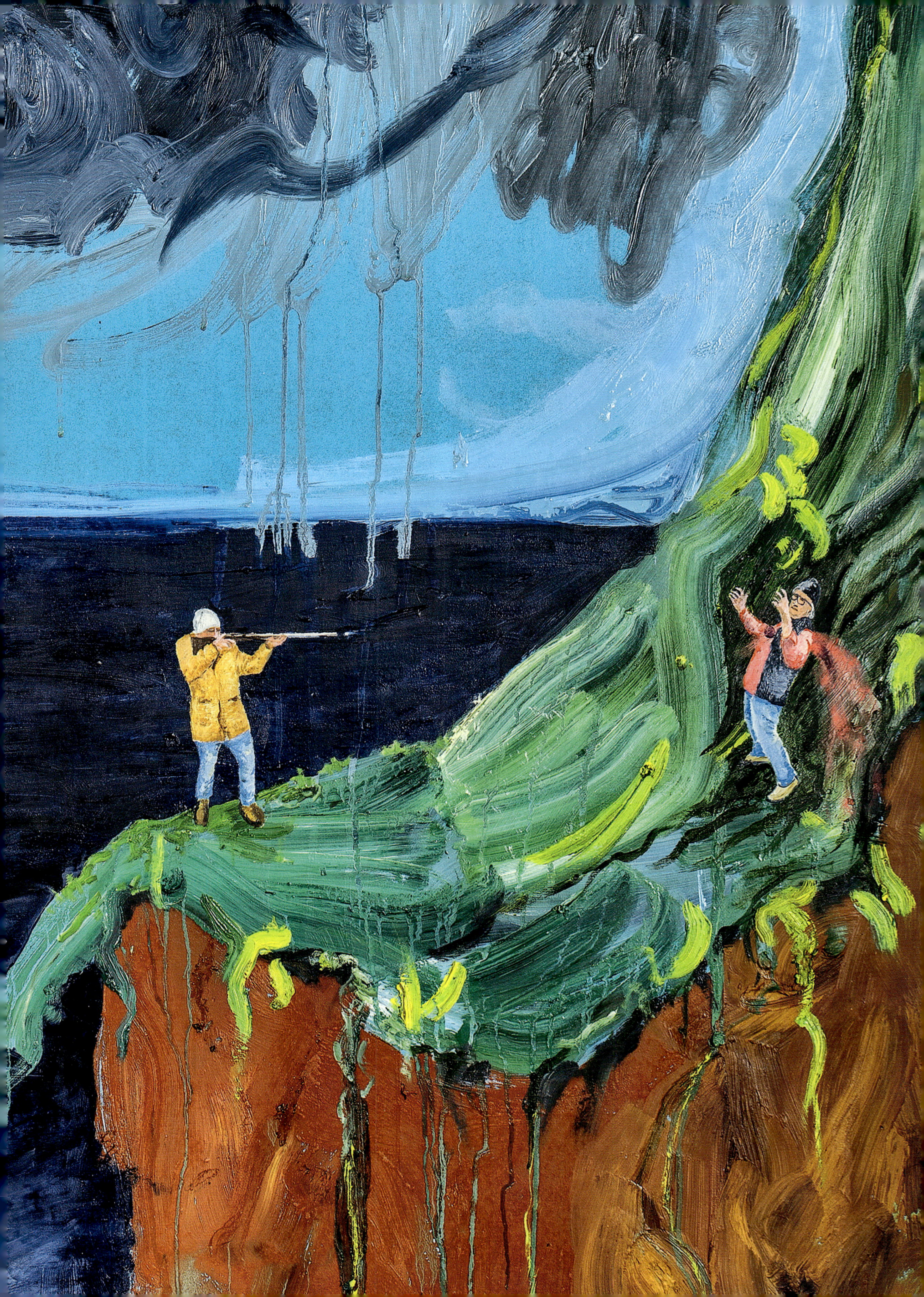

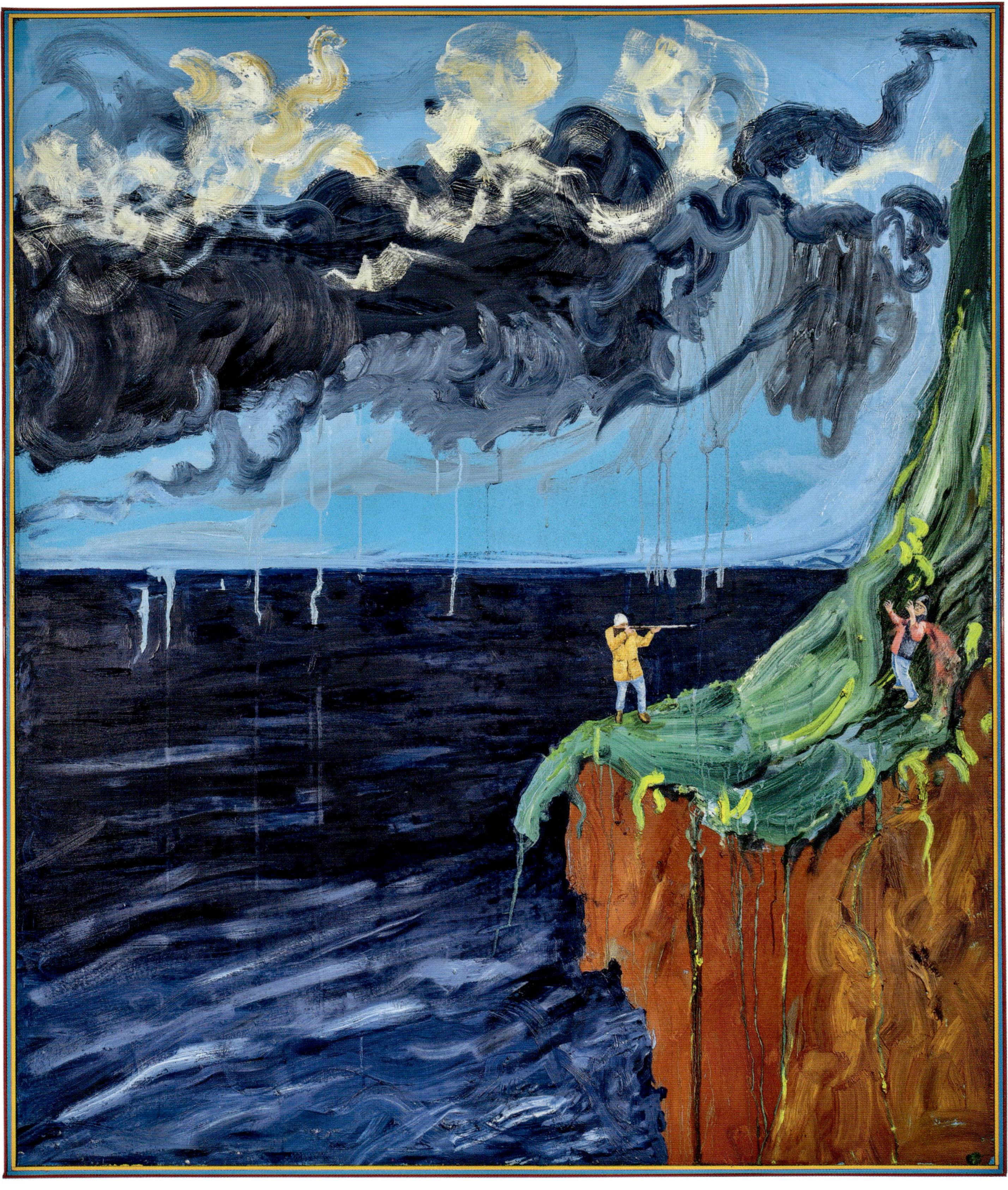

*I Am Shot: A Murder to
Prevent Murder*, 2020
Oil on panel
57 x 49 1/4 in

The Invisible World

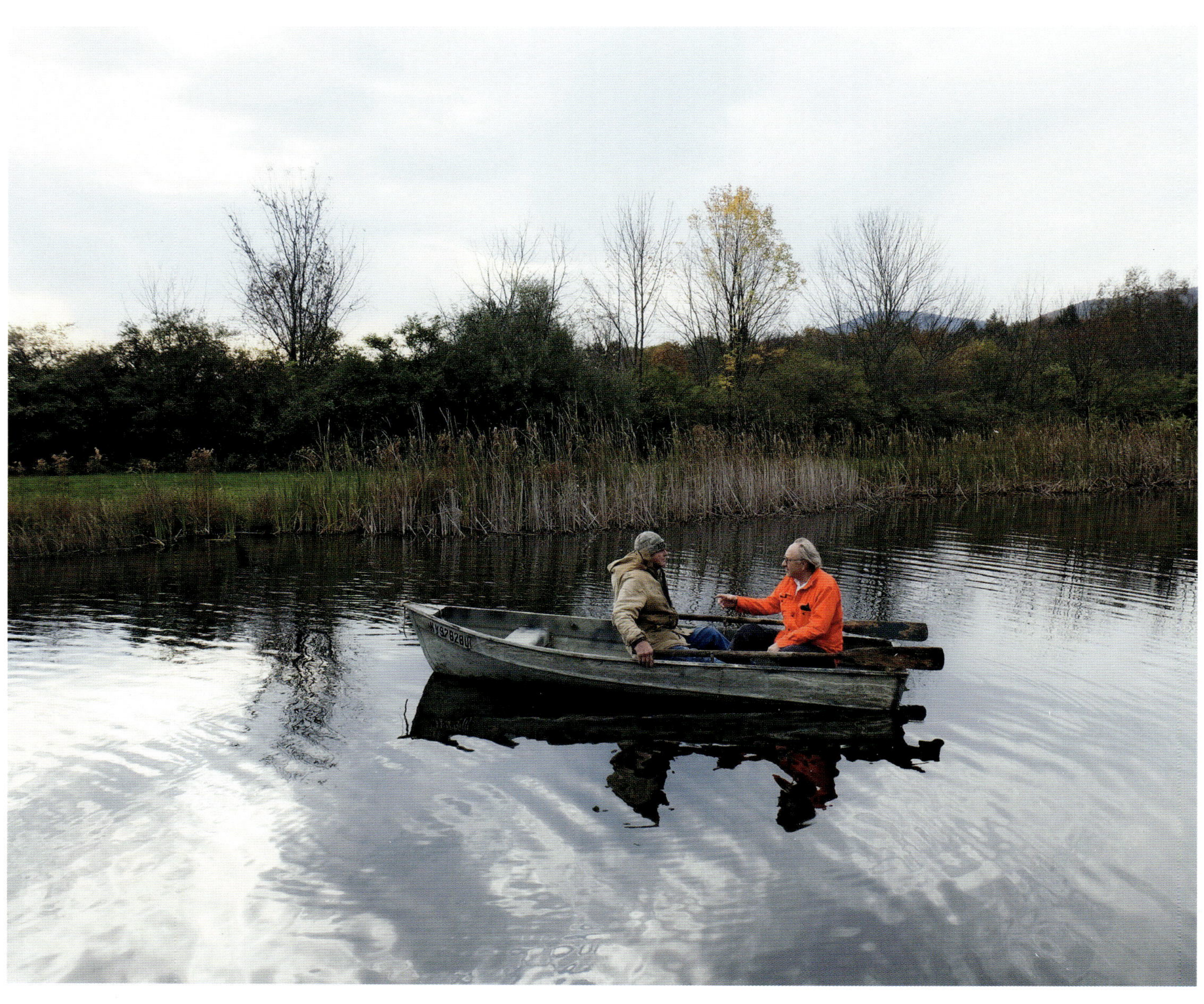

Peter Nadin & Gary on the pond; Old Field Farm, 2022

" ...I look at the pond and see fish...golden orfe swim in the water.
I turn and see Mount Pisgah, and the fish swim in my mind.
I pick up a brush, and the fish swim in the paint..."

The Secret Wedding of the
Invisible Man, 2022
Oil on panel
43 3/4 x 34 7/8 in

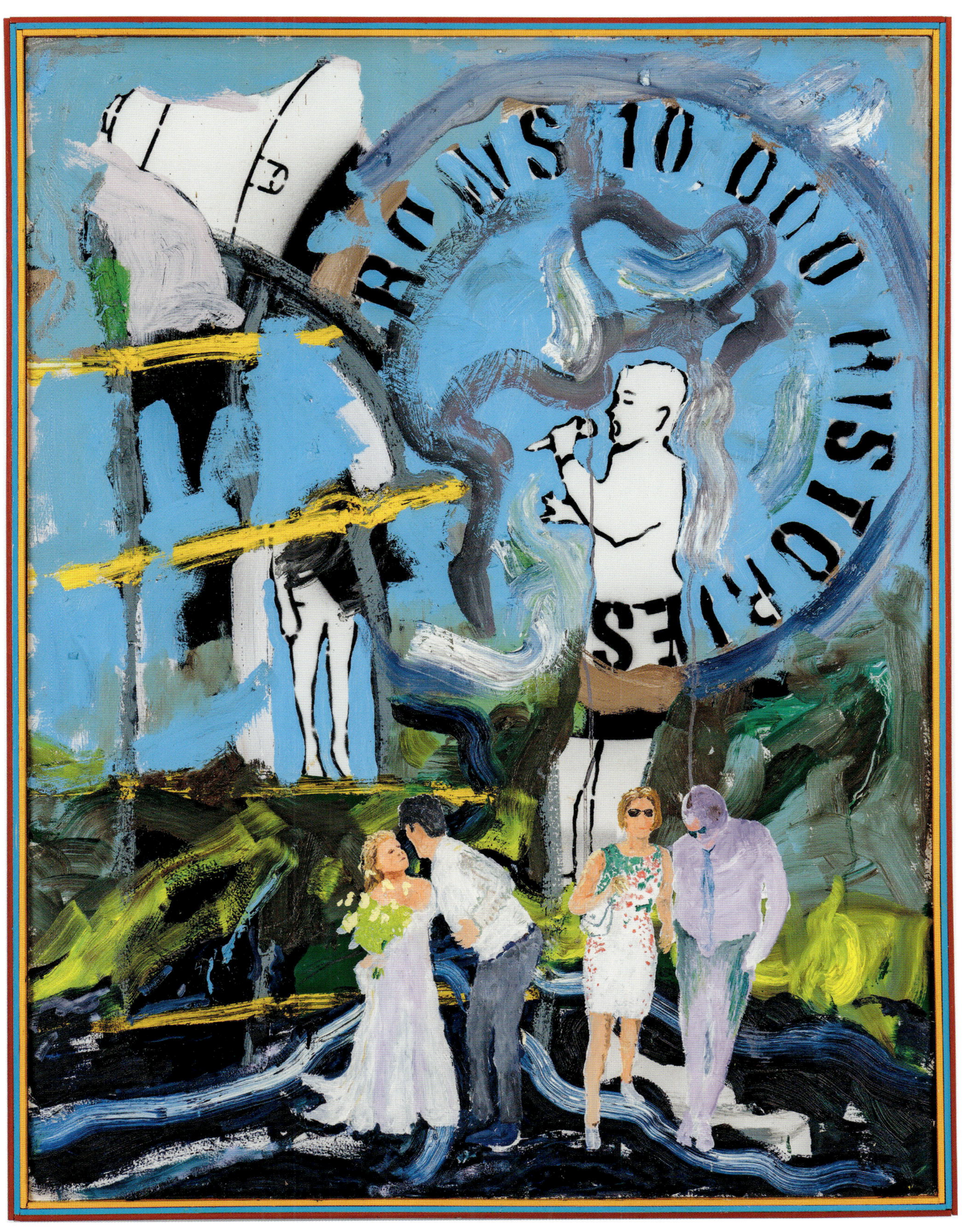
RONS 10.000 HISTOIRES

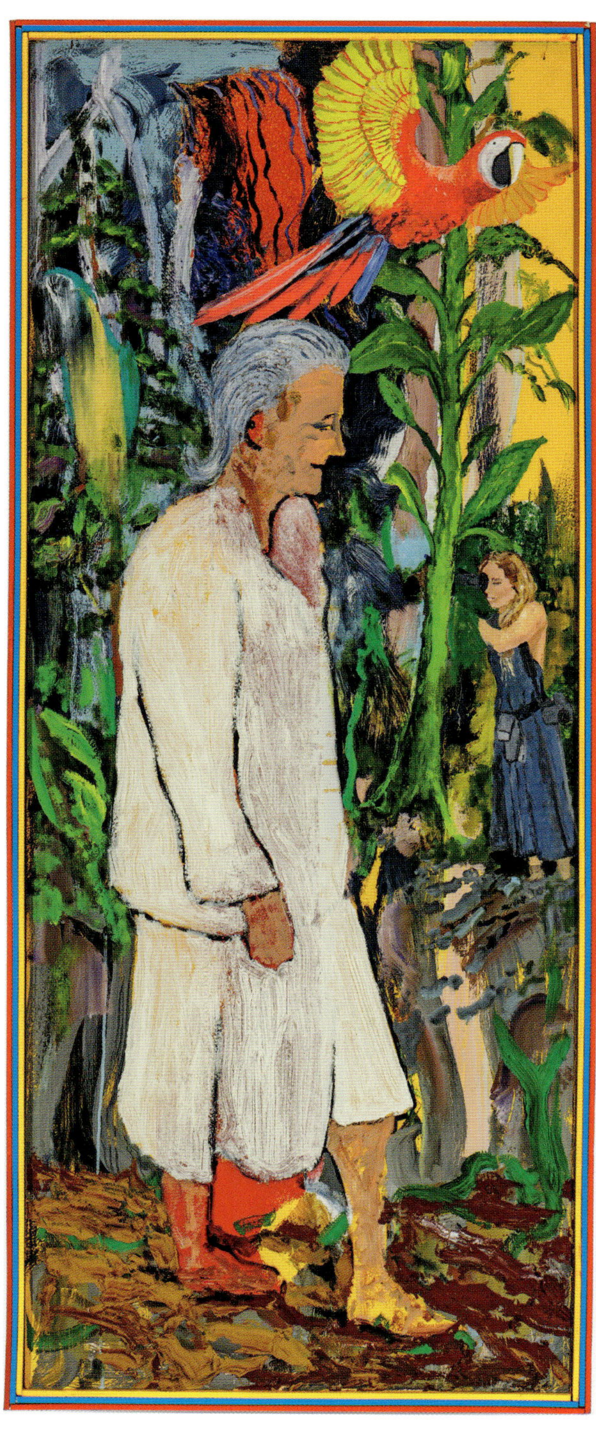

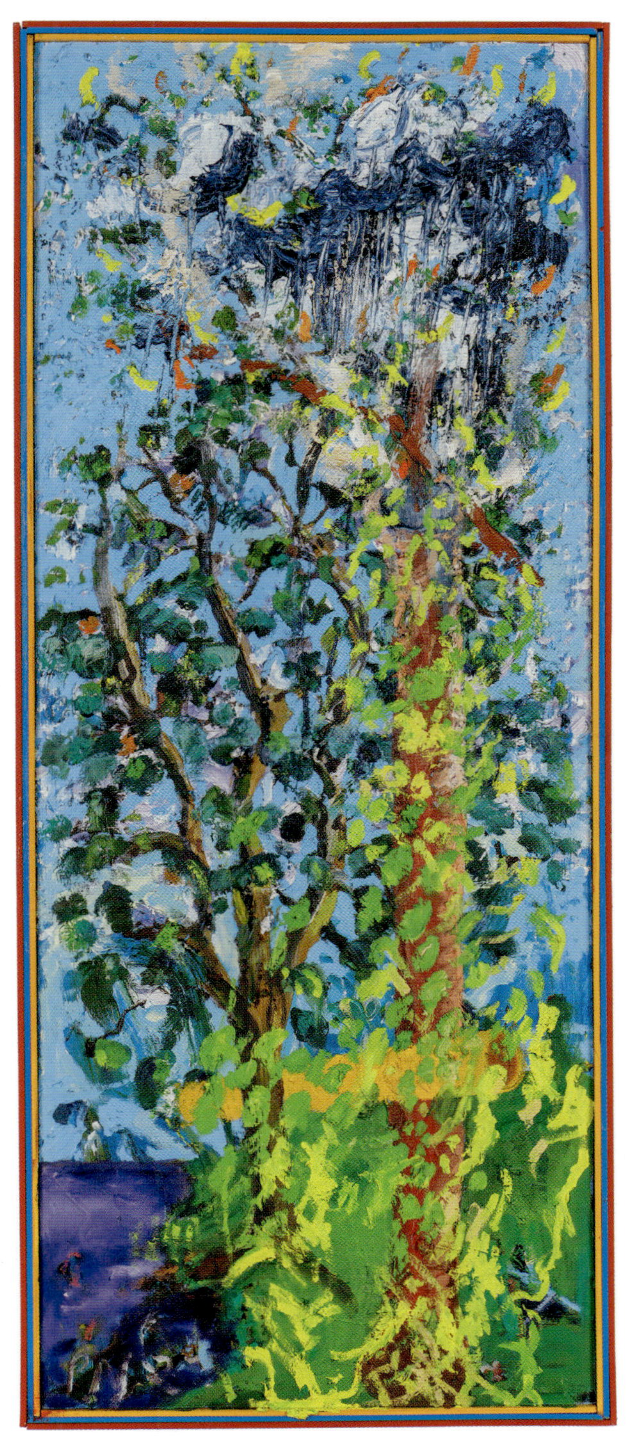

The Programmer, 2022 (left)
Oil on panel
49 1/4 x 20 3/4 in

Landscape with Tree and Storm, 2023 (right)
Oil on panel
48 1/2 x 21 in

Sharkey's Donkey Watching a Fish
(A Migration of Golden Orfe), 2023
Oil on panel
77 5/8 x 49 3/8 in

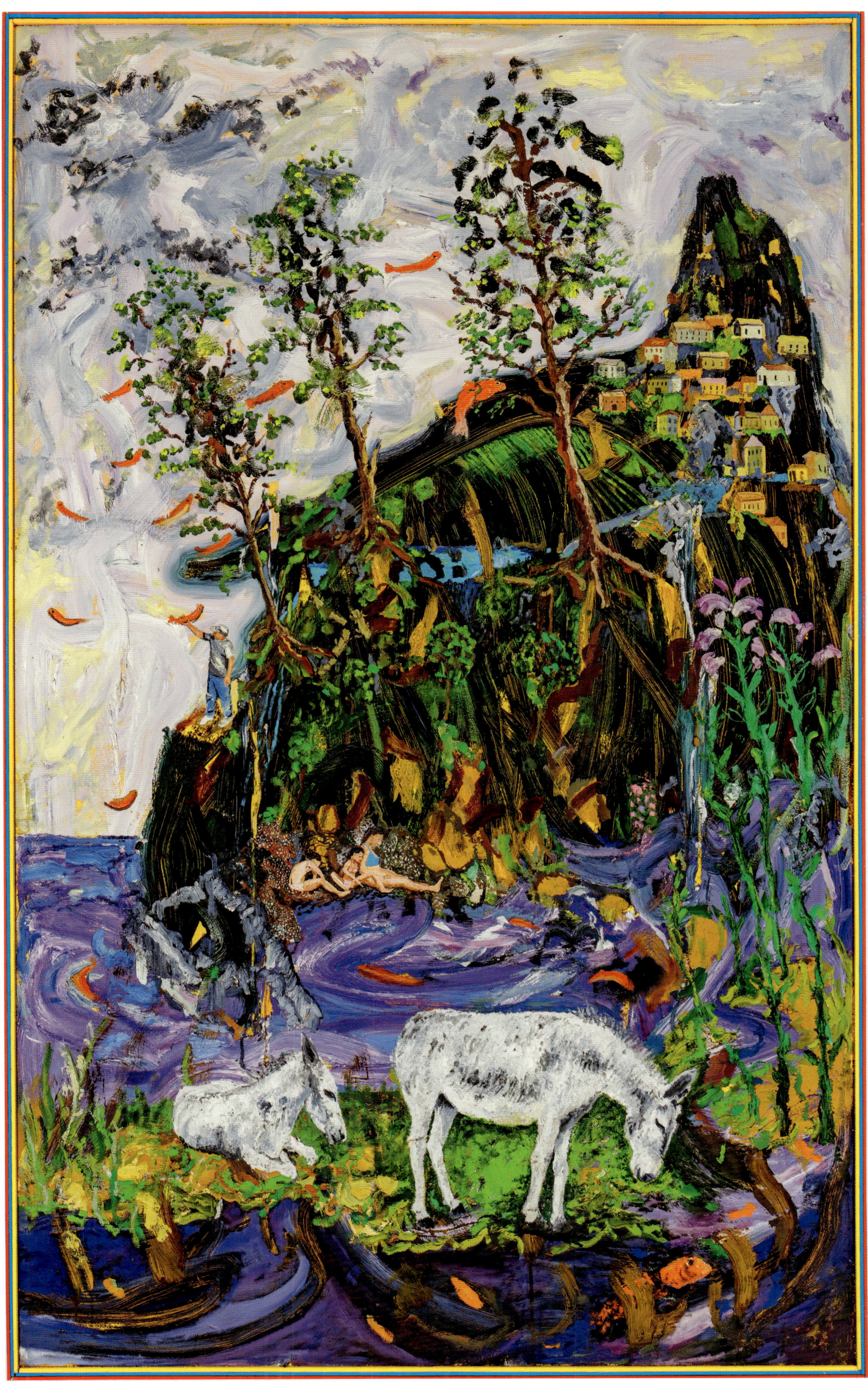

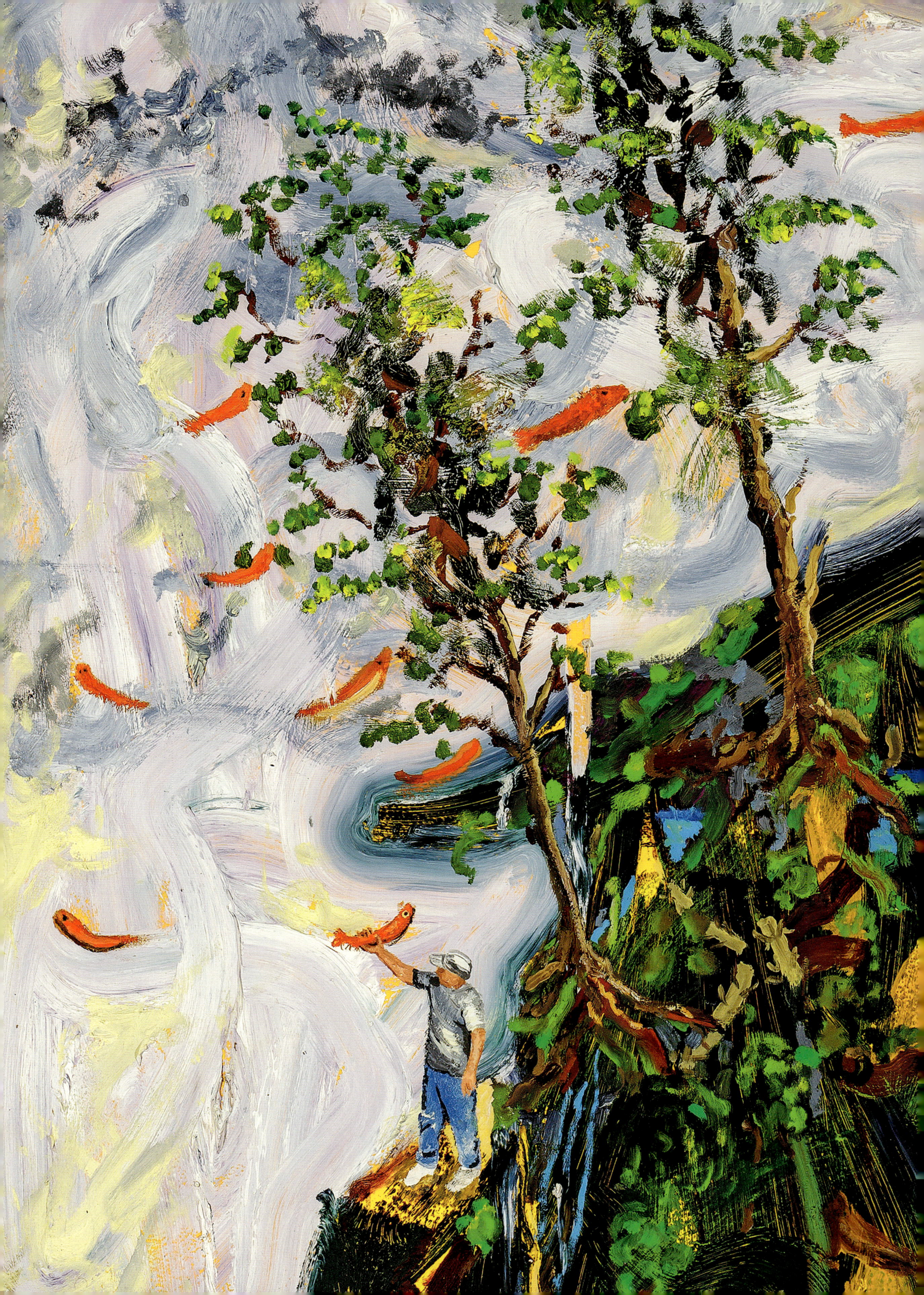

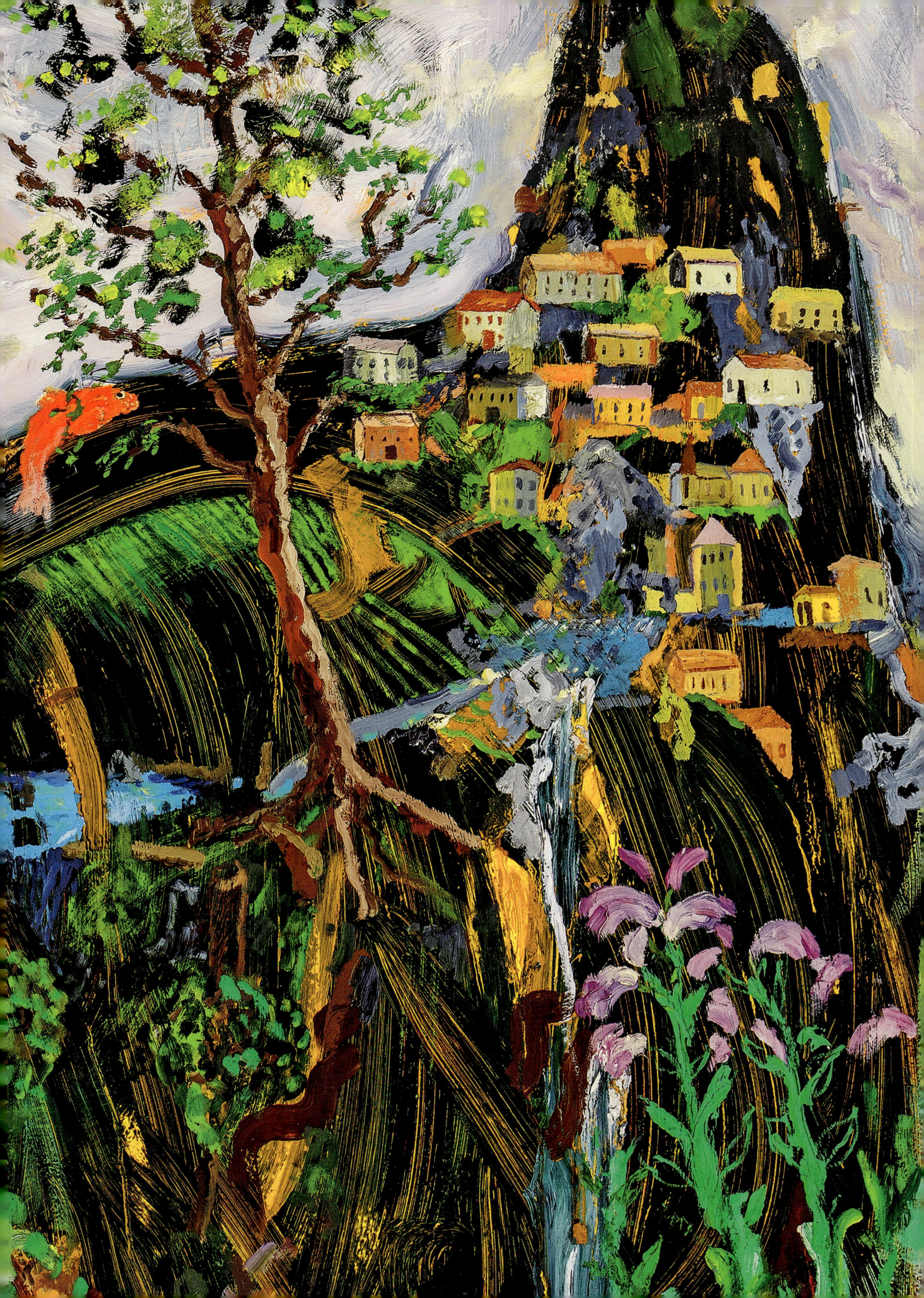

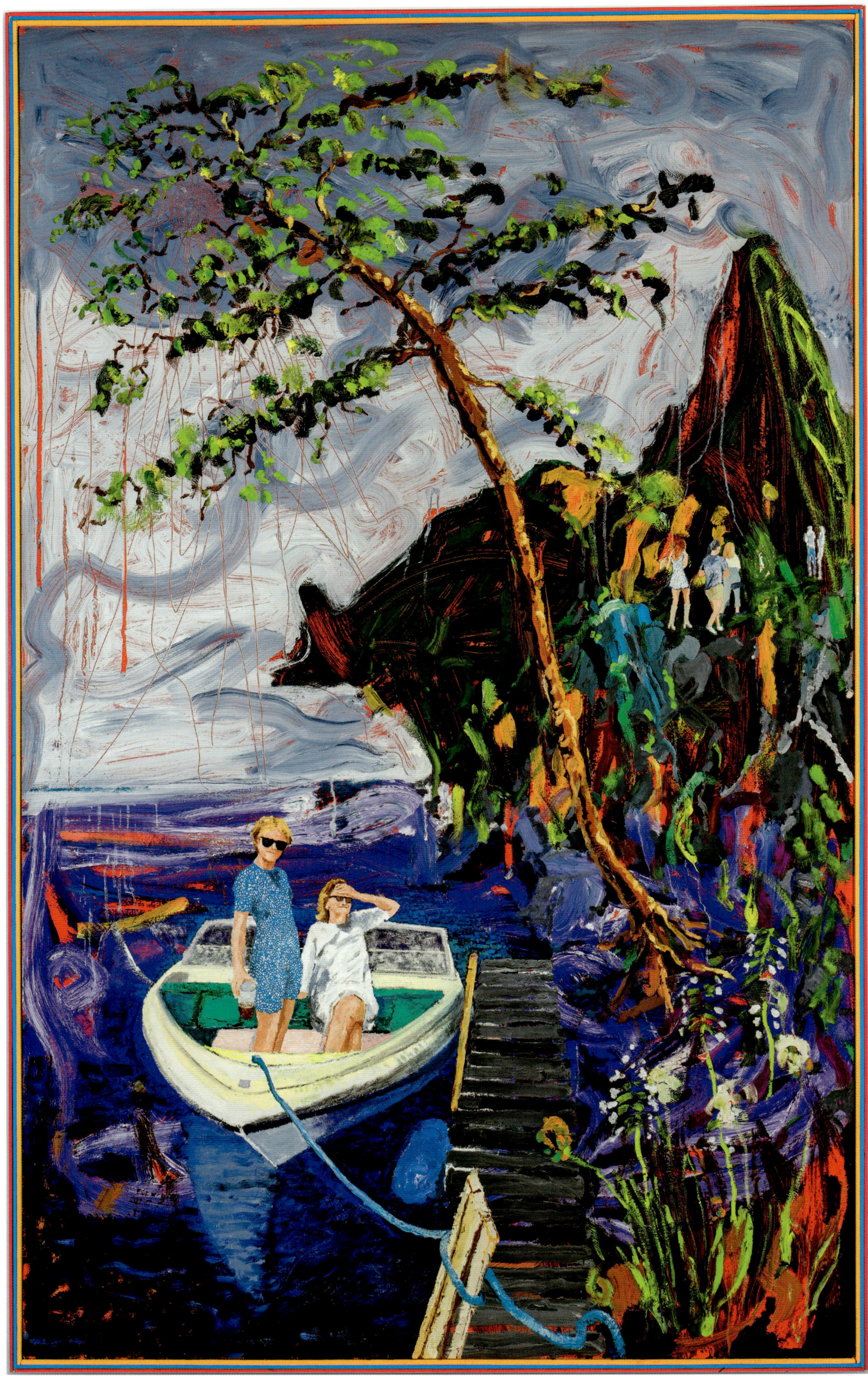

The Blue Rope, 2023
Oil on panel
77 5/8 x 49 3/8 in

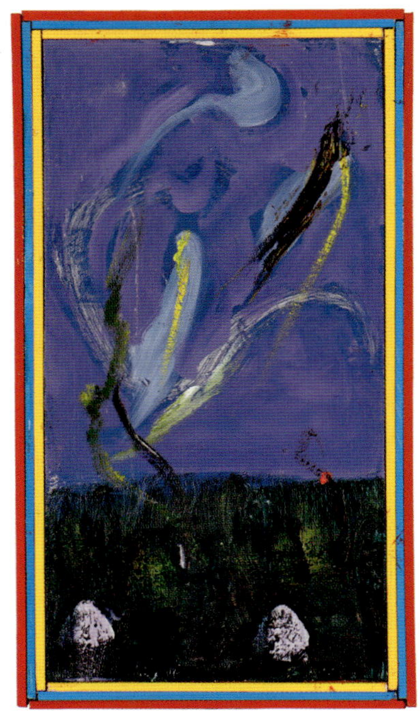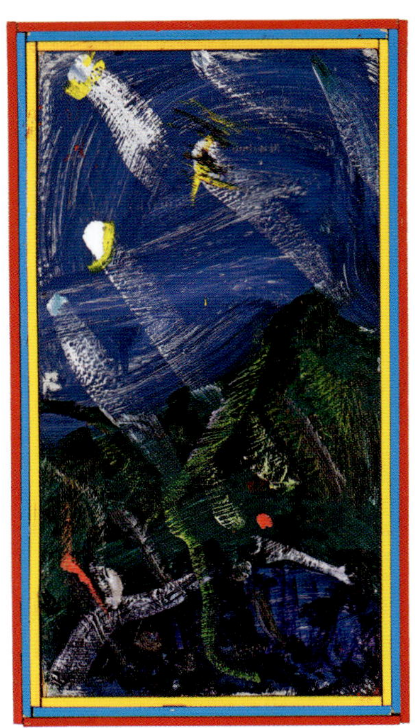

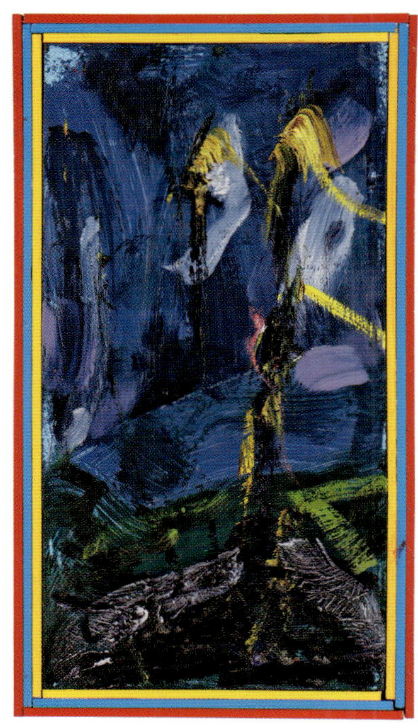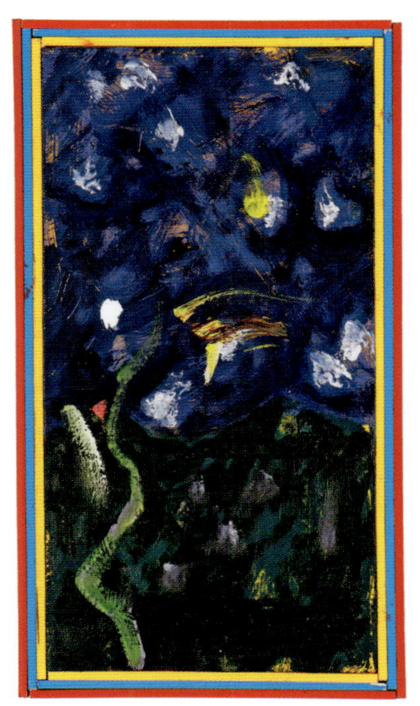

Left to right:

A View East Before Dawn, 2023
Oil on panel
16 1/4 x 9 1/4 in

Looking North, Seeing Mount Pisgah, 2023
Oil on panel
16 1/4 x 9 1/4 in

Seeing Night Sky, 2023
Oil on panel
16 1/4 x 9 1/4 in

Looking at Southern Night Sky, 2023
Oil on panel
16 1/4 x 9 1/4 in

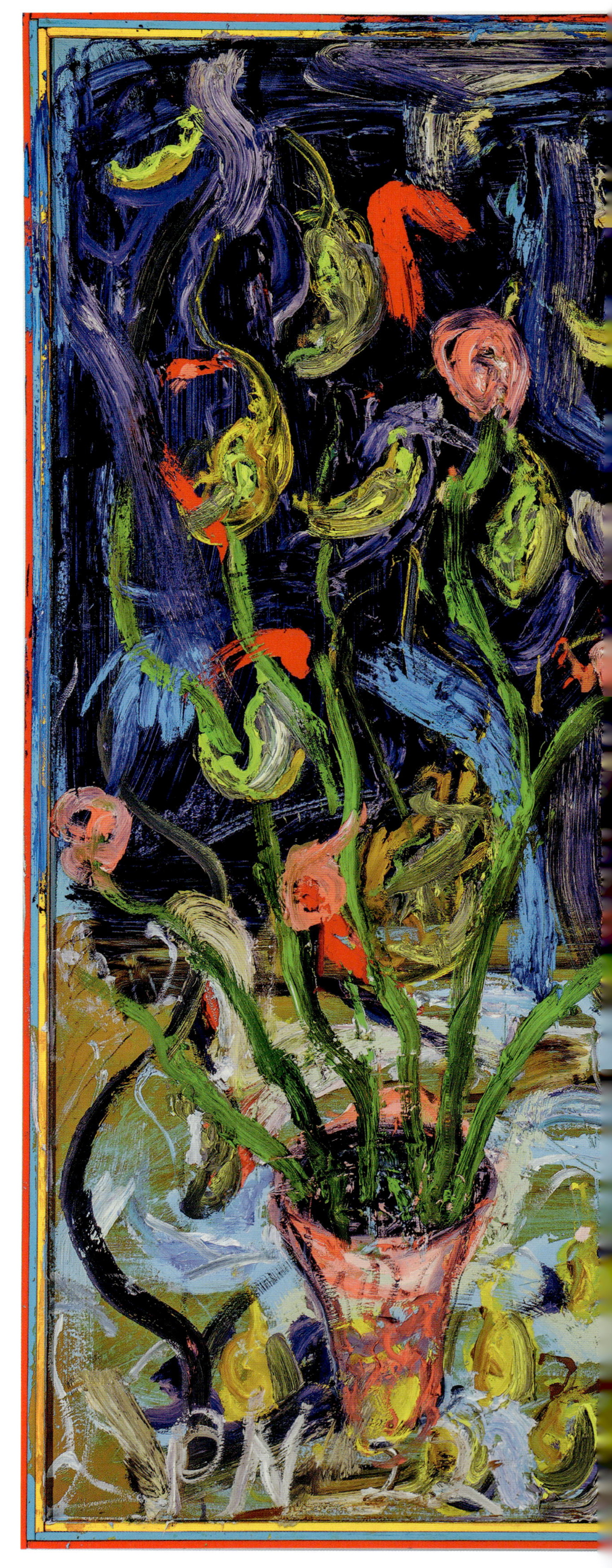

*Dave-Id Looks in a Mirror
(Sees Himself)*, 2022
Oil on panel
49 1/2 x 41 3/8 in

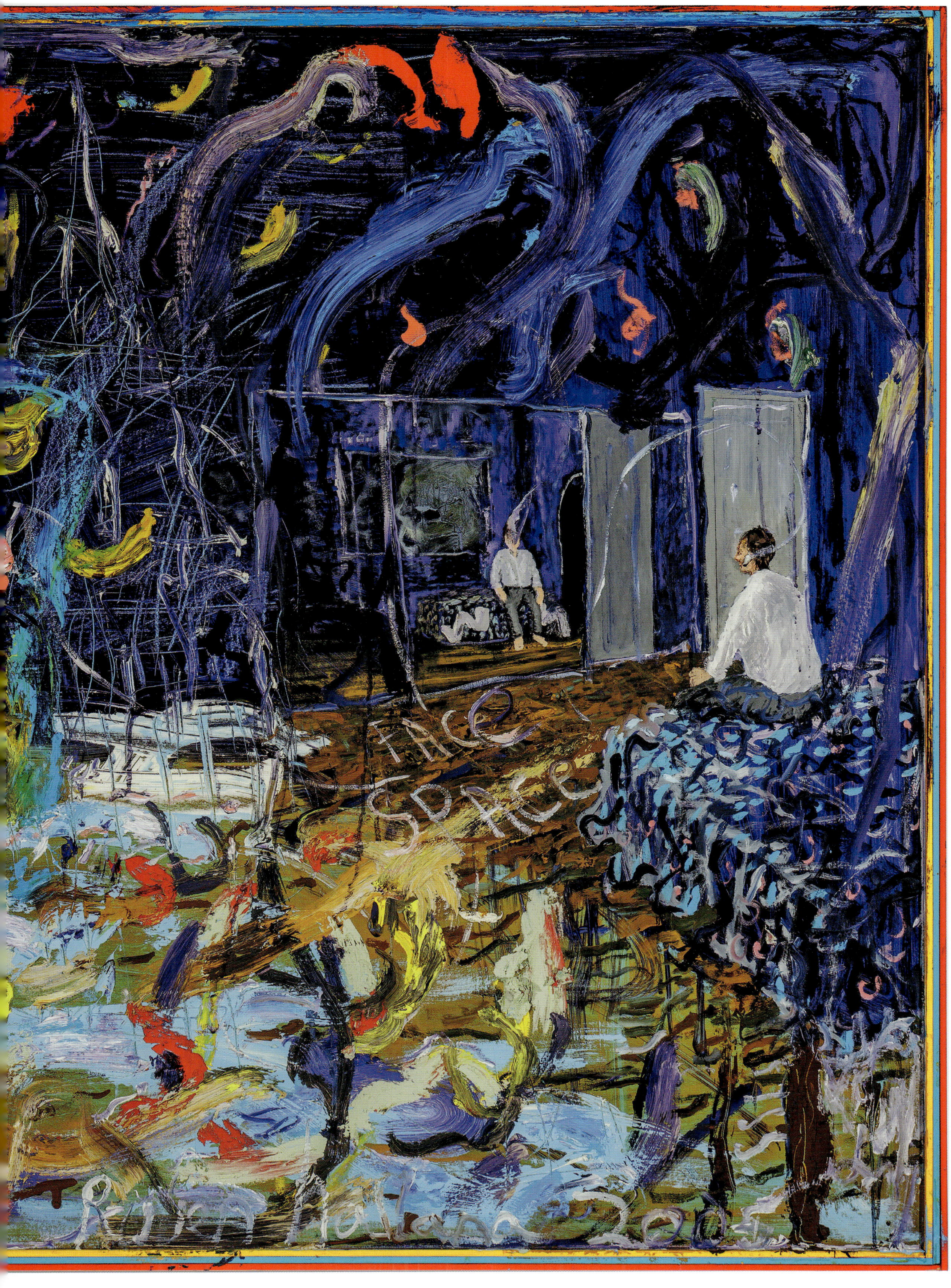

FACE
SPACE
Peter Hallam 2005

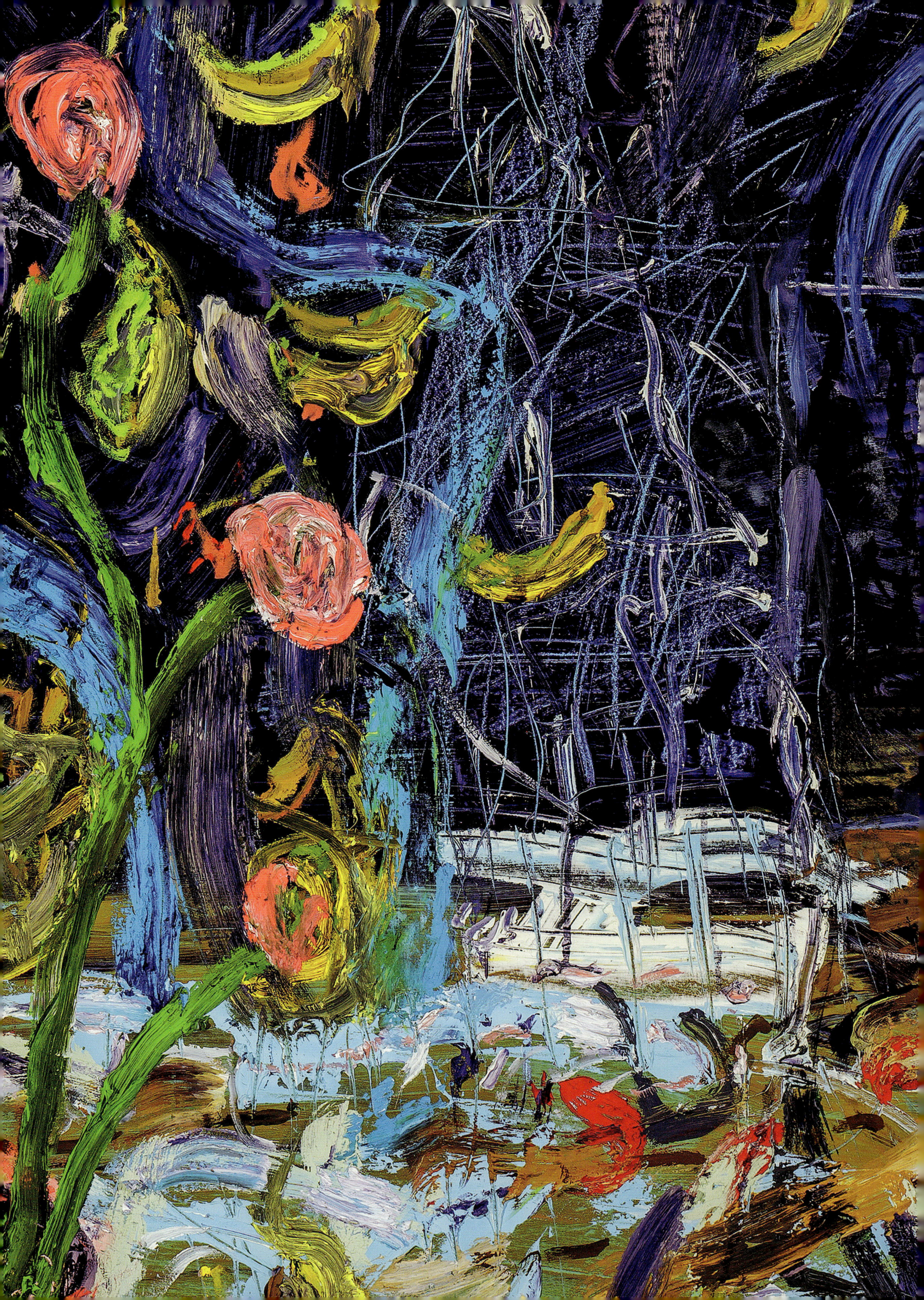

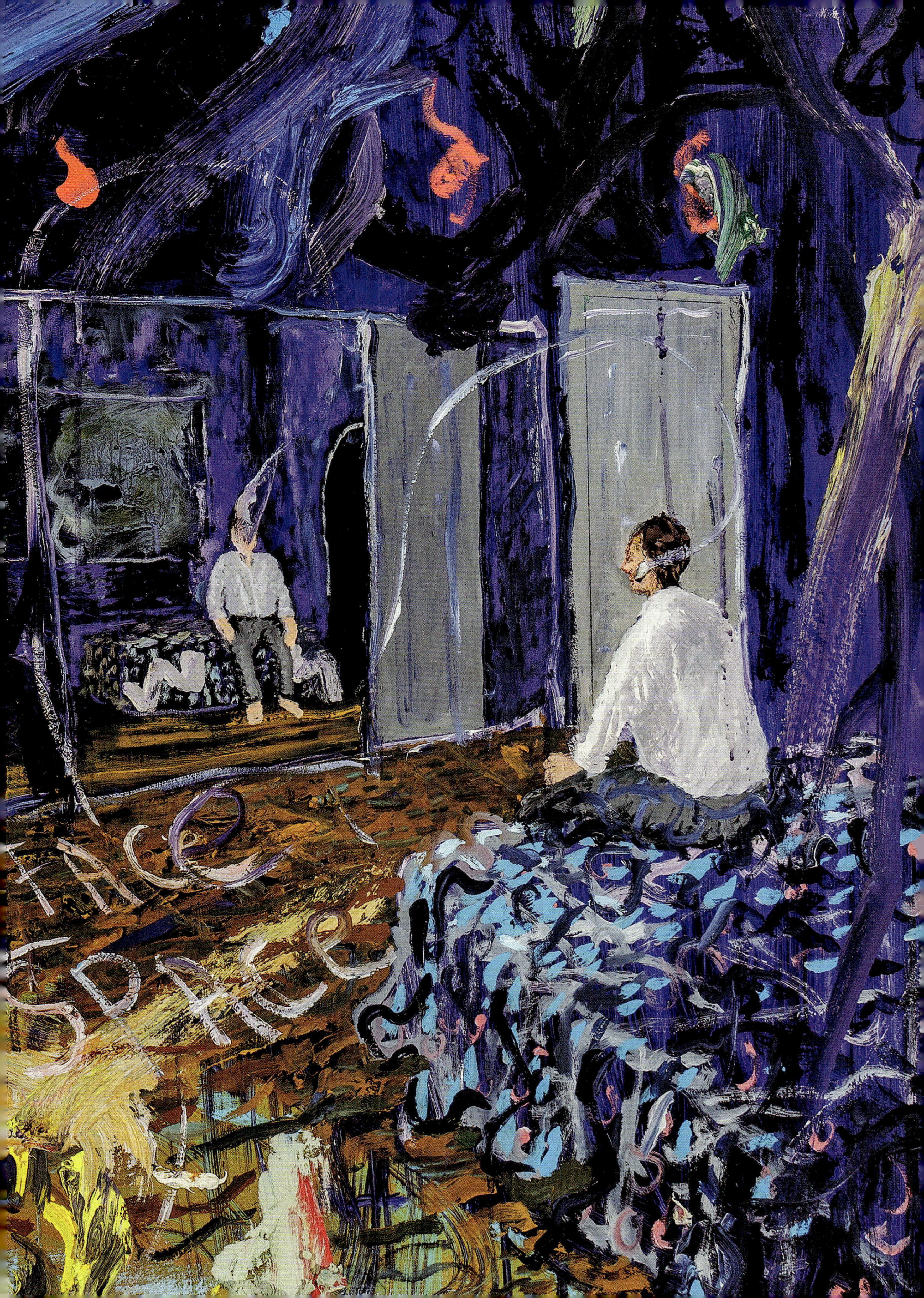
FACe
EDGe

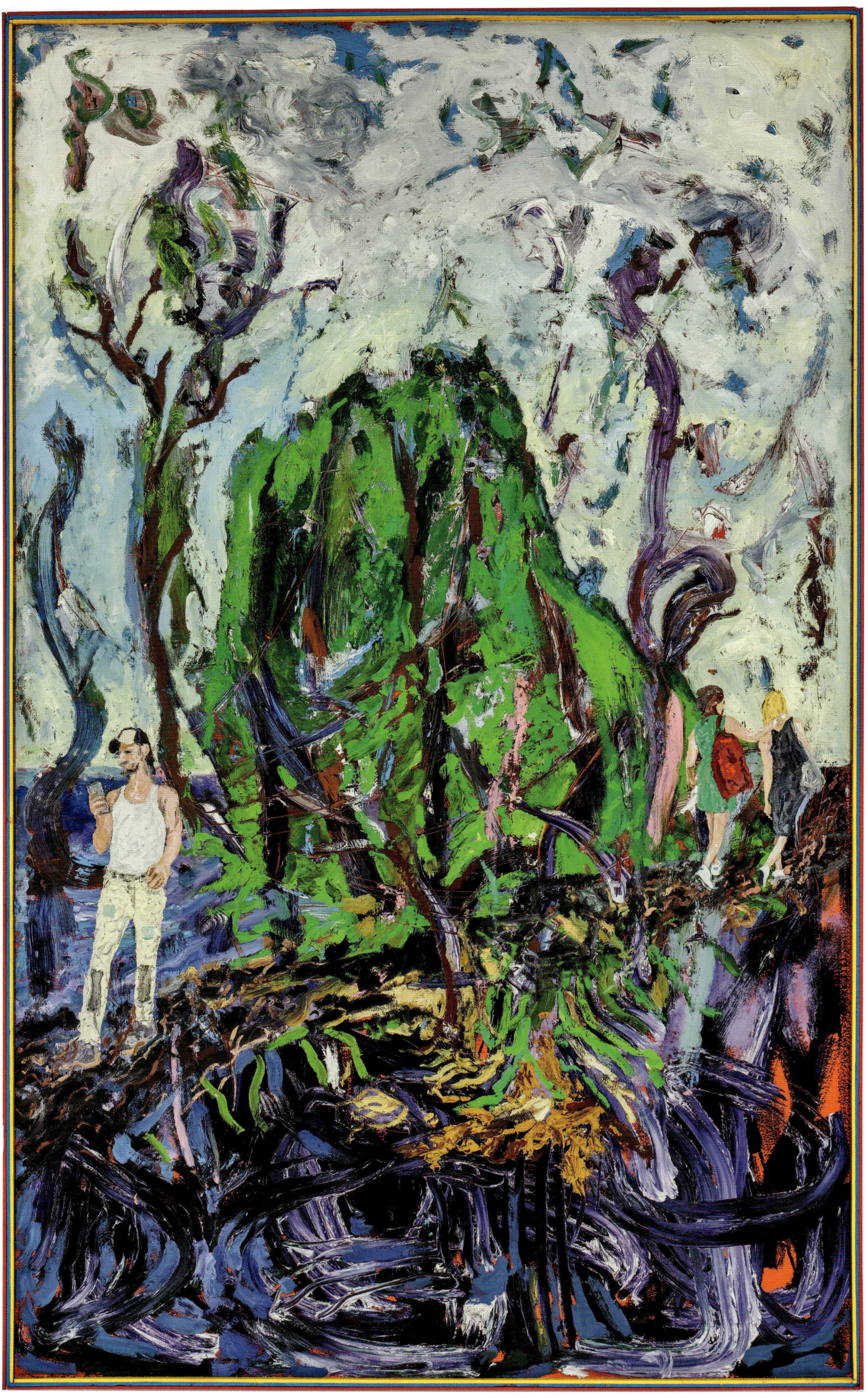

Mount Pisgah with Three
Figures on a Path, 2022
Oil on panel
77 3/4 x 48 3/4 in

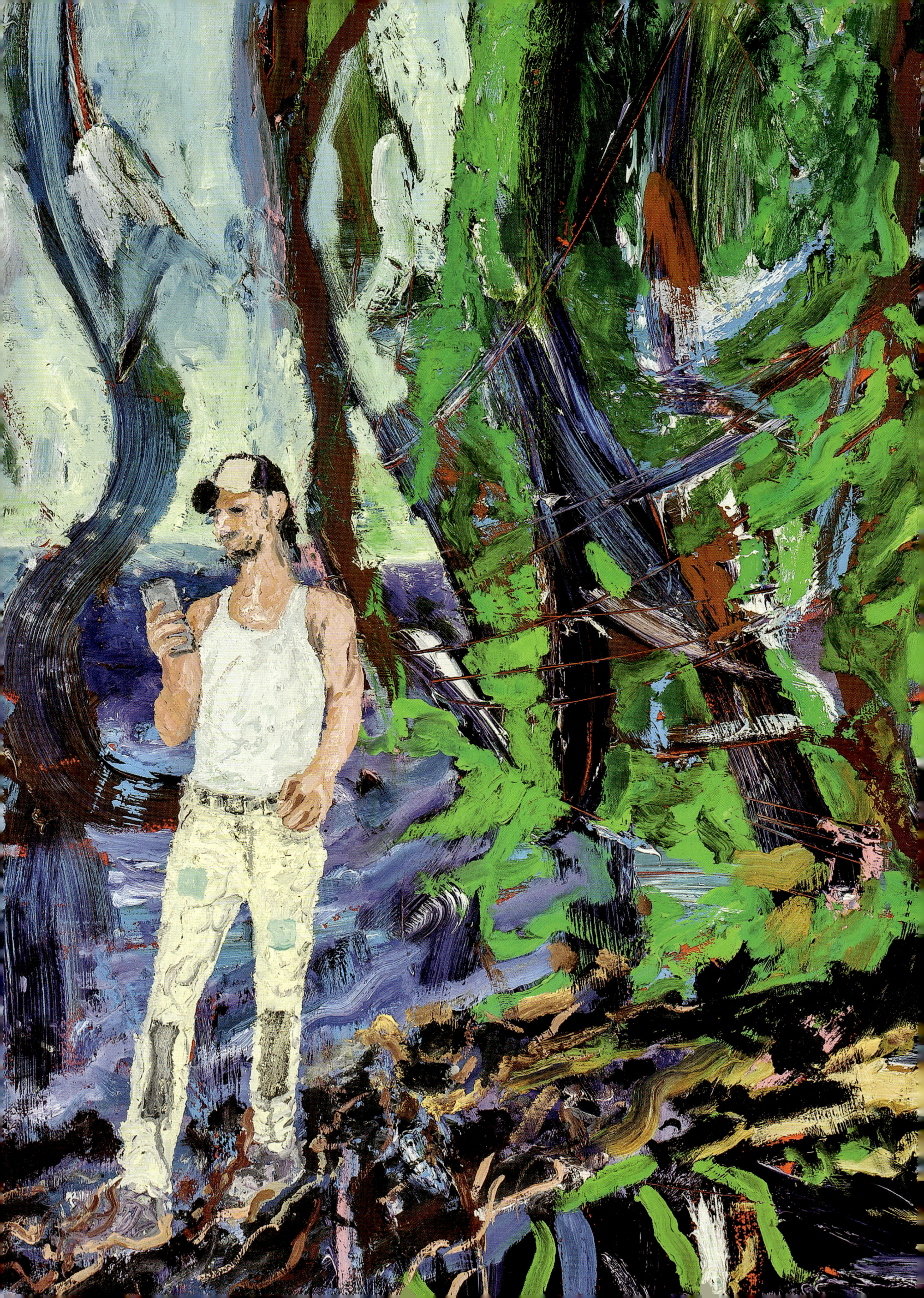

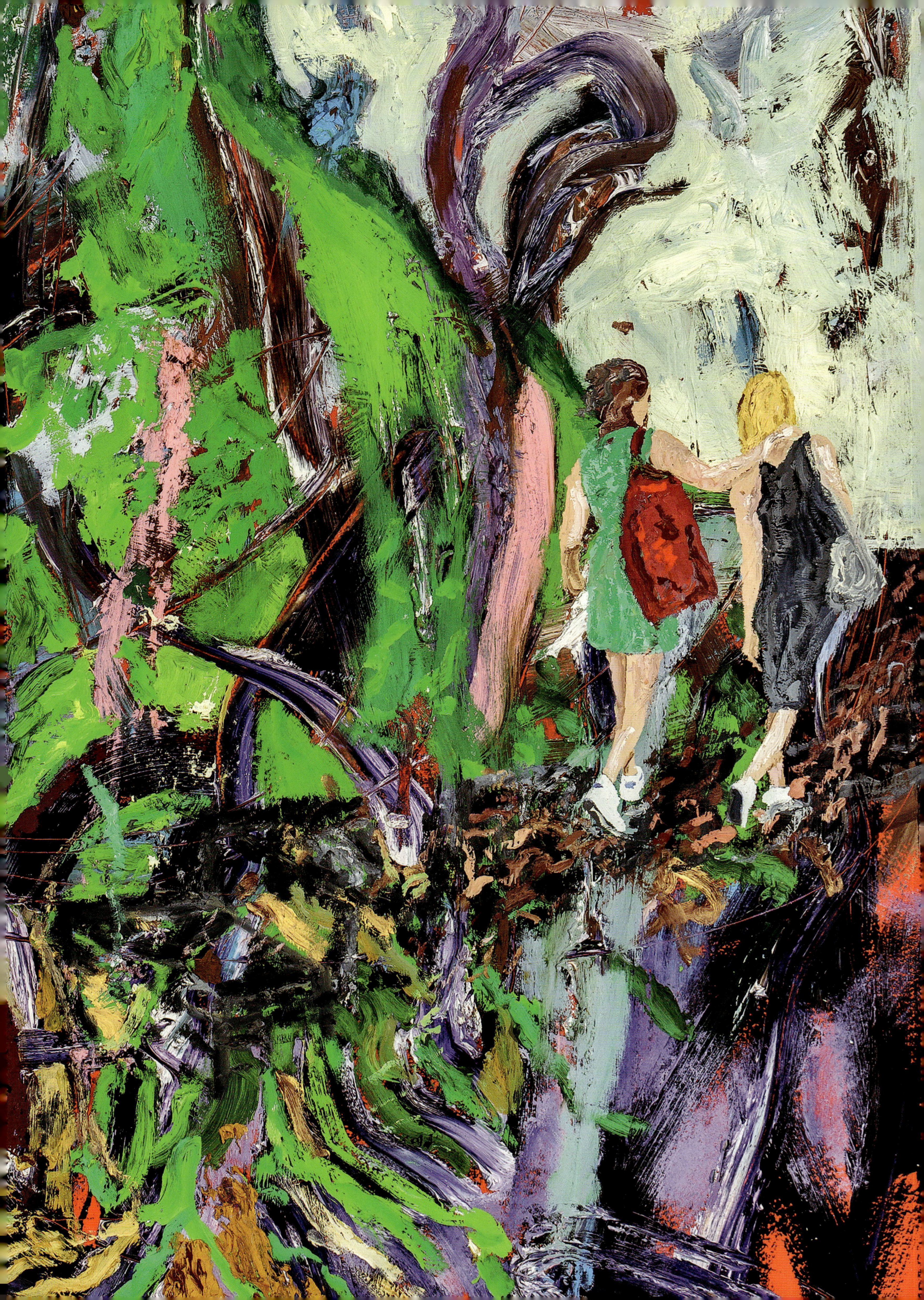

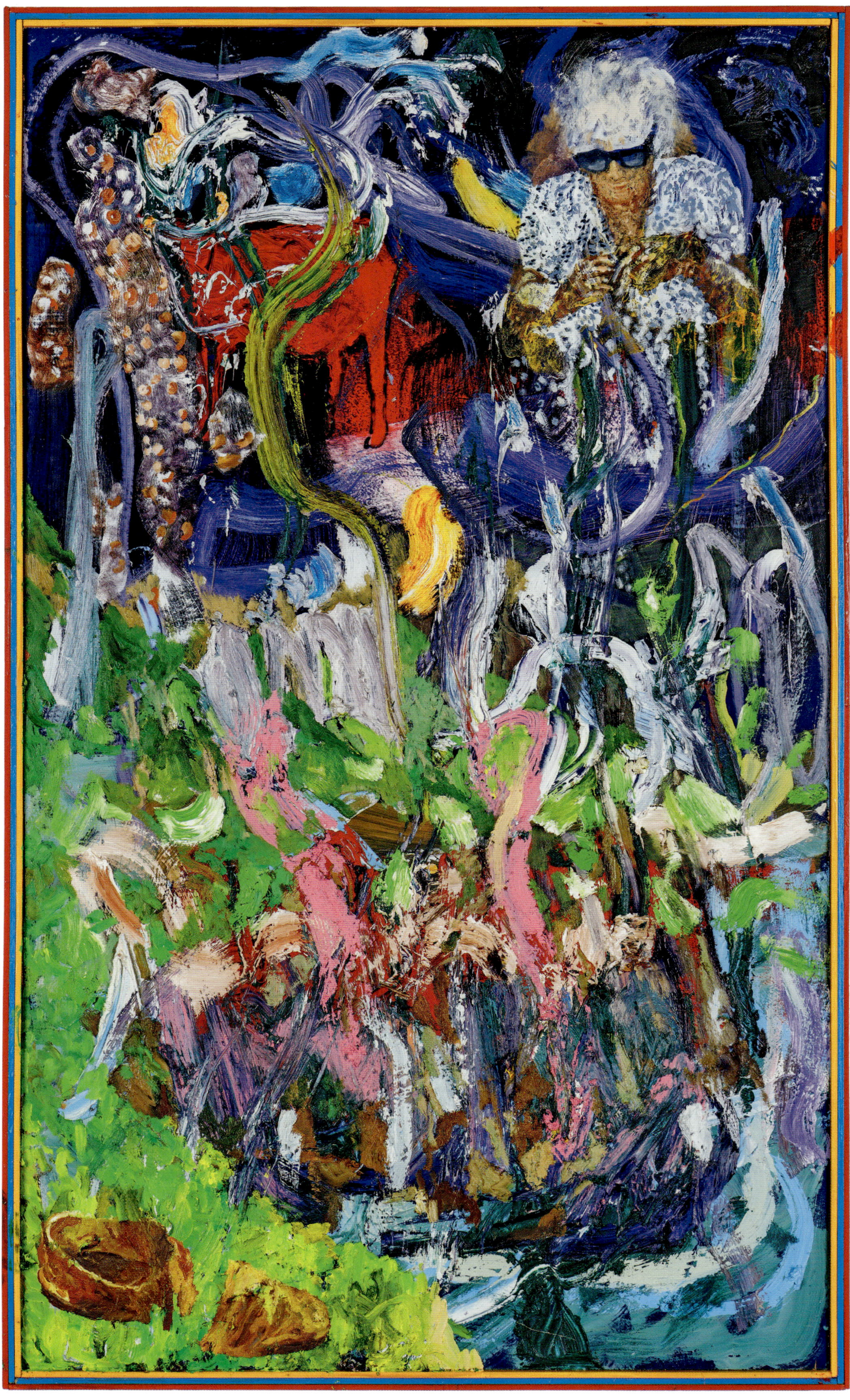

Landscape with Shoe and Ghost, 2023
Oil on panel
49 1/4 x 30 1/2 in

The Crow Catches a Golden Orfe
(Sharkey and Amanda See It), 2023
Oil on panel
78 x 49 in

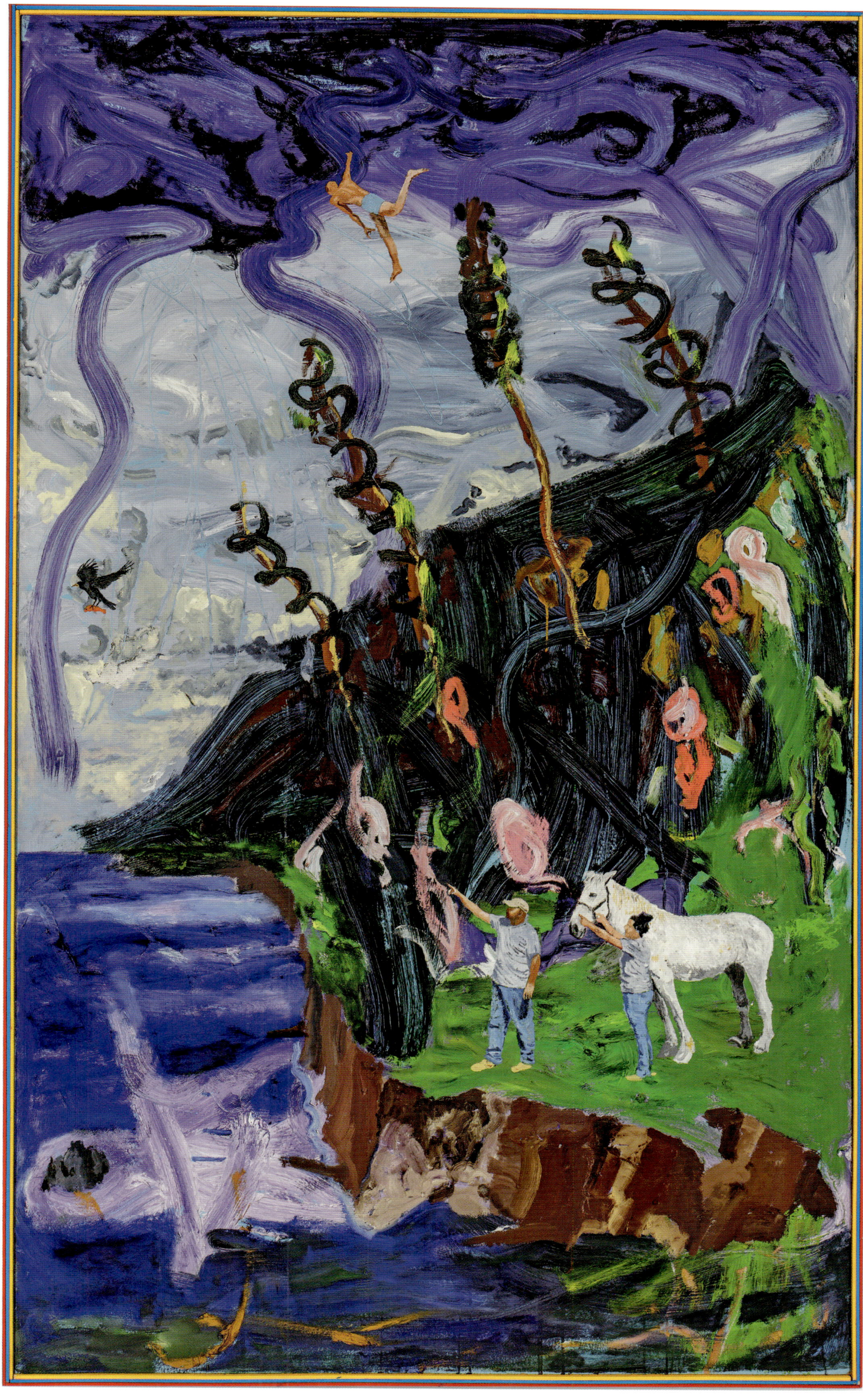

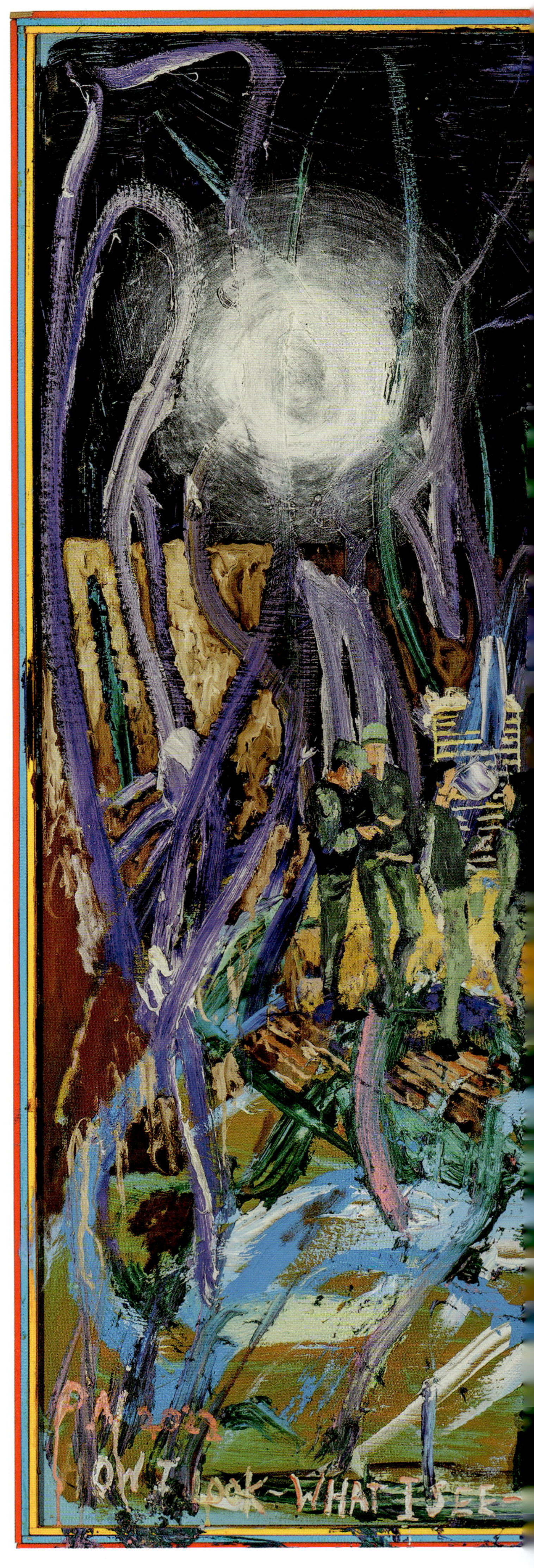

*How I Look, What I See in Baracoa When I'm Not There
(Self Portrait in Absentia)*, 2022
Oil on panel
57 3/8 x 49 1/2 in

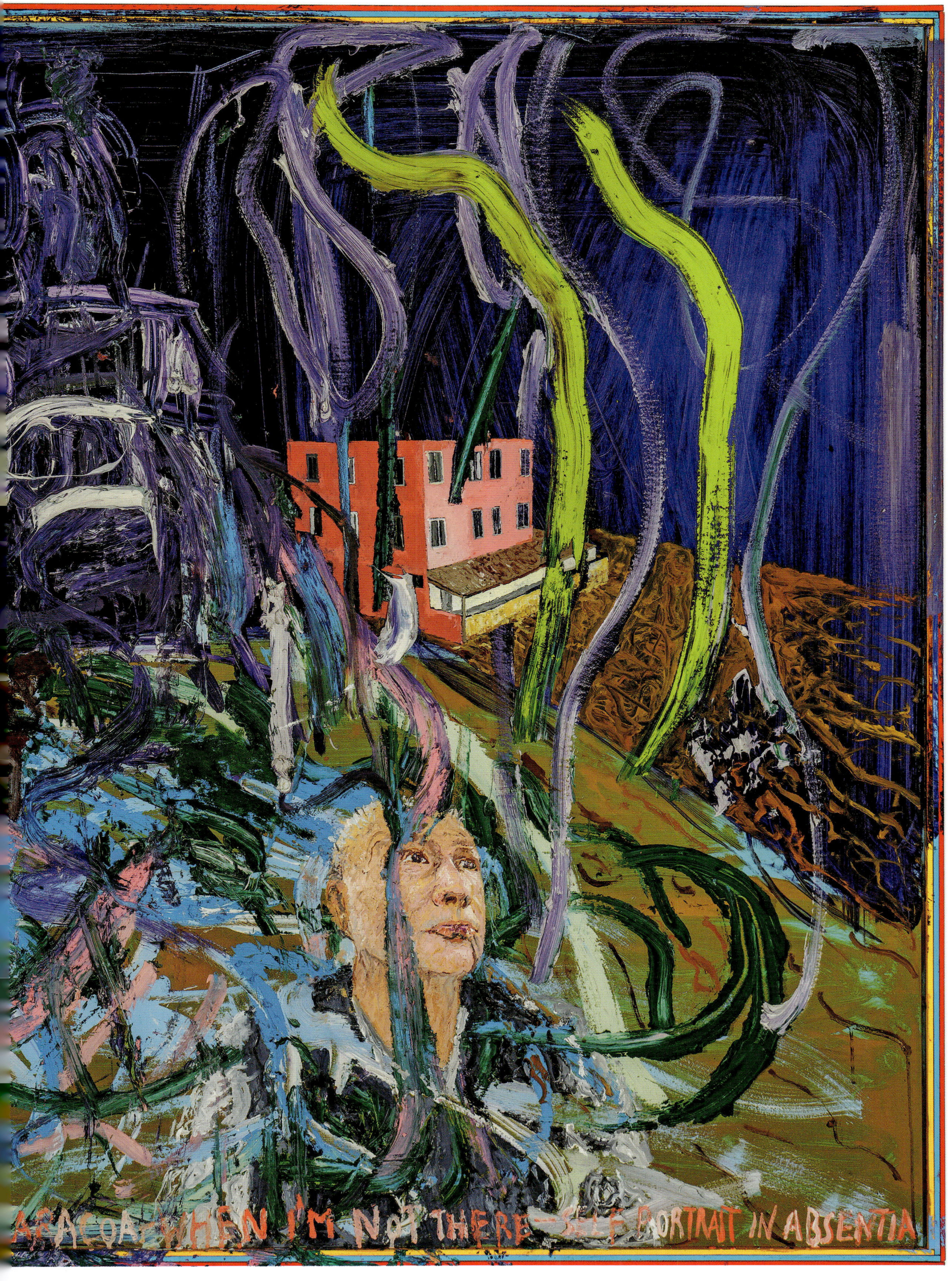

ARAGOA WHEN I'M NOT THERE — SELF PORTRAIT IN ABSENTIA

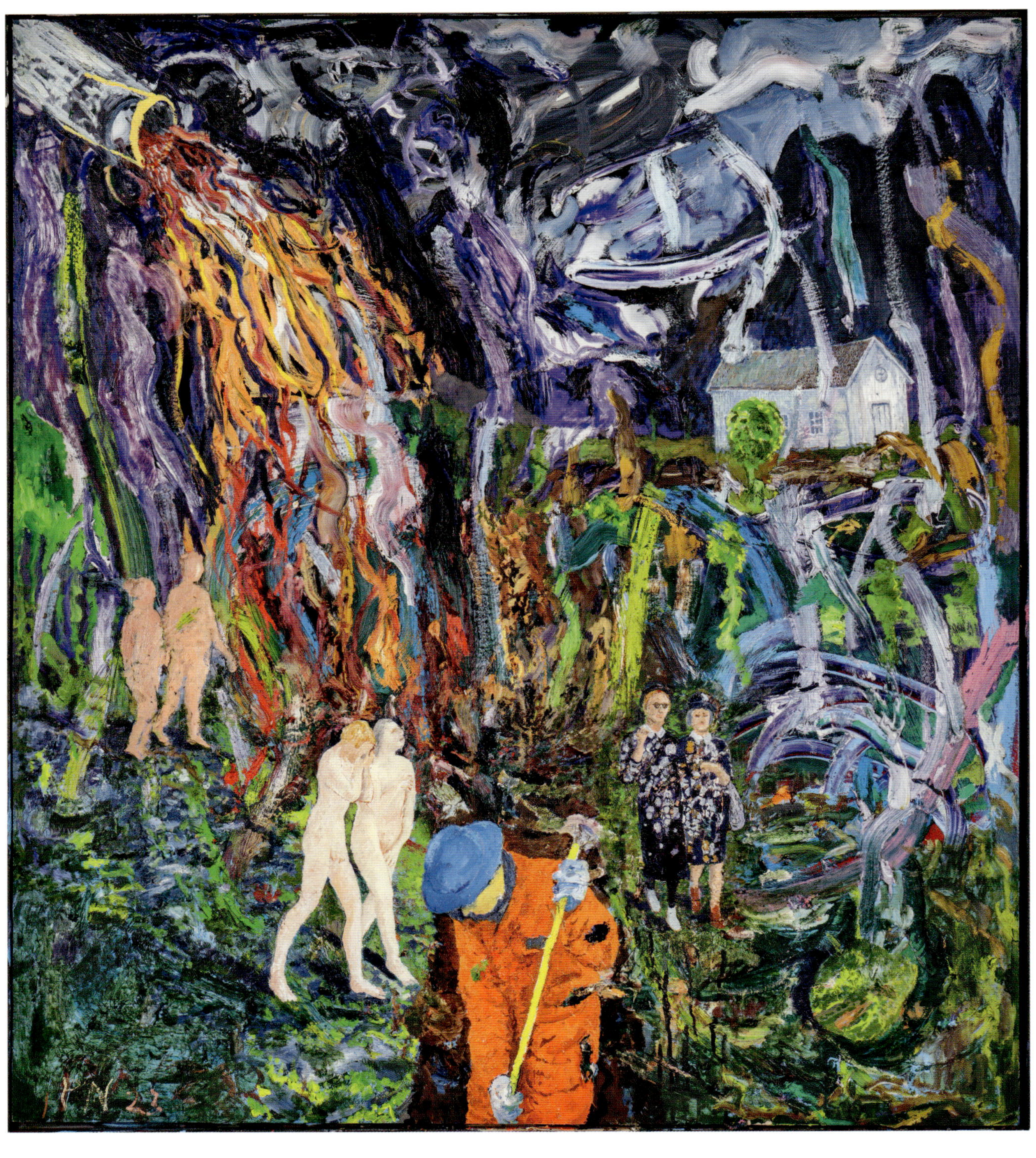

*Adam Installing Utilities in the Garden
of Eden Under the Devil's Fire*, 2023
Oil on panel
48 3/4 x 44 3/4 in

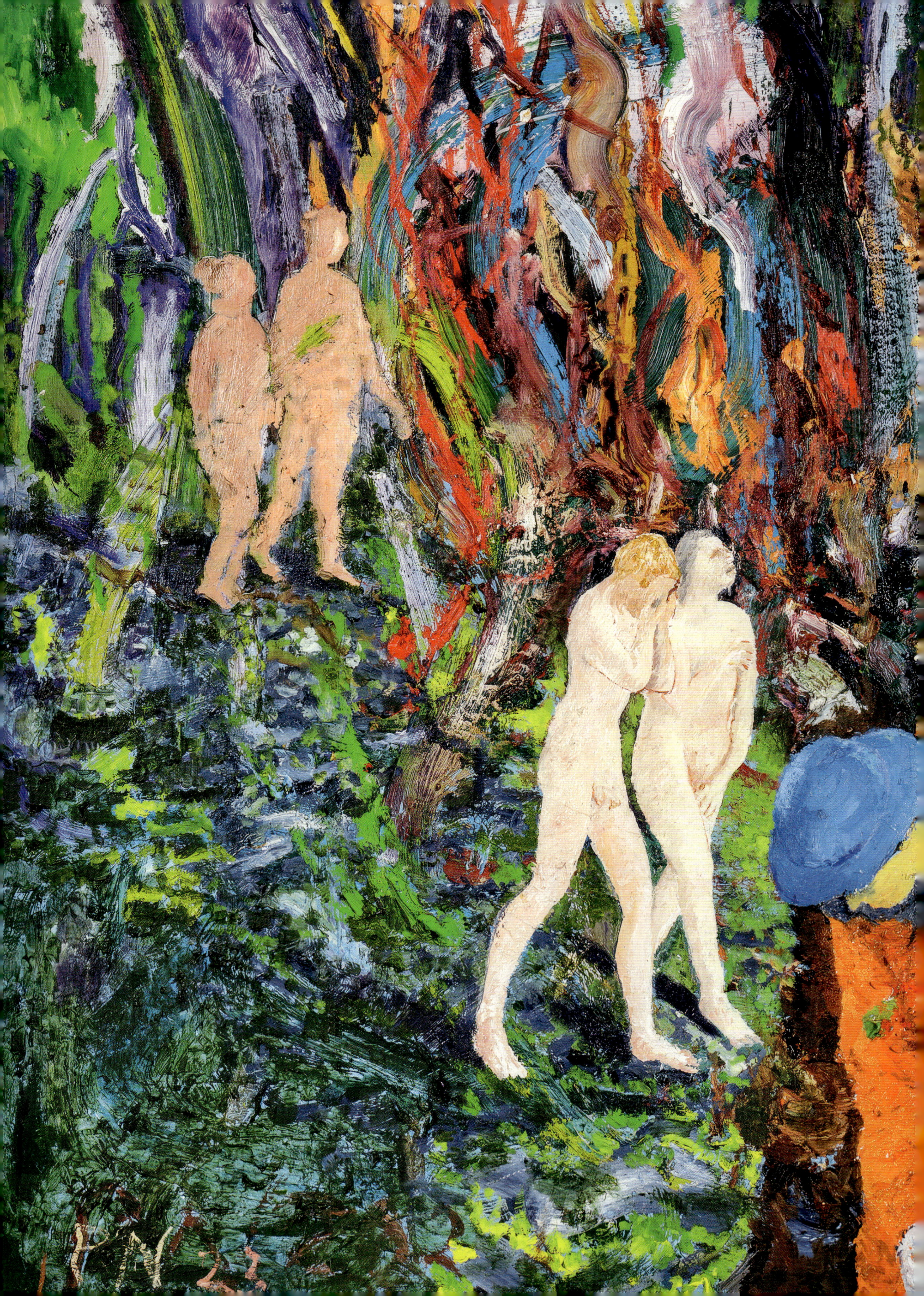

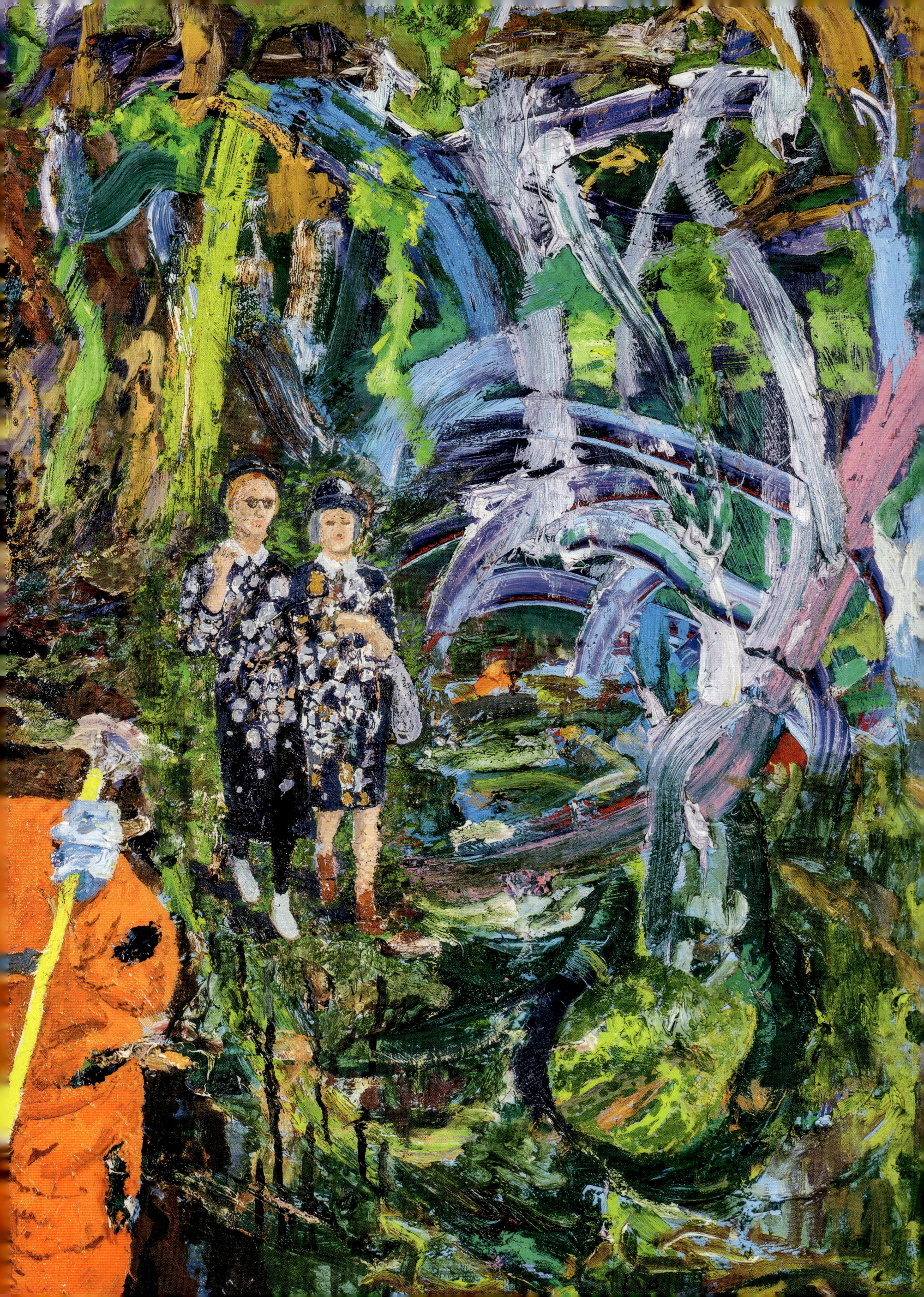

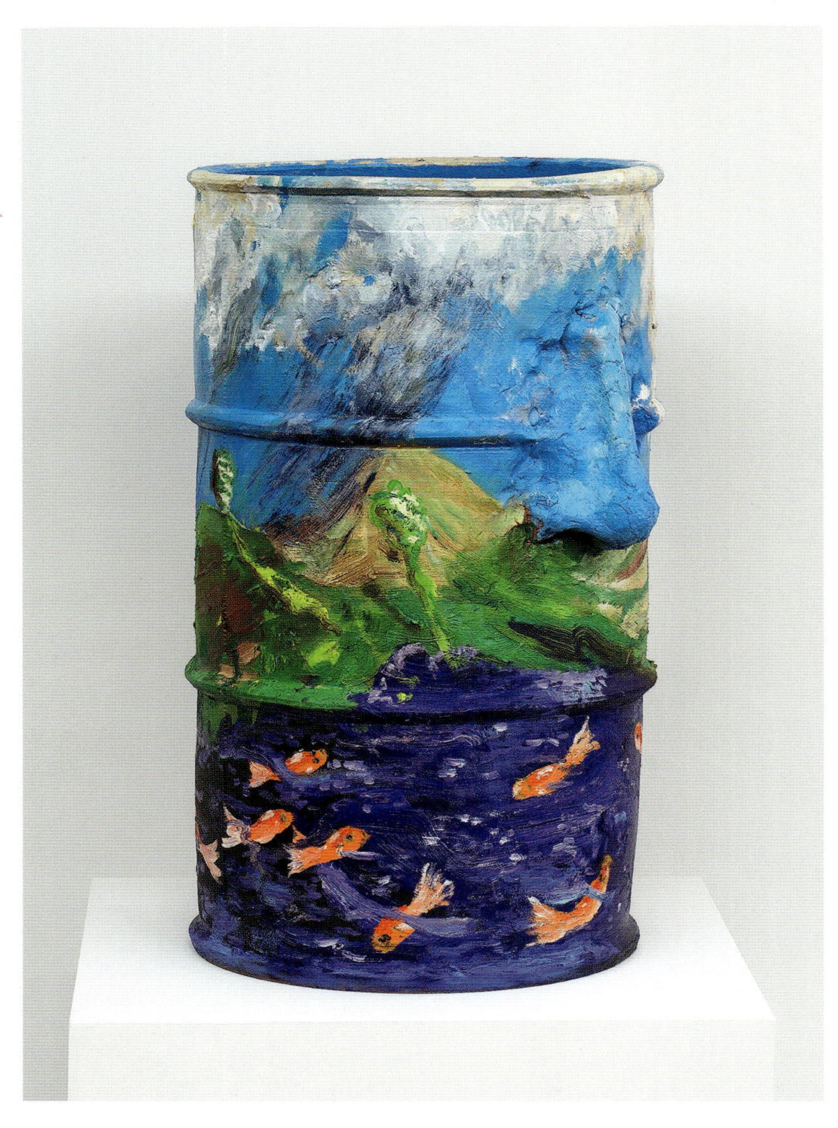

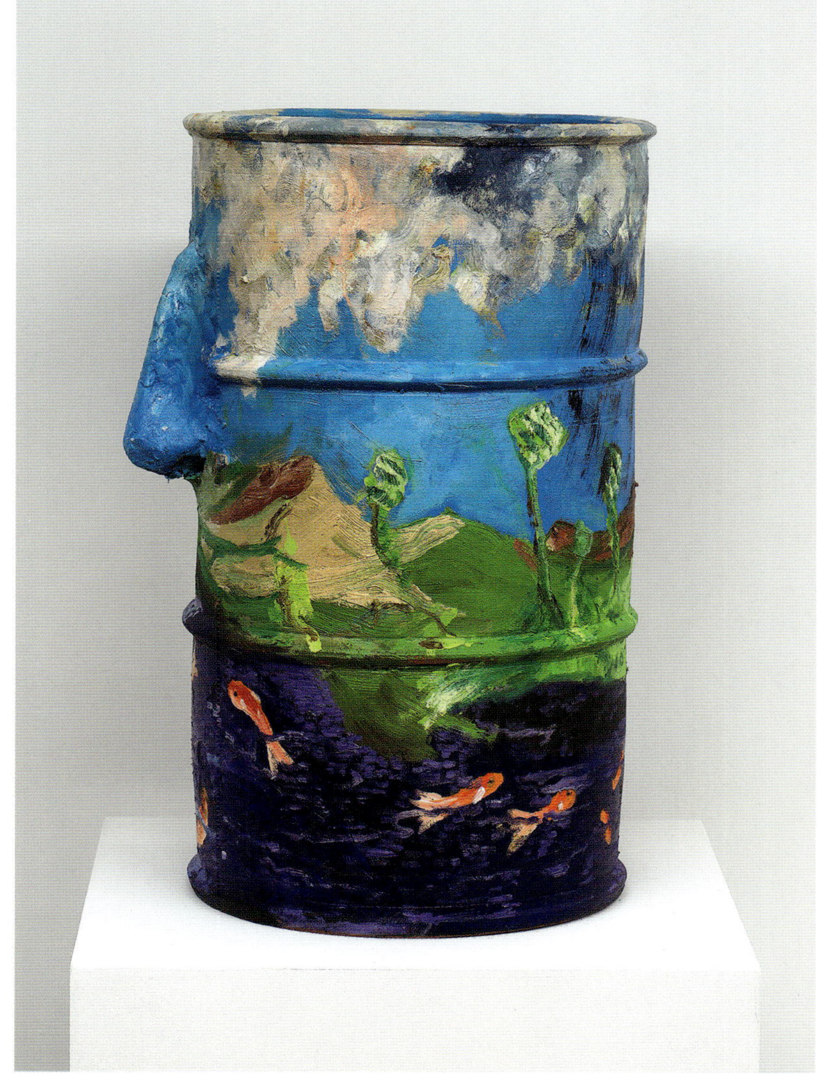

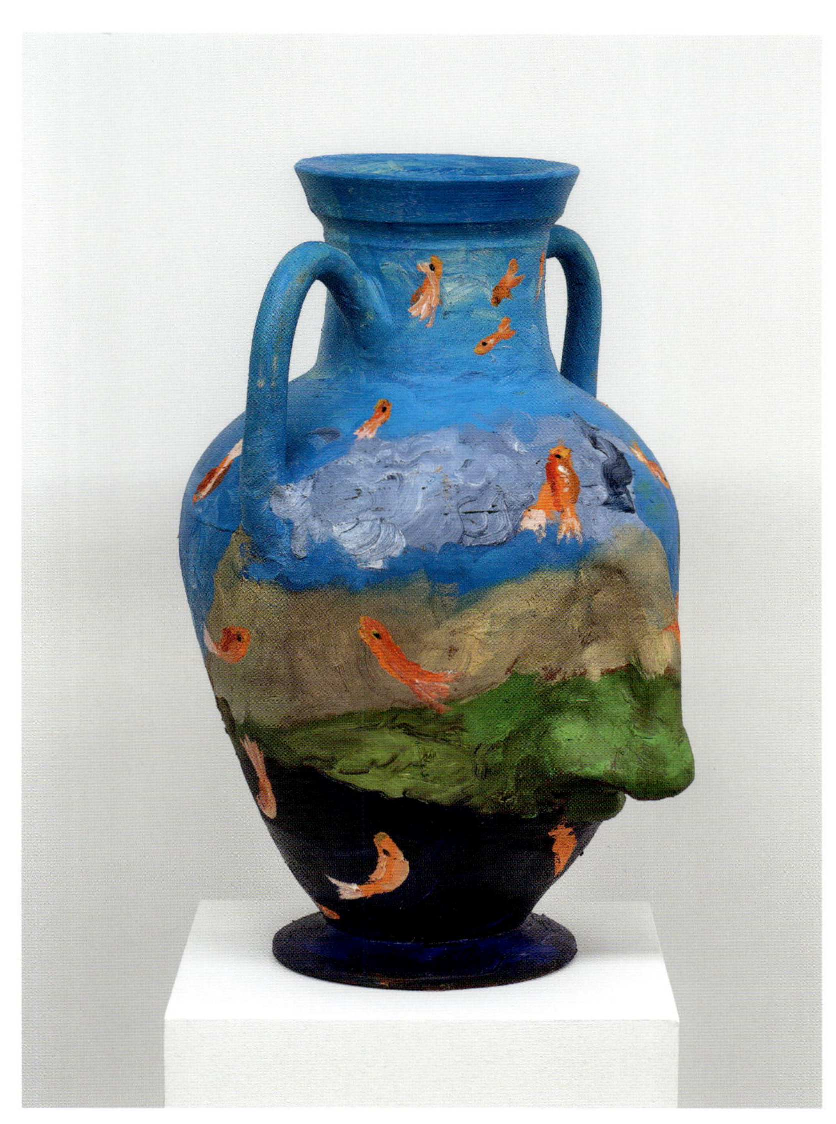

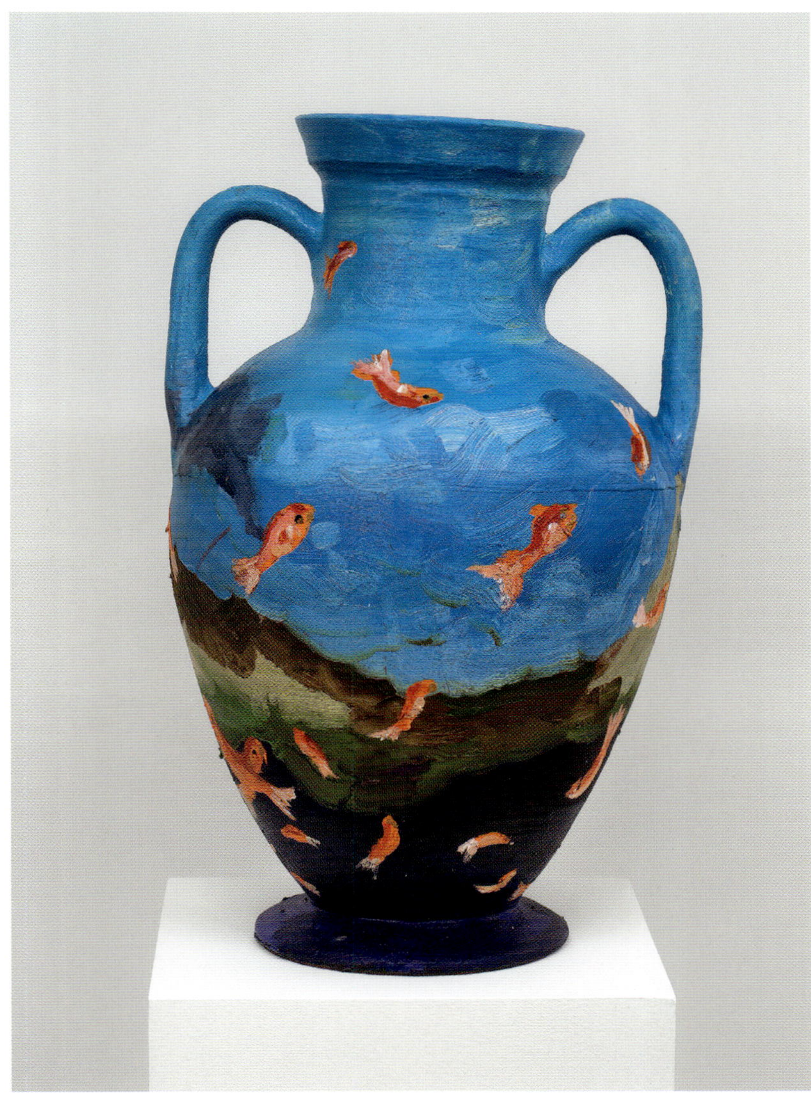

Drum with Nose, 2023 (left)
Painted terracotta
21 1/2 x 11 3/4 x 13 in

Jar with Nose, 2023 (right)
Painted terracotta
20 1/2 x 12 3/4 x 14 1/2 in

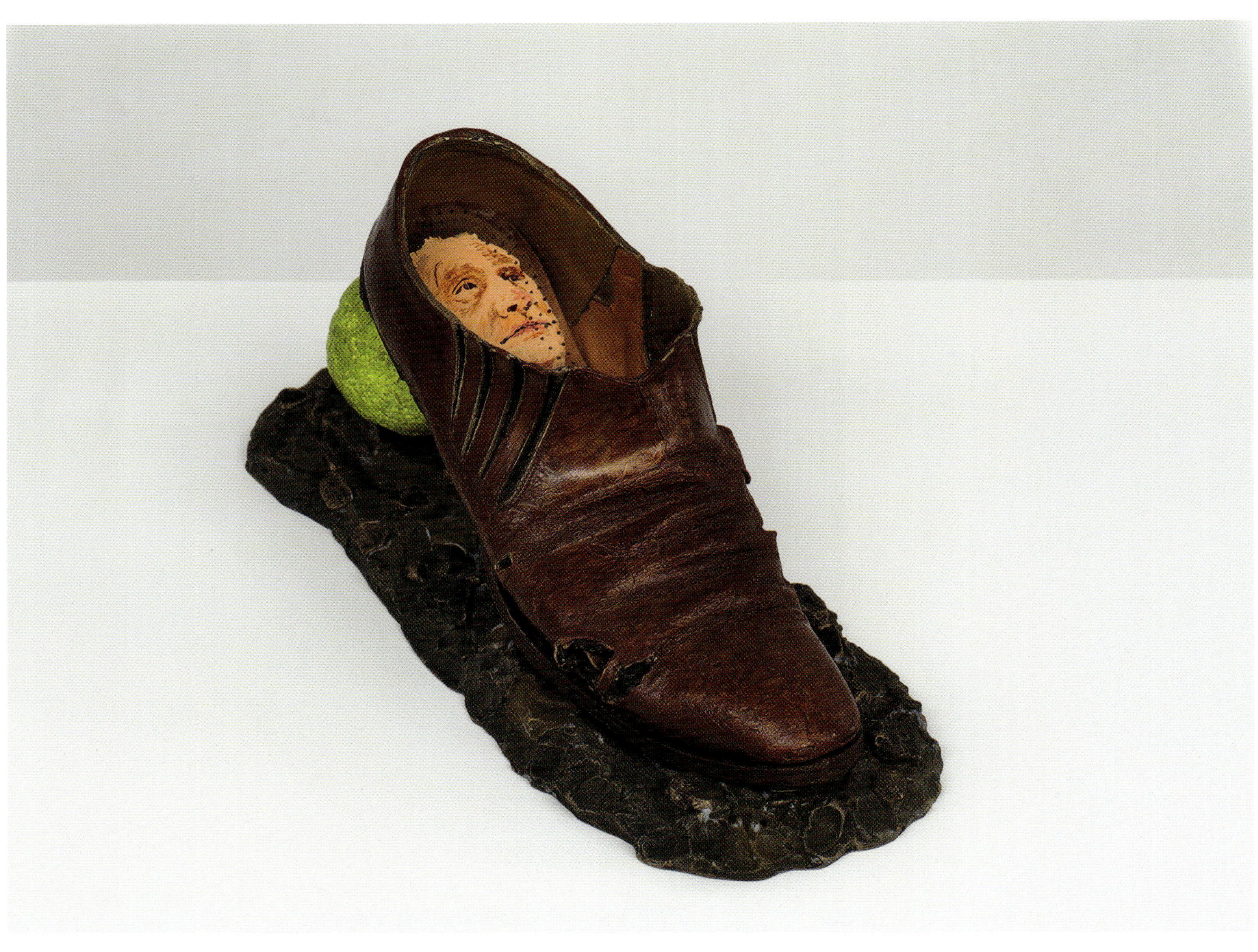

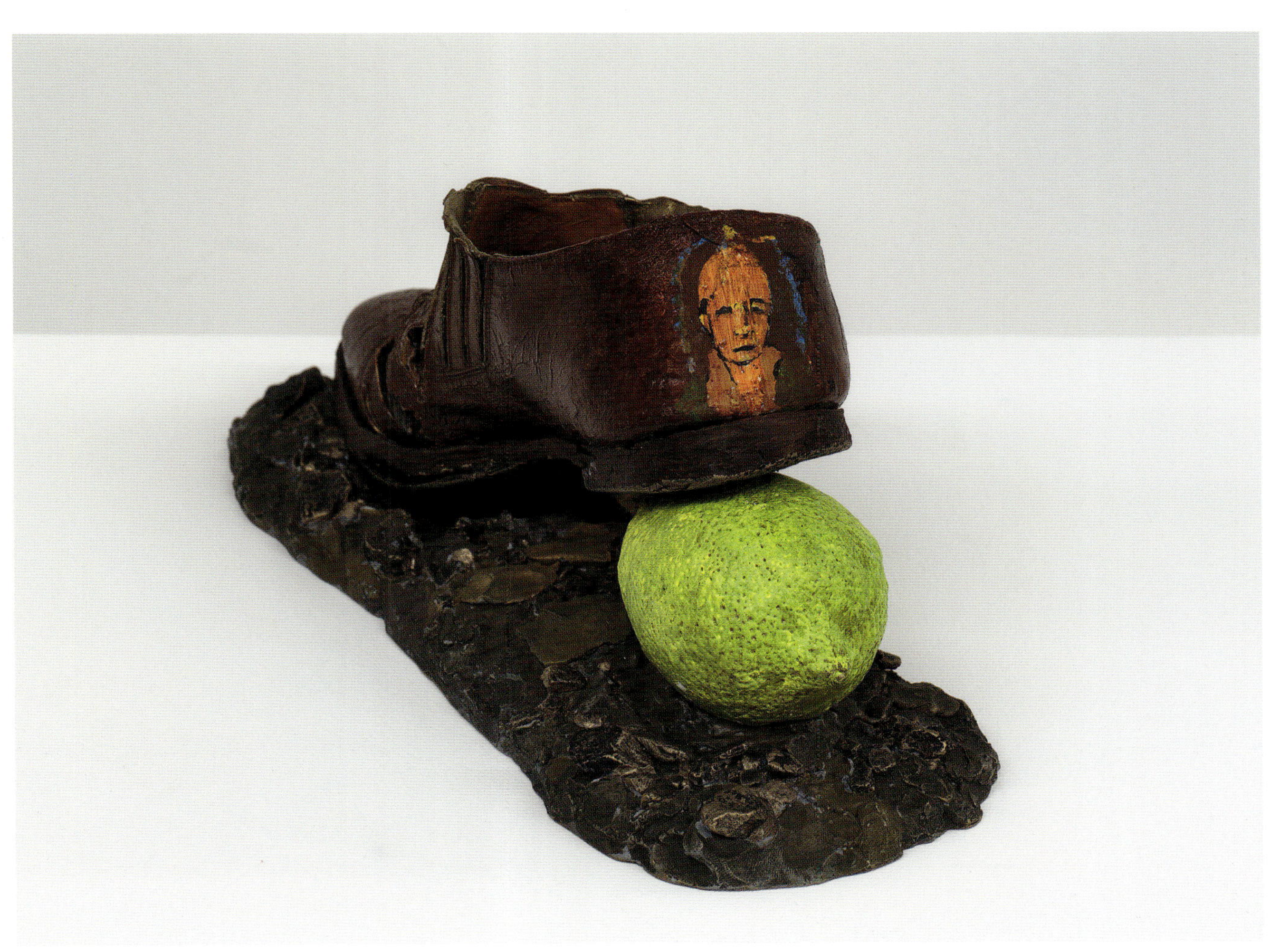

Three Self Portraits with a
Ripening Lemon, 2023
Painted bronze
6 1/4 x 15 x 6 in

Following the Marks
by Natacha Polaert

"You make the marks and let them lead you."
— Peter Nadin

It began—my obsession—a decade ago, soon after I was introduced to the French painter Claude Rutault, the radical inventor of the "de-finitions-methods," who, at age 73, was having at long last his first solo exhibition in America. Rutault (b. 1941; d. 2022) was a painter who did not touch paint or canvas. Instead, over a career of more than half a century, he issued sets of painting instructions to others—curators, collectors, or institutions—who became his "charge-takers." These "de-finitions/methods," as Rutault began calling them in 1973, guided his works, without themselves being works. "I write paintings," Rutault would say.

In the winter of 1978-79, Rutault became the first-ever French artist invited as artist-in-residence at the Institute for Art and Urban Resources, now MoMa PS1. During his time in New York, speaking barely a lick of English, Rutault keenly recorded his encounters with other artists and his obsessions with the city.

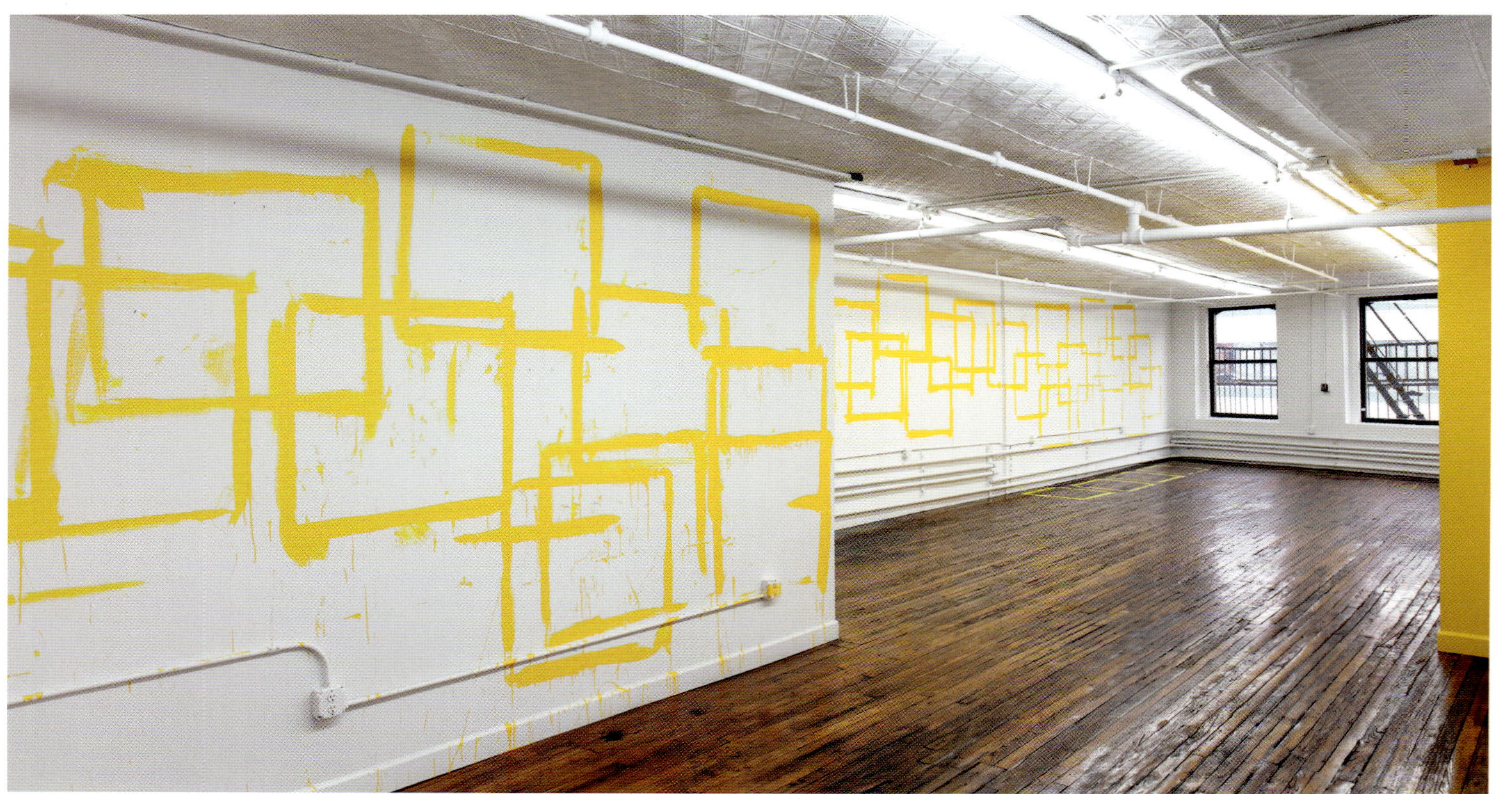

When these journals were donated to the Kandinsky Library at the Centre Pompidou in 2014, I spent time with the archive and, riffling through the files, one, in particular, struck me. It was a rather peculiar three-quarters-of-a-page protocol, never realized, dated June 1979, and written *entirely in French*, addressed to a mysterious Peter Nadin, whose collective art space on West Broadway in TriBeCa, Rutault had visited during his New York stay. In the hundreds of protocols written by Rutault, the "charge takers" were almost never nominal. But this one began: "As the person in charge of a space, Peter Nadin, will have to make a certain number of decisions, just as for any show."

Intrigued, I asked Claude, "Does this Peter Nadin speak French?"

"I don't know," came the answer. Deadpan.

I made a promise to Claude that day to seek Nadin out and ask him to take on the proposal so that it could become, at long last, a work.

I started to ask around. How difficult could finding this Peter Nadin prove to be?

"He left."

"He lives up in the country now."

"He won't be interested."

—

In early spring 2019, I decided to transform my commercial loft on Walker Street in TriBeCa into a space for *one* project, *one good project*, one that might have remained the only project for me. A great hero of mine, Glenn O'Brien, had recently passed away, leaving an extraordinary void in his wake. I organized a tribute exhibition, "Glenn O'Brien: Center Stage," conceived in the manner of a *portrait en creux*. I needed a name for my new space. Off Paradise came into being that fall.

The name evokes the old neighborhood of Five Points, at the center of which was a small, triangular park, full of hopes and grime, called Paradise Square. It also invokes Paradise Alley, the artists' and poets' colony on the then-godforsaken corner of Avenue A and East 11th Street that is referenced in Jack Kerouac's novel The Subterraneans. *Off Paradise is a fictional place, right off Paradise, adjacent to it, but not exactly it.*

Naturally, I invited Claude to be a part of the Glenn O'Brien show, because he and Glenn shared a profound keenness for words. Claude created *Bookshelves (A Portrait from Afar)*, 2019, a striking site-specific installation that reproduced Glenn's overfilled apartment bookshelves as an at-scale "portrait by subtraction."

One November afternoon, a favorite writer of mine, Randy Kennedy, walked into gallery and pulled up a chair. We started to talk and talked some more. Perhaps unsurprisingly, Randy focused much of his attention on the Rutault bookshelves. He was somewhat familiar with Rutault and remembered a trip to Paris where he had seen entire rooms dedicated to Rutault's work at the Pompidou. I brought up the old protocol addressed to Peter, written so many decades ago, by this point mostly a curio.

"Peter's my friend!" Randy said.

I was inching closer.

In early spring 2020, as the world was shutting down, Peter began a return to painting from life, based on close observation in his upstate greenhouse. He focused on his interest in citrus grafting, specifically his efforts to graft a Marrakesh lemon scion onto a sour-orange rootstock and his fascination with how the rootstock's energy allowed for the genetically different scion to produce fruit.

I painted the lemon I'd grafted because I grew it, knew it, trusted it.
Life isn't still—and a still life isn't still—no, it moves.
You just have to know how to follow the tracks.
I first saw the tracks in 1983, followed them—picked them up again in 2020.

An entirely new series was grafted, developed, and completed by the time 2020 drew to a close, marking Peter's return to "unconditional" painting after three decades in which he had withdrawn from the commercial art world and worked to rebuild his conception of painting through an extensive experimental body of work called the "Mark Series."

In the spring of 2022, Off Paradise hosted a pair of sequential exhibitions "A Proposal to Peter Nadin, 1979; realized 2022," Peter's fulfillment of the Rutault protocol, and "The Distance from a Lemon to Murder," works from his new series, exemplifying two inextricably interwoven aspects of Peter's career: his early conceptual projects and his ongoing exploration of pictorial conventions and mark-making.

During his realization of the Rutault proposal, Peter said:

I remember meeting Rutault in 1978, maybe start of '79. I remember him coming into the space at 84 West Broadway that I had with Chris D'Arcangelo. And he came in and looked around and we said "Hi" and what have you. Then some time later he came back, and we started to talk. I realized we had a lot of ideas in common and areas to explore. And another time later—I think the third visit—he came and handed me a proposal. And the proposal is what I'm executing now. It's taken forty-three years, not that long really. But now seems like the right time to do it. Before, I don't know why I didn't do it. But now, I want to do it. And I think that the space is the right place for it.

I feel grateful to have provided that space to Peter. I see Off Paradise as an homage to pioneering New York art spaces such as 84 West Broadway, operating in their spirit.

To know Peter is to love Peter. Ours is one of the single most rewarding and energizing relationships of my career. This book is the cartography, intaglio, of our friendship. I am profoundly grateful to Claude Rutault for having guided me to Peter, to Glenn O'Brien for inspiring Off Paradise, to Gina Nanni for making its debut possible, and to Randy Kennedy for making the vital introduction to this *seer*.

84 West Broadway final announcement card, 1979

The Work shown in this space is a response to the existing conditions and/or work previously shown within the space.

Nov. 9—
30 days work:
1,450 sq. ft.
Function by Peter Nadin
Design by function
Execution by Peter Nadin , Christopher D'Arcangelo and Nick Lawson
Materials: Compound, Drywall, Wood, Nails, Paint.

We have joined together to execute functional constructions and to alter or refurbish existing structures as a means of surviving in a capitalist economy.

Dec. 12 1978—

FOLLOWING AND TO BE FOLLOWED.
A work in situ by DANIEL BUREN
Opening Tuesday, Dec. 12 7-9 pm.

Feb 1 1979—

PAINTING FOR ONE PLACE
SEAN SCULLY

Mar 28 1979—

JANE REYNOLDS

Apr 19-25 1979

A PLACE TO STAY / CONCERNING A DUALITY
OF FUNCTION

APRIL 26, 1979 —

AROOM
DEFIN
EDNOT
BYITS
WALLS
BUTBY
APUMP   PETER FEND

MAY 16, 1979
8PM
RHYS CHATHAM

performance with
GLENN BRANCA
and NINA CANAL

MAY 30, 1979

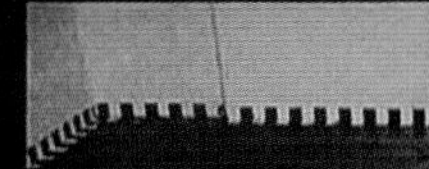

This Work may be seen every thurs thru sat 1-6pm at Peter Nadin, 3n 84 West Broadway, N.Y., N.Y. 10007.

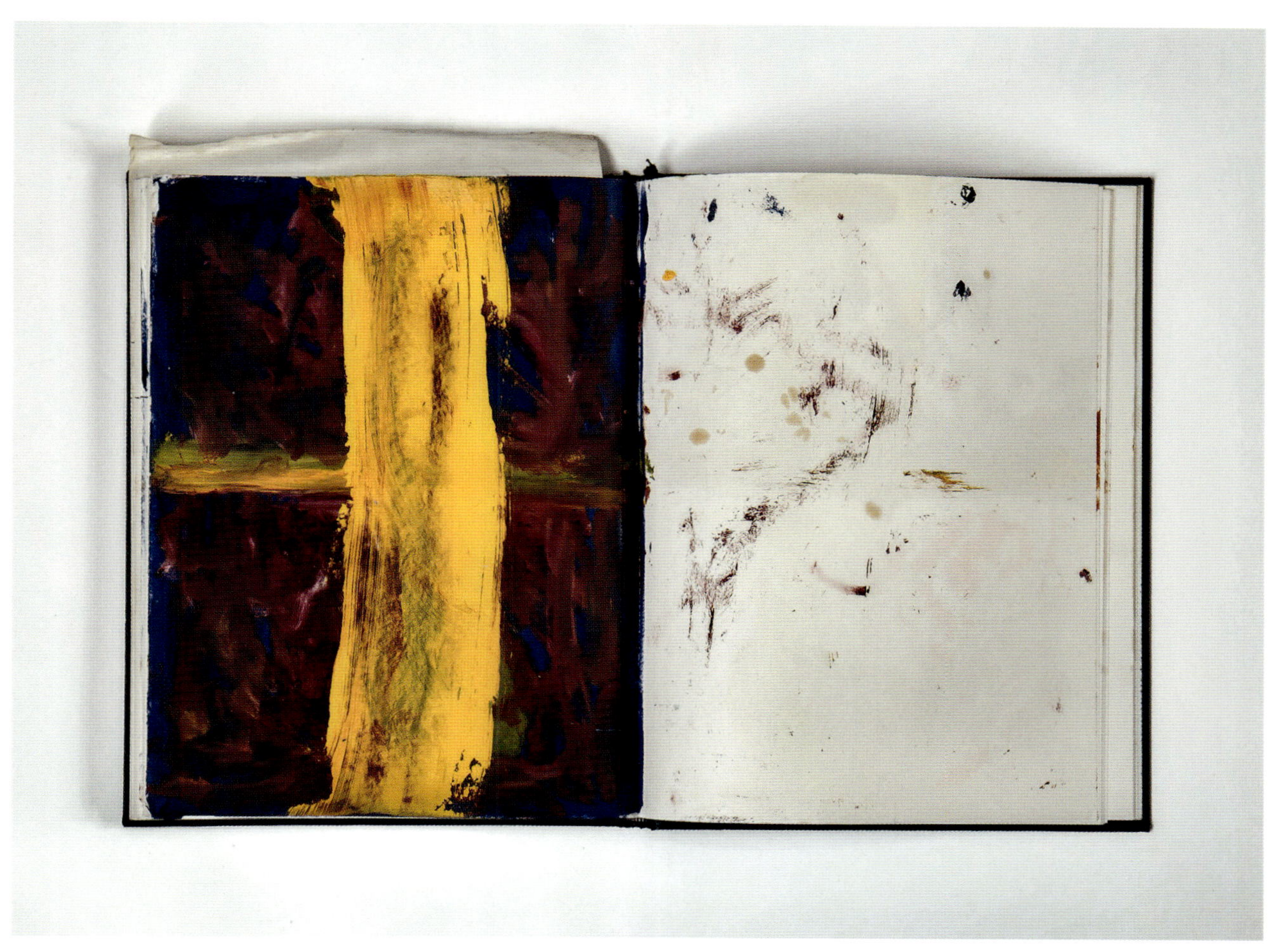

Notebook entry, 1978

Works Index

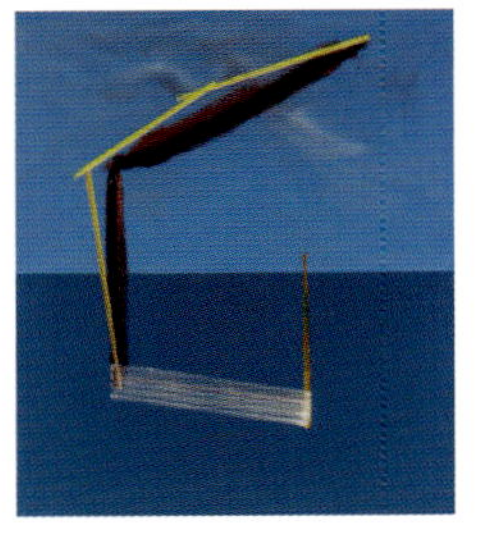

8

View II / The Artist, 1986
Oil, acrylic, and enamel on canvas
72 x 63 1/2 in

Gift of Raymond J. Learsy to the
American Friends of the Centre
Pompidou

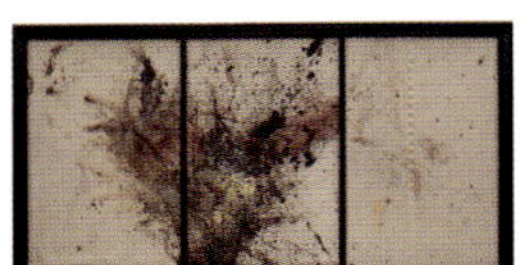

16

Landscape and Instinct, 2011
Wax, honey, black walnut and cashmere wool on linen
82 x 165 in

Collection of the artist

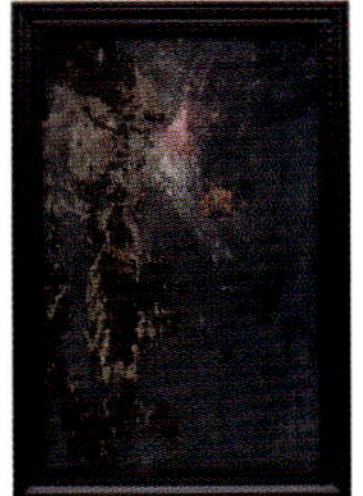

19

House and Dream III, 2010
Wax, honey, black walnut, indigo flake
white on linen
82 x 55 in

Collection of the artist

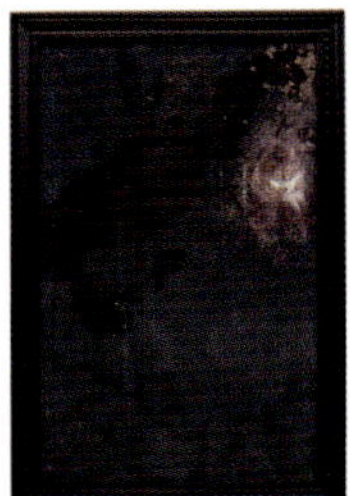

19

House and Dream IV, 2010
Wax, honey, black walnut, indigo flake
white on linen
82 x 55 in

Collection of the artist

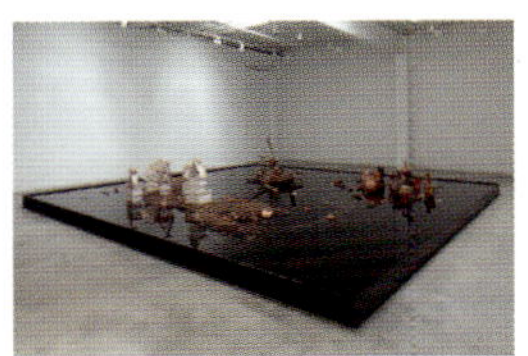

20

Raft, 2010
Honey, terracotta, wood, twine, bank
run, wax, ham
24 x 24 ft

Collection of the artist

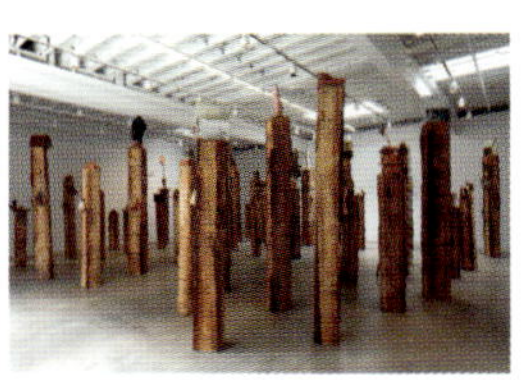

21

The Bo'sun's Chair, 2010
Hemlock trees, terracotta, wood,
string, nutria fur, wax, fabric, indigo
pigment, bronze, galvanized nails
5 ft – 10 ft 2 in

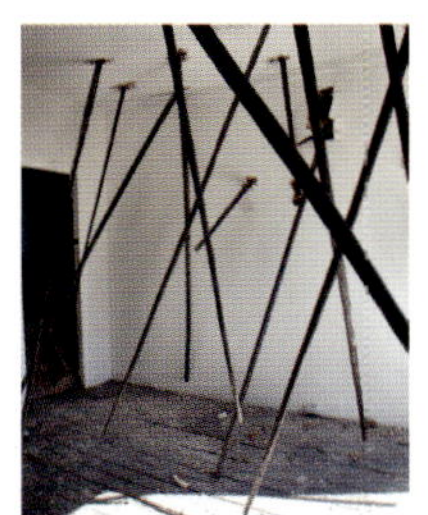

25

First Mark installation
New Orleans, 1991

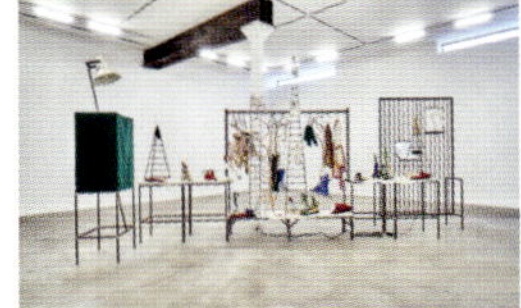

27

Off the Rack, 2019
Various materials, video
111 × 218 × 80 in

Collection of the artist

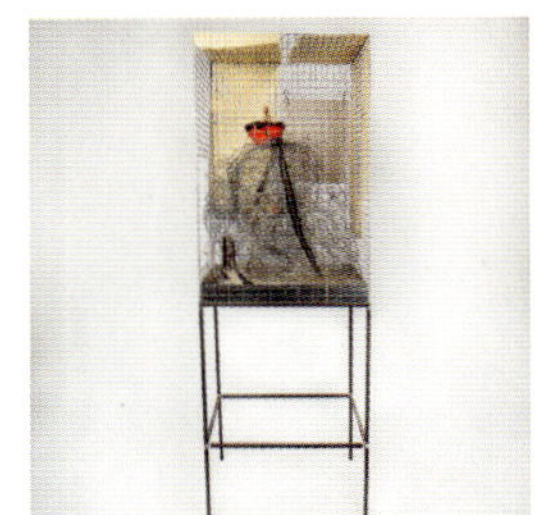

30

Off the Rack (detail), 2019
Various materials
111 × 218 × 80 in

Collection of the artist

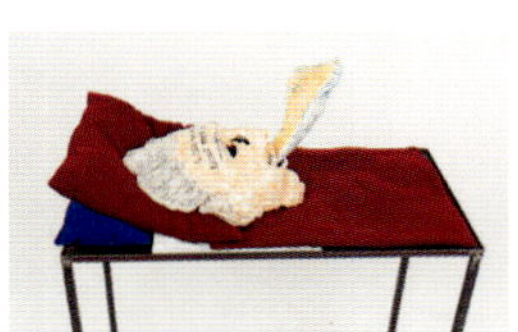

31

Off the Rack (detail), 2019
Metal, ceramics, fabric
111 × 218 × 80 in

Collection of the artist

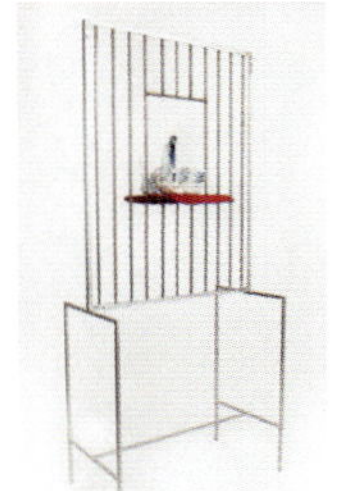

32

Off the Rack: The Programmer
(detail), 2019
Metal, ceramics, fabric
74 3/4 x 33 1/2 x 18 in

Collection of the artist

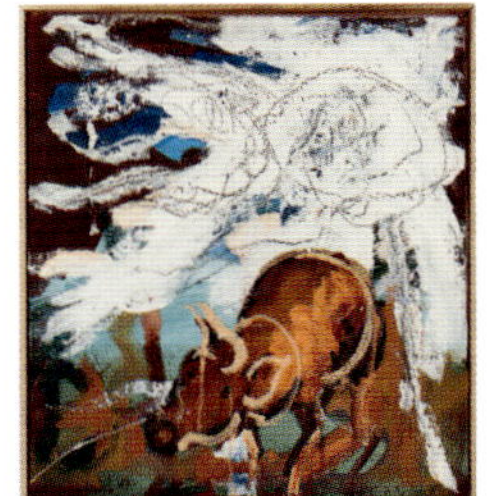

35

Abe in Landscape Rooting, 2015
Oil on panel
21 x 19 in

Courtesy Off Paradise

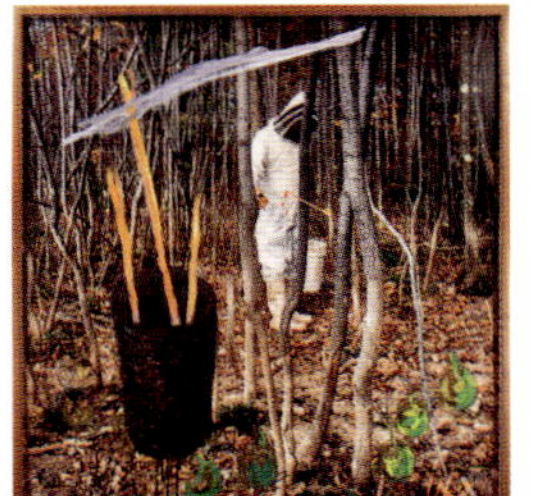

36

Heracles, 2015
Oil on photograph
36 1/2 x 36 1/2 in

Courtesy Off Paradise

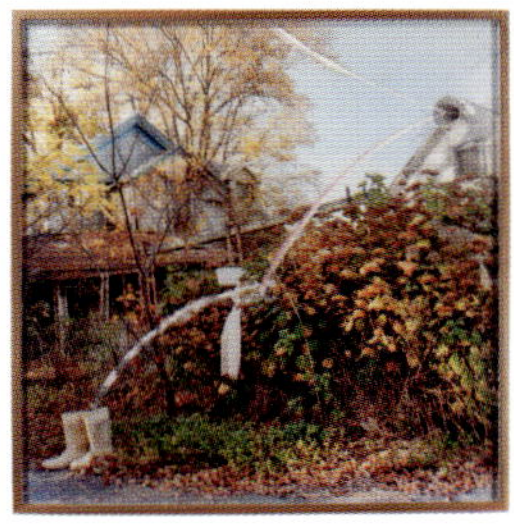

38

Cedrini's Lodge with Mark, 2015
Oil on photograph
36 1/2 x 36 1/2 in

Courtesy Off Paradise

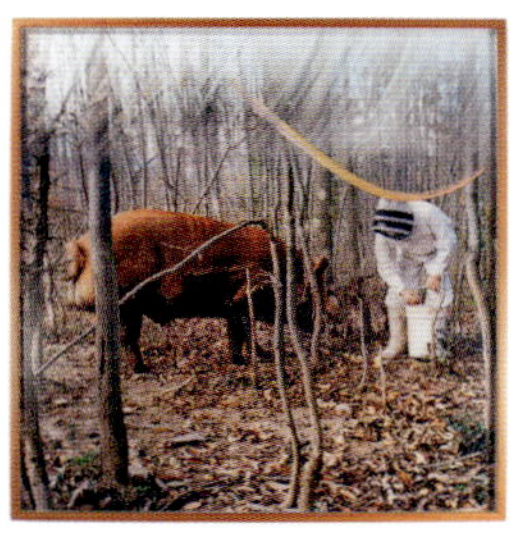

38

Feeding Abe, 2015
Oil on photograph
36 1/2 x 36 1/2 in

Courtesy Off Paradise

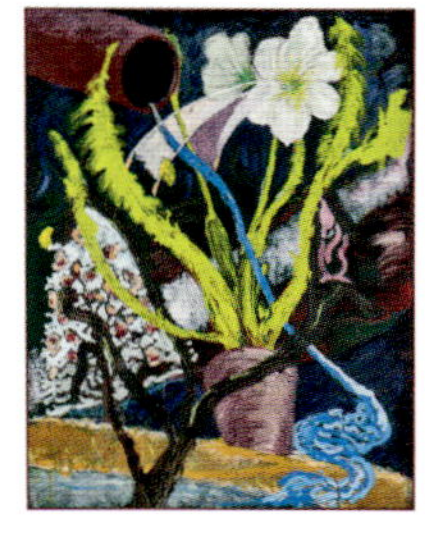

53

The Culvert Drains into the Pond While the Lilies Blossom in a Pot, 2020
Oil on panel
43 3/8 x 34 in

Collection of Shezad & Miranda Dawood

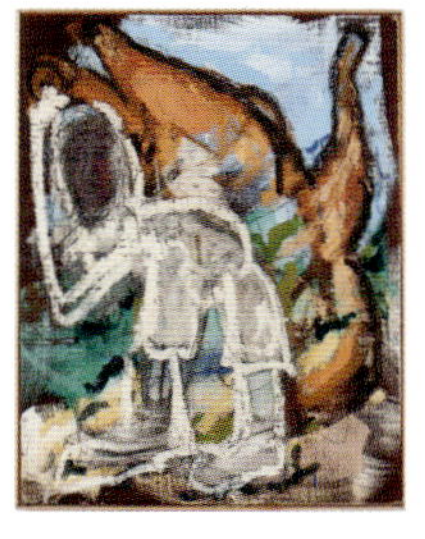

39

Abe and Me, 2015
Oil on panel
43 x 33 in

Courtesy Off Paradise

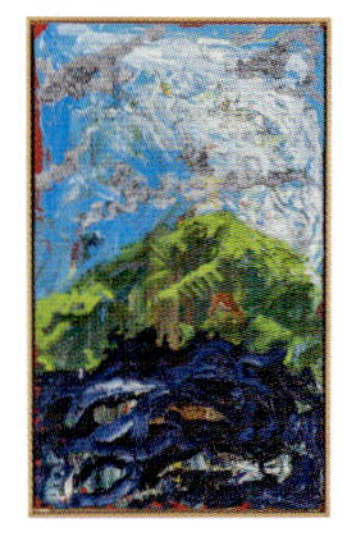

54

Young Deer by the Pond, 2020
Oil on panel
30 15/16 x 18 7/8 in

Collection of Ryan Sloan

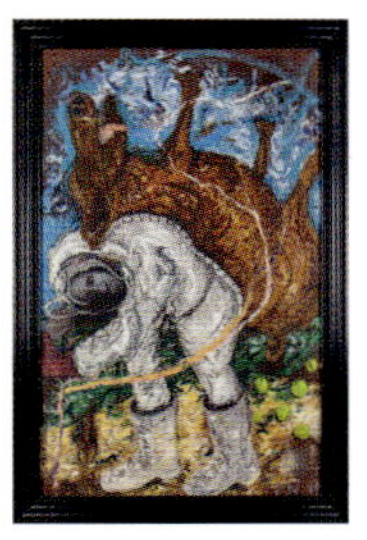

40

Abe and Me / Heracles and the Erymanthian Boar, 2015
Oil on panel
82 x 55 in

Collection of the artist

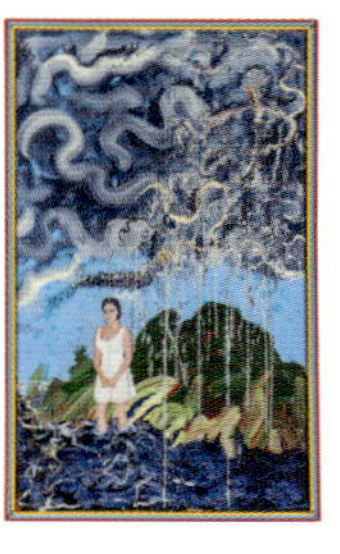

55

Annaliet Quero Standing in the Water, 2020
Oil on panel
32 1/2 x 20 11/16 in

Collection of Raymond J. Learsy

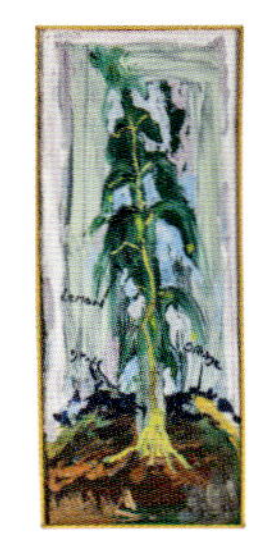

47

A Graft of Marrakesh Lemon onto Sour Orange Rootstock, 2020
Oil on panel
18 1/2 x 7 11/16 in

Collection of Robert Becker

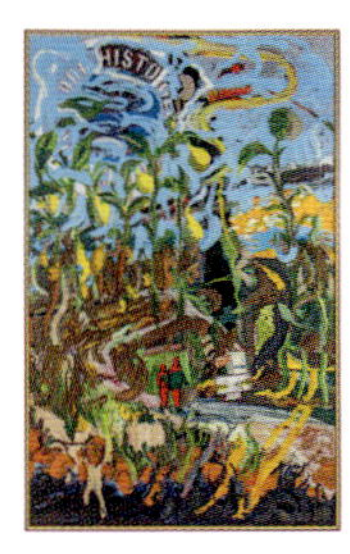

56

Two Figures Walking Past Dimitrios the Greek's Possessions on Cornwallville Road, 2020
Oil on panel
77 3/4 x 49 3/8 in

Collection of Diane L. Ackerman

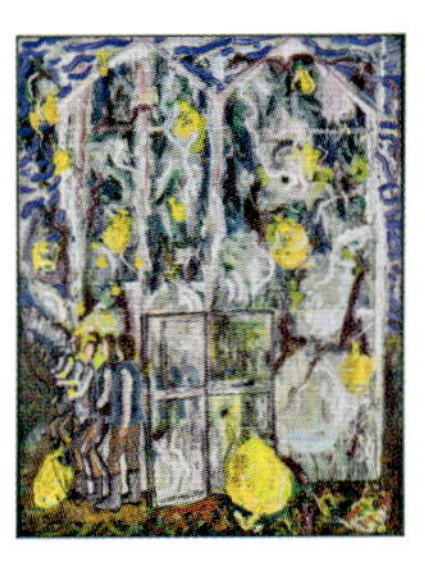

49

Anne and Lemons Leaving the Greenhouse, 2020
Oil on panel
43 3/8 x 34 1/8 in

Collection of Raymond J. Learsy

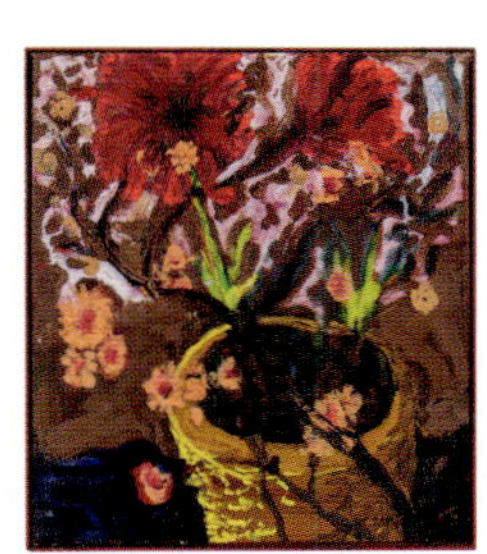

59

Amaryllis in a Pot, 2020
Oil on panel
20 3/4 x 18 3/4 in

Courtesy Off Paradise

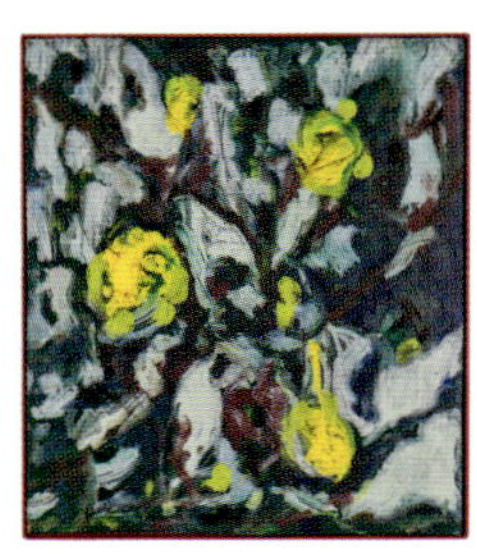

50

Lemon or Yellow, 2020
Oil on panel
20 3/4 x 18 3/4 in

Collection of Solveig Fernlund

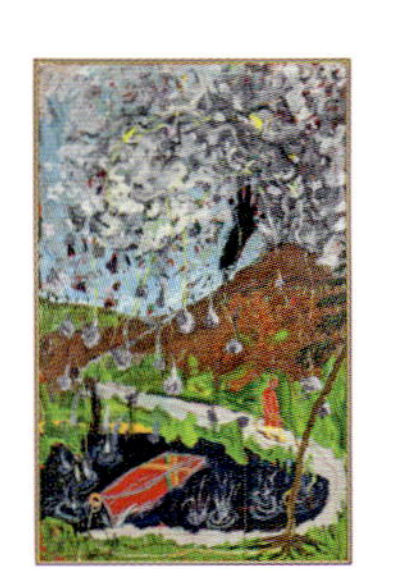

62

Red Figure Walking to Red Boat (Volcano Erupting), 2020
Oil on panel
77 7/8 x 49 1/2 in

Courtesy Off Paradise

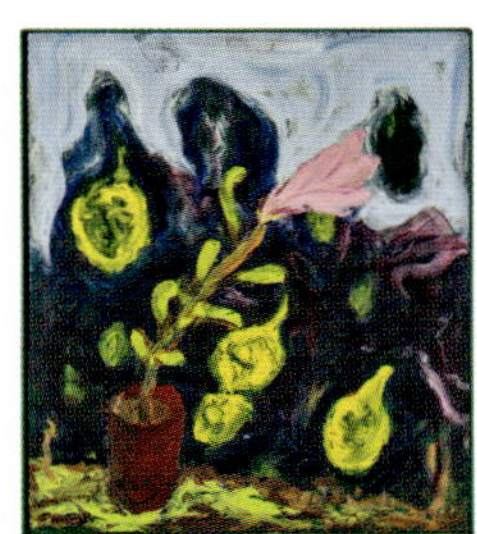

51

Lemons and Mountains, 2020
Oil on panel
20 3/4 x 18 3/4 in

Collection of Natacha Polaert

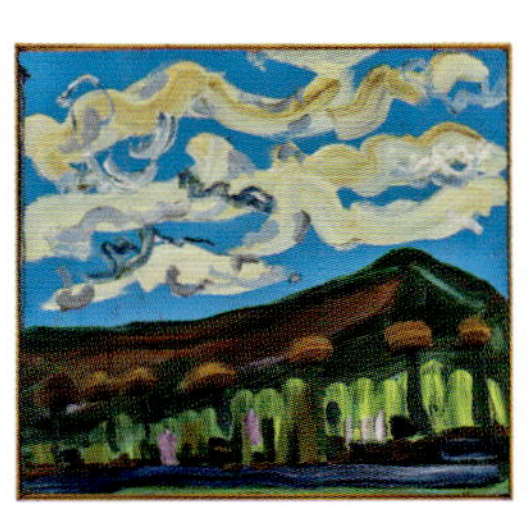

64

The Water Flows From the Culvert to the Pond, to Catskill Creek, to the Hudson River, 2020
Oil on panel
18 13/16 x 20 3/4 in

Courtesy Off Paradise

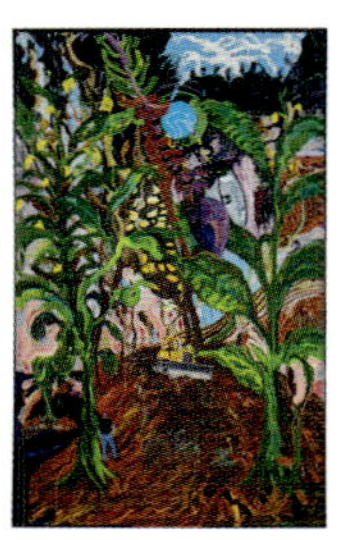

67

Curt and Mert Landscaping, 2020
Oil on panel
77 3/8 x 48 1/2 in

Gift of Raymond J. Learsy to
the American Friends of the
Centre Pompidou

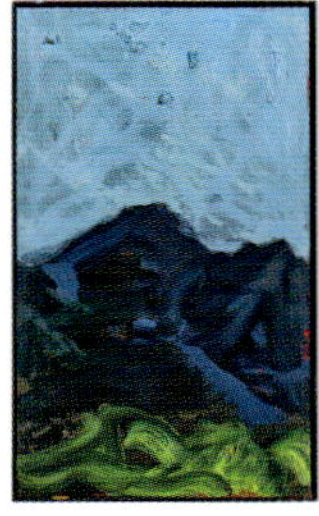

70

Mount Pisgah at Dusk, 2020
Oil on panel
20 3/4 x 12 3/4 in

Collection of Janet & Randy Kennedy

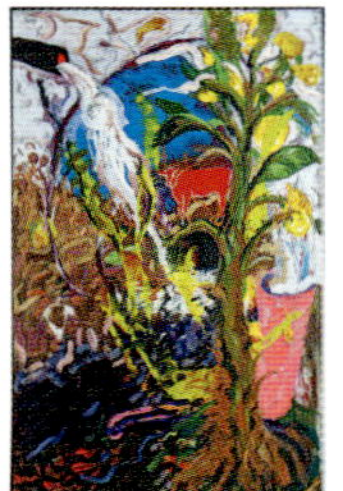

73

Sharkey's Cow Beneath a Culvert, 2020
Oil on panel
77 3/8 x 48 3/8 in

Courtesy Off Paradise

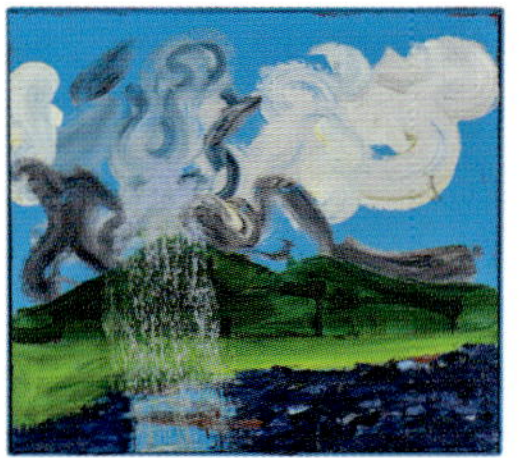

75

*Cloud Burst of Wax Rain Falls onto the
Pond*, 2020
Oil on panel
18 13/16 x 20 3/4 in

Courtesy Off Paradise

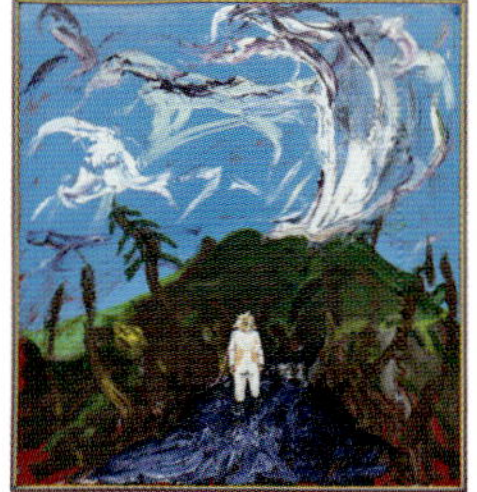

77

Stu Sugar Standing in the Water, 2020
Oil on panel
34 3/4 x 32 in

Collection of Raymond J. Learsy

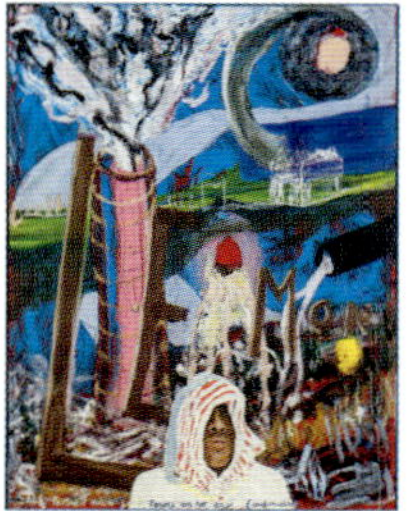

78

*Self Portrait with Wet Towel on a Hot Day
(unfinished)*, 2020
Oil on panel
42 3/4 x 33 3/4 in

Collection of Beth Rudin DeWoody

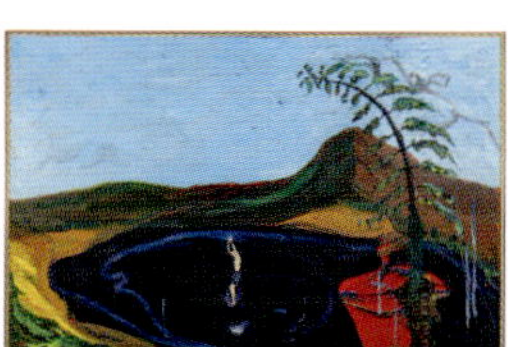

80

Johan Jumps from a Tree into the Pond, 2020
Oil on panel
49 7/16 x 77 5/8 in

Collection of Johan Svensson

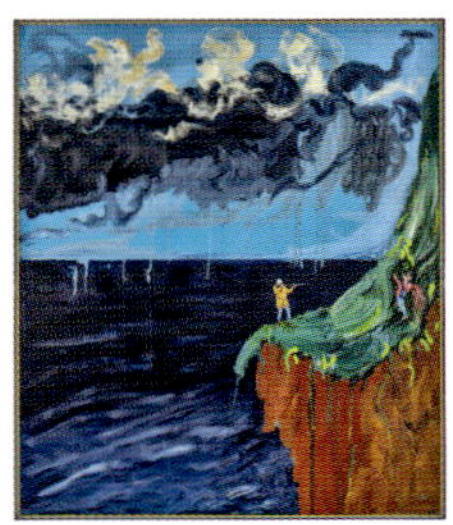

82

I Am Shot: A Murder to Prevent Murder,
2020
Oil on panel
57 x 49 1/4 in

Collection of the artist

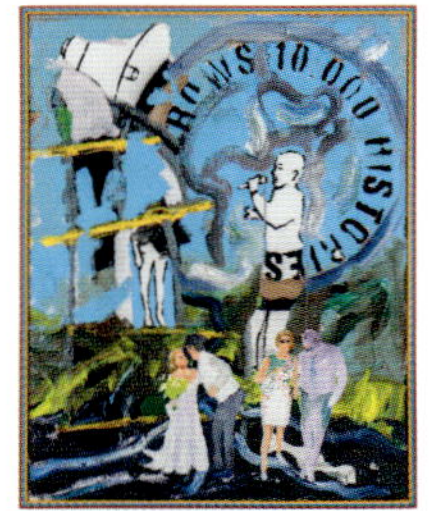

91

The Secret Wedding of the Invisible Man,
2022
Oil on panel
43 3/4 x 34 7/8 in

Collection of Natacha Polaert

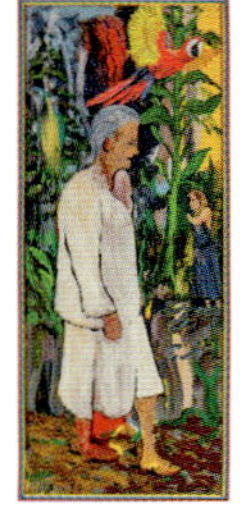

92

The Programmer, 2022
Oil on panel
49 1/4 x 20 3/4 in

Courtesy Off Paradise

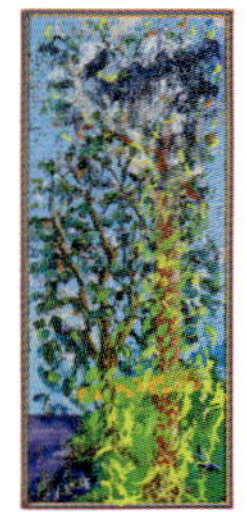

93

Landscape with Tree and Storm, 2023
Oil on panel
48 1/2 x 21 in

Courtesy Off Paradise

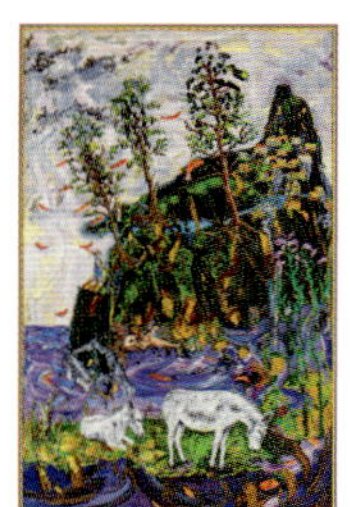

95

*Sharkey's Donkey Watching a Fish
(A Migration of Golden Orfe)*, 2023
Oil on panel
77 5/8 x 49 3/8 in

Courtesy Off Paradise

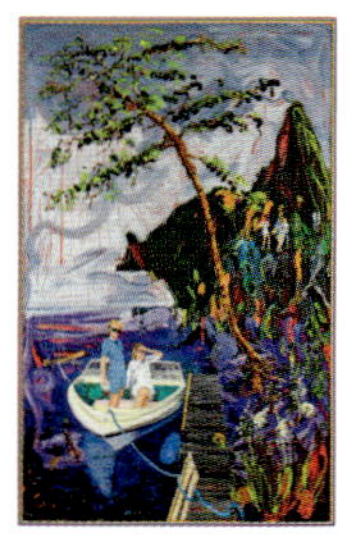

98

The Blue Rope, 2023
Oil on panel
77 5/8 x 49 3/8 in

Courtesy Off Paradise

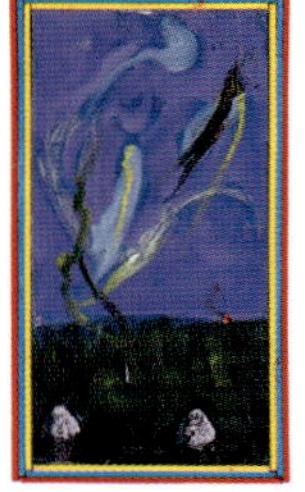

100

A View East Before Dawn, 2023
Oil on panel
16 1/4 x 9 1/4 in

Courtesy Off Paradise

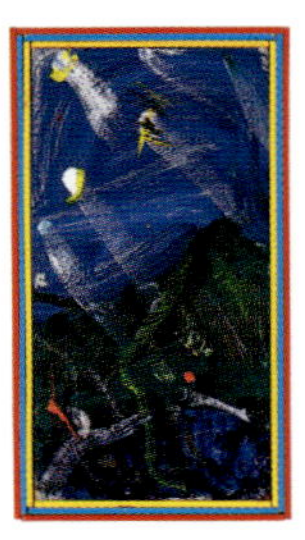

100

Looking North, Seeing Mount Pisgah, 2023
Oil on panel
16 1/4 x 9 1/4 in

Courtesy Off Paradise

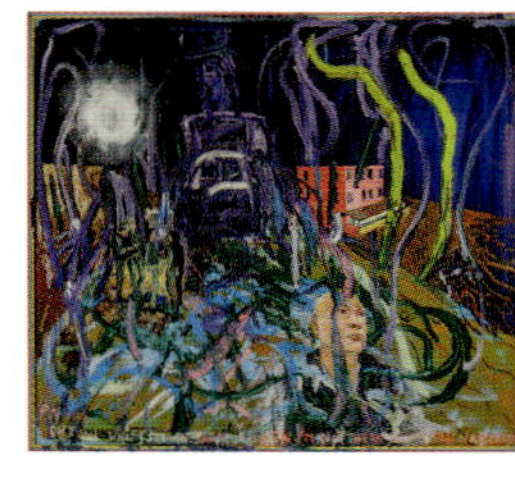

114

*How I Look, What I See in Baracoa When
I'm Not There (Self Portrait in Absentia)*,
2022
Oil on panel
57 3/8 x 49 1/2 in

Courtesy Off Paradise

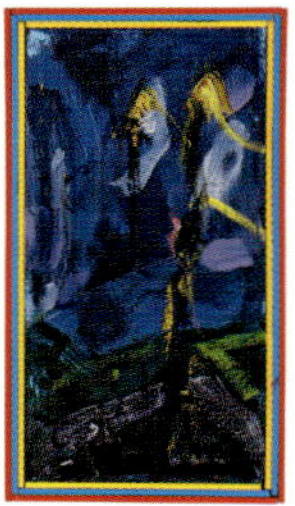

101

Seeing Night Sky, 2023
Oil on panel
16 1/4 x 9 1/4 in

Courtesy Off Paradise

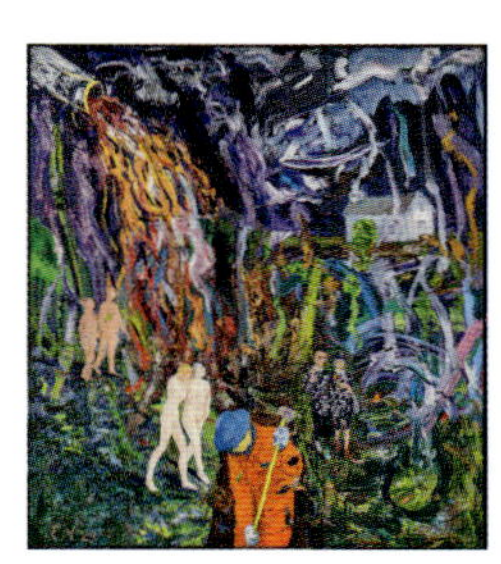

116

*Adam Installing Utilities in the Garden of
Eden Under the Devil's Fire*, 2023
Oil on panel
48 3/4 x 44 3/4 in

Courtesy Off Paradise

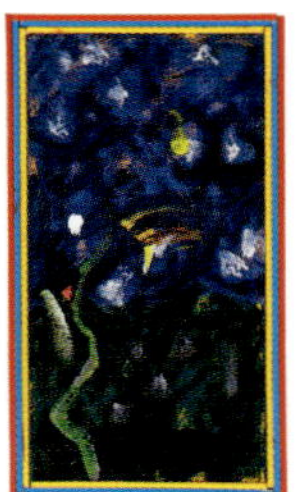

101

Looking at Southern Night Sky, 2023
Oil on panel
16 1/4 x 9 1/4 in

Courtesy Off Paradise

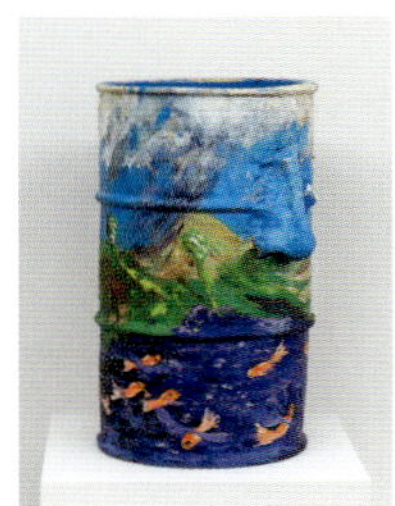

120

Drum with Nose, 2023
Painted terracotta
21 1/2 x 11 3/4 x 13 in

Courtesy Off Paradise

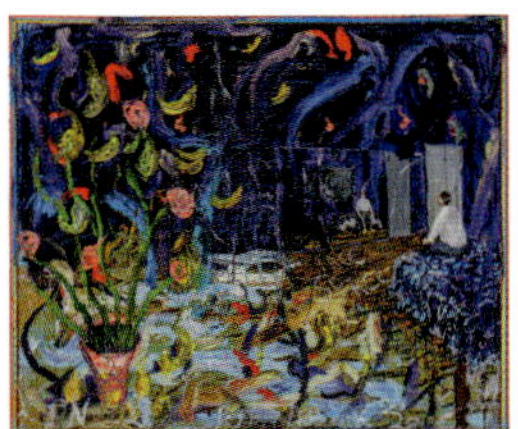

102

Dave-Id Looks in a Mirror (Sees Himself),
2022
Oil on panel
49 1/2 x 41 3/8 in

Courtesy Off Paradise

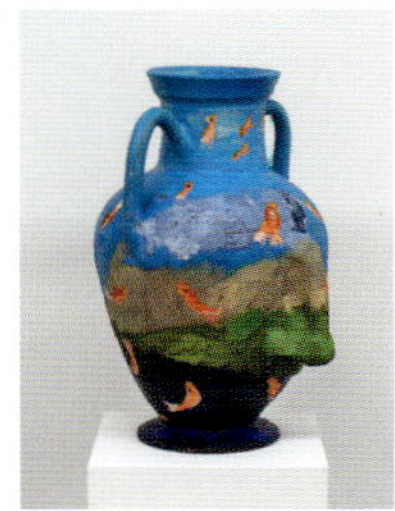

121

Jar with Nose, 2023
Painted terracotta
20 1/2 x 12 3/4 x 14 1/2 in

Courtesy Off Paradise

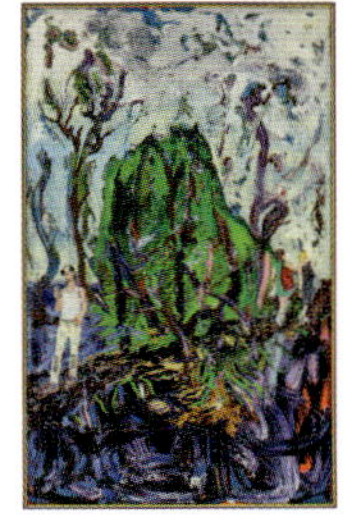

106

Mount Pisgah with Three Figures on a Path,
2022
Oil on panel
77 3/4 x 48 3/4 in

Courtesy Off Paradise

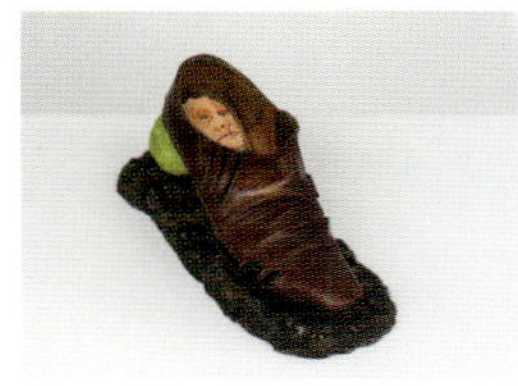

122

Three Self Portraits with a Ripening Lemon,
2023
Painted bronze
6 1/4 x 15 x 6 in

Courtesy Off Paradise

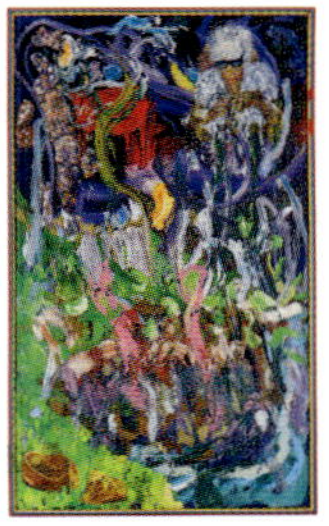

110

Landscape with Shoe and Ghost, 2023
Oil on panel
49 1/4 x 30 1/2 in

Courtesy Off Paradise

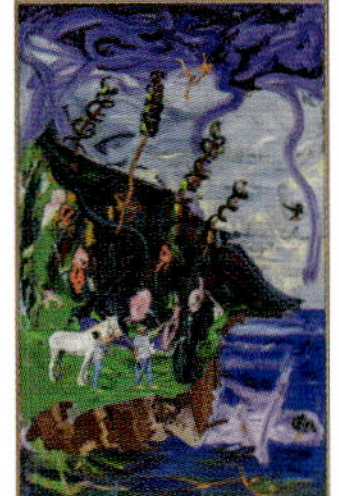

113

*The Crow Catches a Golden Orfe (Sharkey
and Amanda See It)*, 2023
Oil on panel
78 x 49 in

Courtesy Off Paradise

Bibliographical Notes

Peter Nadin

1954 Born in Bromborough, England

Education

1972-76 Newcastle-upon-Tyne University, England

Solo Exhibitions

2024 "The Invisible World", Off Paradise, New York
2023 "Views, Independent 20th Century", Battery Maritime Building, New York
2022 "The Distance From A Lemon to Murder", Off Paradise, New York
Claude Rutault, A Proposal to Peter Nadin, 1979; realized 2022, Off Paradise, New York
2019 "The Mark Series: The Speaker...Off The Rack", James Fuentes Gallery, New York Third 2017-18 Mark / El Tercer Trazo, Centro de Desarrollo de las Artes Visuales, Havana, Cuba
"Third Mark", Galería Provincial Arte Soy, Santiago de Cuba, Cuba Third Mark, Galería Provincial de Artes Plásticas, Guantánamo, Cuba Third Mark, Galería Provincial de Pedro Esquerré, Villa Clara, Cuba Third Mark, Centro Provincial de Artes Plásticas Galería, Pinar del Río, Cuba
2015 "Still Life", Half Gallery, New York
2013 "Taxonomy Transplanted", Horticultural Society of New York
2011 "First Mark / El Primer Trazo", Gavin Brown's Enterprise, New York
2007-09 "First Mark / El Primer Trazo", San Francisco de Asis Convento, Havana, Cuba, organized by Wilfedo Lam Center
"First Mark", Museo Municipal de Arte Moderno Museo de Gibara, Cuba First Mark, Finca Correa Jovellanos, Matanzas, Cuba
"First Mark", Galeria Jose Miguel Gonzalez, Colon, Matanzas, Cuba First Mark, Museo de Holguin, Holguin, Cuba
"First Mark", Museo de Matanzas, Matanzas, Cuba
"First Mark", San Antonio de los Baños, Cuba
"First Mark", Museo de Arte de Pinar (MAPRI), Pinar del Rio, Cuba
"First Mark", Cuenca, Ecuador
1993 "Peter Nadin", Brooke Alexander Gallery, New York
1992 "Recent Work: Selection from Six Series", Yale Center for British Art, Yale University, New Haven
1991 "A Tide of Tongues, Peter Nadin", Thea Westreich, New York
"Seven Sisters, Peter Nadin and Jessica Stockholder", Adelson Galleries, New York
"Poetry Room", one-year installation, American Fine Art, New York 1990 The Double, Jay Gorney Modern Art, New York
"Time Between Waves", Jablonka Galerie, Cologne
1989 "Studio Window", Brooke Alexander Gallery, New York
"Currents: Peter Nadin", Institute of Contemporary Art, Boston 1988 Views, Jay Gorney Modern Art, New York
1987 "Peter Nadin, Views XI & XII", Cash/Newhouse Gallery, New York
"Peter Nadin, Still Life Paintings 1982-83", Amelie A. Wallace Gallery, State University of New York, College at Old Westbury, Long Island
"Views", Brooke Alexander Gallery, New York
1986 "The Symmetry of Night and Day", Brooke Alexander Gallery, New York Peter Nadin, Jay Gorney Modern Art, New York
1985 "State of the Mind", Cash/Newhouse Gallery, New York 1984 Fountain City, Jack Tilton Gallery, New York
1983 "Still Life", Hallwalls, Buffalo
"Still Life, Spiritual America", New York
1982 "Eating Friends", (with Jenny Holzer), Artists Space, New York
"Living", (with Jenny Holzer), Chantal Crousel Gallery, Paris Living, La Coin de Miroir, Dijon
1981 "Living", Le Nouveau Musée, Lyon Living, Museum Für (Sub)Kultur, Berlin
1980 "Living", Rudiger Schottle Gallery, Munich Living, Onze Rue Clavel, Paris

Selected Group Exhibitions

2022 "Symbiosis", curated by Beth Rudin DeWoody, Berkshire Botanical Garden, Massachusetts
2022 "Peter Nadin and Maximilian Schubert", Independent New York, Spring Studios, New York
2021 "NOTHNG OF THE MONTH CLUB", an exhibition under the sign of Ray Johnson curated by Randy Kennedy and Natacha Polaert, Off Paradise, New York
2020 "The Penumbral Age in the Time of Planetary Change", The Museum of Modern Art, Warsaw

2016 The "Value of Food", The Cathedral Church of Saint John the Divine, New York
2015 "Family Business", New York
2014 Flag Art Gallery, New York
2010 "One Leading Away from Another", 303 Gallery, New York Huis Clos, Galleria Elba Benitez, Madrid, Spain
2008 The Havana Biennial: Punto de Encuentro, Havana, Cuba
2008 The New Orleans Biennial: Prospect 1, KKProjects, New Orleans
1991 "Drawings", Brooke Alexander Gallery, New York
"One Hundred Years of European and American Art", Adelson Galleries, New York
1990 "The Unique Print: '70s into the '90s", Lois & Michael Torf Gallery
"The Unique Print", Museum of Fine Arts, Boston
"All Quiet on the Western Front", Galerie Antoine Candau, Paris
1989 "Landscapes", Brooke Alexander Gallery, New York
1988 "Eroffnungsausstellung", Joblonka Galerie, Cologne
The Venice Biennial: Aperto XLIII
"Art at the End of the Social", Rooseum, Stockholm 12 From New York, Grey Art Gallery, New York Group Exhibition, Jay Gorney Modern Art, New York Paintings, Michael Klein, Inc., New York
1987 "Similia/Dissimilia", Stadtische Kunsthalle Düsseldorf
"Similia/Dissimilia", Columbia University, New York
"Similia/Dissimilia", Leo Castelli Gallery, New York
"Similia/Dissimilia", Sonnabend Gallery, New York
"Major Acquisitions, Small Appliances", Solo Gallery, New York
1986 "Emerging Artists", Cleveland Center for Contemporary Art The Moral Essays, Castelli Graphics, New York
Group Show, Brooke Alexander Gallery, New York
Group Show, Cash/Newhouse Gallery, New York
"Odd and Intense", Pictogram Gallery, New York
Group Show, Jay Gorney Modern Art, New York
1985 "Alles und Noch Viel Mehr", Kunstmuseum, Bern Persona Non Grata, Daniel Newburg Gallery, New York
"Thought Objects, JAA #7", Cash/Newhouse Gallery, New York From Organism to Architecture, Studio School, New York Final Love, Cash/Newhouse Gallery, New York
"Smart Art", Carpenter Center, Harvard University, Cambridge Cult and Decorum, Tibor de Nagy Gallery,
"New York Inside/Out", DeFacto, New York
Group Show, Jay Gorney Modern Art, New York
1984 "Natural Genre", Florida State University, Tallahassee
"Recent Prints", Minneapolis Society of Fine Art
"A Pierre et Marie", Rue D'Ulm, Paris
"Civilization and the Landscape of Discontent, Nature Morte", New York Still Life with Transaction, International with Monument, New York Still Life with Transaction, Gallery Jurka, Amsterdam
1983 Festival of Language, M.C.A.D. and Walker Art Center, Minneapolis
"A Pierre et Marie", Rue D'Ulm, Paris
Group Show, Cleveland Contemporary Arts
1982 Group Show, Barbara Gladstone Gallery, New York Group Show, Le Nouveau Musée, Lyon
Presence Discret, Dijon Musée, France
1981 "A New Sensibility", Young Hoffman Gallery, Chicago
"Addressed", Annina Nosei Gallery, New York
"Represent, Representative, Representation", Brooke Alexander Gallery, New York Westkunst, Heute Section, Museen der Stadt, Cologne
1980 "Collaborative Projects", Brooke Alexander Gallery, New York 14
"New Artists", Lisson Gallery, London
"Times Square Show", New York
"The Offices of Fend, Fitzgibbon, Holzer, Nadin, Prince, and Winters", 305 Broadway, New York
"The Offices of Fend", White Columns, New York
"The Offices of Fend", Anna Leonowens Gallery, Halifax
1978-79 Gallery, 84 West Broadway
1977-78 Collaboration with Chris D'Arcangelo

Selected Film Screenings

2019 "Taxonomy Transplanted," Serpentine Cinema & General Ecology: On Earth at The Long Now, Kraftwerk Berlin, Germany
"First Mark," Host: Abstractions, Land, Water, Enclosures, Distance, Sea and Seed,
Kunsthal Aarhus, Denmark
2018 "First Mark," Cinema Zagara, Athens, Greece
2017 "Third Mark," Gibara International Film Festival, Gibara, Cuba

Bibliography

2022 Kennedy, Randy. "The Distance from a Lemon to Murder: A Conversation with Peter Nadin," The Paris Review (May 17)
Murtha, Chris. "Claude Rutault & Peter Nadin," The Brooklyn Rail, April 2022
2019 Kennedy, Randy. "Design by Function: An oral history of the experimental art space 84
West Broadway 1978-79," Ursula, Issue 3 (Summer) 2017 Hoffman, Laura. "Peter Nadin," Artforum (February)
Arias, Martha Cabrales. "English Artist Exhibits the Third Mark in Santiago de Cuba," Sierra Maestra (April)
Pupo, Erian Peña. "The Third Mark by Peter Nadin," La Union de Escritores y Artistas de Cuba (April)
Tejeda, Darion Martinez. "Unconventional Exhibition is Shown in Guantanamo,"
Venceremos (November)
2016 D'Aurizio, Michele. "The Gesture that Makes the Mark," Flash Art (January)
2013 Wallace, Ian. "Peter Nadin at the Horticultural Society of New York," Artforum
2011 Kennedy, Randy. "Farm to Gallery: Peter Nadin's Comeback," New York Times Magazine
(June)
Cashdan, Marina. "The Taming of Peter Nadin," Art in America (June)
Yablonsky, Linda. "Peter Nadin: The Muse of Old Field Farm," Artnet (July)
Hurst, Howard. "Caring About Peter Nadin," Hyperallergic (July)
Scrimgeour, Alexander. "Peter Nadin at Gavin Brown's Enterprise," Artforum (October)
1991 Jones, Alan. "Books in Artists' Lives, Part II Peter Nadin" Arts (February) Jones, Alan. "The Space for
Poetry," Tema Celeste (June)
Princenthal, Nancy. "Artist Book Beat: Tide of Tongues, Peter Nadin," Print Collectors Newsletter, vol. XXII No. 3
Frankel, Stephen Robert. "Poetic Despensation," Art & Auction (April)
Bessler, Gabriele. "Peter Nadin at Jablonka Gallery," Kunstforum (March-April) Beuth, Rein. "Peter Nadin at
Jablonka Gallery," Die Welt (27 January)
Cyphers, Peggy. "Peter Nadin at Jay Gorney Modern Art," Arts (December) Graw, Isabelle. "Peter Nadin at
Jablonka Gallery," Artscribe (May)
Koether, Jutta. "Peter Nadin at Jablonka Gallery," Artforum (May)
Tager, Alisa. 'Peter Nadin at Jay Gosrney Modern Art," Lapiz (November)
1989 Hornung, David. "Peter Nadin Brooke Alexander," ArtNews (October) McCoy, Pat. "Peter Nadin,"
Artscribe (March/April)
1988 Brea, Jose Luis. "Peter Nadin, La Torre de Babel," Sur Expres (July)
Dunning, Jennifer. "The World's Last Act has a Latin Beat," The New York Times (October 31)
Jones, Alan. "A Visit with Peter Nadin," Arts (December)
Kreigsman, Alan. "Jansen Skills That Shock," The Washington Post (November 7) Miller, John. "Peter Nadin
Jay Gorney Modern Art," Artforum (September)
Russell, John. "25th Anniversary Exhibition to Benefit the Foundation for Contemporary Performance Art,
Leo Castelli, Brooke Alexander," The New York Times (December 9) Saltz, Jerry. "Beyond Boundaries," pub-
lished by Van der Marck
1987 Morgan, Robert C. "Peter Nadin: Styles and Sign," Arts (May) Sturman, John. "Peter Nadin," ArtNews
(October)
1986 Collins, Tricia and Milazzo, Richard. "Tropical Codes," Kunstforum (April/May) Cotter, Holland. "Re-
views: Peter Nadin," Flash Art (October/November) Decter, Joshua. "Cult and Decorum," Arts (March)
"Peter Nadin," Arts (February)
Indiana, Gary. "Peter Nadin," The Village Voice (March 25)
Jones, Alan. "Up Against the Wall--Day for Night," NY Talk (June)
Levin, Kim. "Group Show," The Village Voice (September 17)
Perl, Jed. "Winter Notebook," The New Criterion (April)
Raynor, Vivien. "Beyond Stylish Considerations," The New York Times (September 12) Raynor, Vivien "Ste-
phen Buckley and Peter Nadin," The New York Times (May 30)
1985 Collins, Tricia and Milazzo, Richard. "Neutral Trends," East Village Eye (July) Frazer, Andrea. "In and
Out of Place," Art in America (June)
Indiana, Gary. "Peter Nadin," The Village Voice (December)
"Peter Nadin at Casa/Newhouse," Art in America (November)

Gary Indiana, "From Organism to Architecture," The Village Voice (February 24) Morgan, Robert. "Peter Nadin," Arts (November)
1984 Collins, Tricia and Milazzo, Richard. "From the Neutral Subject to the Hypothesis of World Objects," Natural Genre, Florida State University, Tallahassee
Masheck, Joseph. "Peter Nadin," Point 1, Willis, Locker & Owens Publishing, New York Morgan, Robert. "Still Life," AfterImage Magazine (April)
O'Brien, Glenn. "Peter Nadin, Jack Tilton Gallery," Artforum (November)
1983 Skelly, Jack. "Beyond Baroque," Magazine (Winter)
1982 Morgan, Robert. "Eating Through Living," AfterImage Magazine (Winter) 1981 Armstrong, Richard. "Cologne: HeuteWestkunst," Artforum (September)
Marmer, Nancy. "Isms on the Rhine," Art in America (November)
Schjeldahl, Peter. "Anxiety as a Rallying Cry," The Village Voice (September 16) 1980 Davidow, Joie. "Beyond Conceptual Art," L.A. Weekly (February 7)
Fend, Peter. "Peter Nadin," Umbrella Magazine (January)
Rein, Ingrid. Suddeutsche Zeitung (December 18)
1979 Fend, Peter. "New York Byline," Umbrella Magazine (September)
VonBrandenberg, Peter. "Continuning Work: Peter Nadin," Flash Art (June) Zimmer, William, "Art Picks," SoHo Weekly News (September 1)

Anthologies, Periodicals, and Books

"Bodiless Ceremonies," Sur Expres, No. 11, 1988
"Poems," Effects Magazine, No. 3, New York, 1986
"The Live Pool," Wild History, Tanam Press, New York, 1984
"Songs," J.A.A. Book, New York, 1984
"Still Life," Effects Magazine, No.2, New York, 1984
"The Offices of Fend," Fitzgibbon, Holzer, Nadin, Prince & Winters, New York, 1984 "A Moment of Truth," New Observations, No. 20, New York, 1984
"Still Life," Real Life Magazine, No. 10, New York, 1980
"Living," Hotel, Tanam Press, New York, 1980
"Work Death," L.A.I.C.A. Journal, Los Angeles, Summer, 1979
"Position Papers," Artforum, New York, December 1979
The Mark Series: Method and Manual – Art, Poetry, Farming, Ceramics, Film, 2003-2018, Edgewise Press, New York, 2019
Taxonomy Transplanted: Art, Language, Farming, Edgewise Press, New York, 2013
First Mark / El Primer Trazo, Charta, Milan, 2007
First Mark: Unlearning How to Make Art, Edgewise Press, New York, 2007 Twelve Prints and Poems, Grenfell Press, New York, 1995
Tide of Tongues, Thea Westreich and Adelson Galleries, New York, 1991 Still Life, Tanam Press, New York 1983
Eating Through Living, Tanam Press, New York, 1981 (with Jenny Holzer) Eating Friends, Top Stories #7, New York, 1981 (with Jenny Holzer) Living, self-published, New York, 1980 (with Jenny Holzer)

Selected Museum Collections

The Metropolitan Museum of Art, New York
The Museum of Modern Art, New York
Yale University Art Gallery, New Haven
Yale Center for British Art, New Haven
Fitzwilliam Museum, Cambridge, United Kingdom
Centre Pompidou, Paris, France
Parrish Art Museum, Watermill, New York

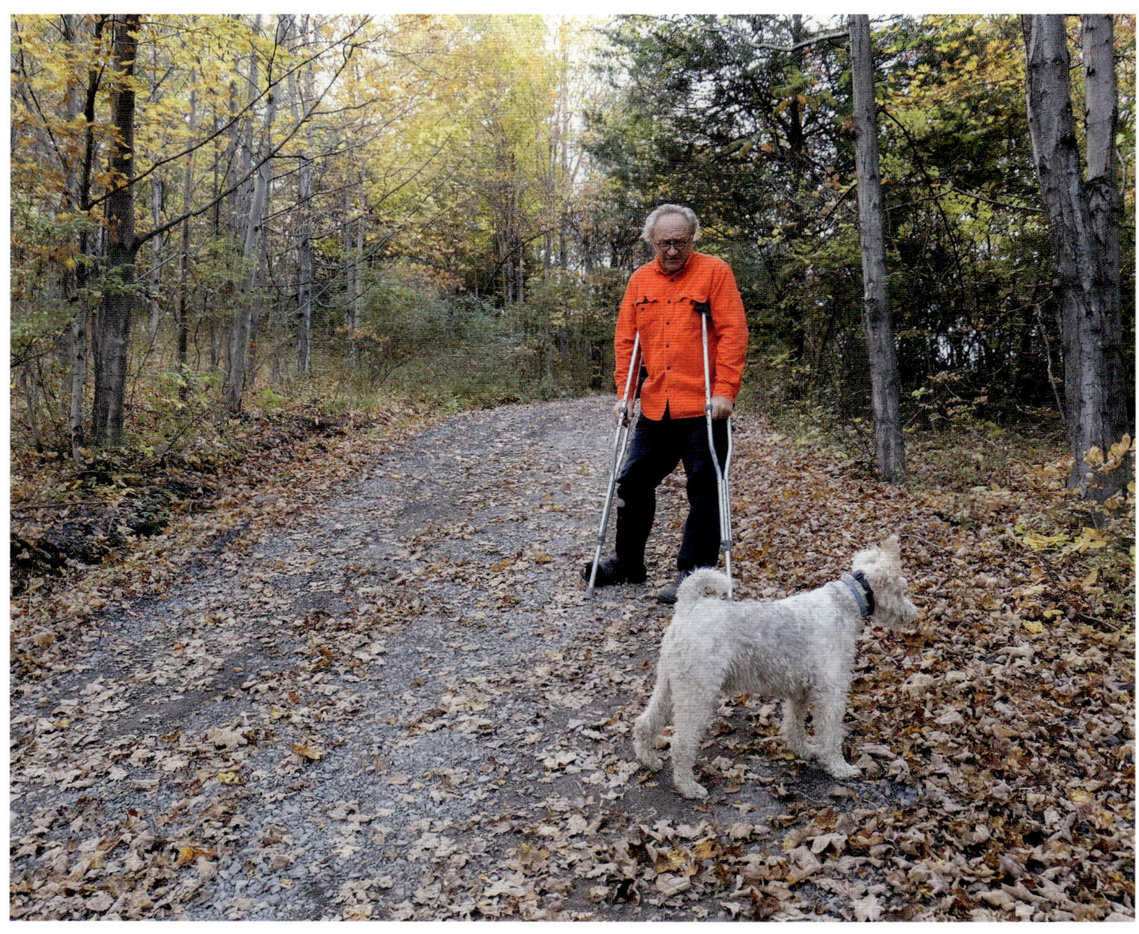

Peter Nadin & Lu; Old Field Farm, 2022

Biography

Peter Nadin (b. 1954 in Bromborough, England) is an artist, farmer, and poet based in New York City and Upstate New York. A key figure of the downtown New York art scene of the late 1970s and 1980s, his work explores the practice of mark and image making as evolutionary human functions. He arrived in New York in 1976. In 1978, with the help of Chris D'Arcangelo, he founded the artist-run space 84 West Broadway, located in his own Tribeca loft. Two years later, he became a founder of an artists' collective called "The Offices of Fend, Fitzgibbon, Holzer, Nadin, Prince & Winters," whose members offered up their talents as critical thinkers to solve real-world problems for clients.

In 1993, Nadin left the commercial art world, while continuing to quietly paint on his farm in an isolated part of the Catskill Mountains, working closely with the land and showing only occasionally in unexpected settings such as The Museum of Modern Art, Cuenca, Ecuador (2008) and Galería Provincial Arte Soy, Santiago de Cuba, Cuba (2009).

Over many years, Nadin worked on a cycle of conceptual paintings, known as the "Mark Series", in which he sought to break down his previous conceptions of the genre, effectively "unlearning how to make art."

In early spring 2020, as the world was shutting down, Nadin began a return to "painting from life," observing the plants in his upstate greenhouse. He began to focus on the grafting of a Marrakech lemon scion onto a sour-orange rootstock—specifically, on how the graft of the scion joins the rootstock and how the rootstock's energy allows for the genetically different scion to produce fruit.

From January through June 2022, Off Paradise hosted a pair of sequential exhibitions, "A Proposal to Peter Nadin, 1979; realized 2022" and "The Distance from a Lemon to Murder", exemplifying two very singular aspects of Nadin's career: his early conceptual projects and his ongoing exploration of pictorial conventions and mark making.

The first exhibition realized, at long last, an instructions-based proposal that French artist, Claude Rutault, wrote in 1979 specifically for Peter's artist-run space 84 West Broadway. The second presented his return to unconditional painting—painting "from life"—for the first time in thirty years.

In Nadin's newest series, "The Invisible World," the rational world of ocular representation is reassembled into poetic form. For many years, Nadin has accompanied his artwork with poetry. Here, the poem is no longer separate from the painting but is embedded in the paint and composition of the artwork. In this new series, Nadin is looking at the unseen—or maybe seeing the previously seen, now invisible, but indivisible from observation.

Peter Nadin *The Invisible World*

—

Acknowledgments from Old Field Farm

Natacha Polaert, Off Paradise
Roman Spataro, *Design Direction*
Johan Svensson, *Design Consultant*
Anna Heyward, *Copy Editor*

Contributors:

Randy Kennedy
Chris Murtha
Natacha Polaert

Photographs:

© Alon Koppel, pg: 3, 8, 35, 36, 38, 39, 40, 47, 49, 50, 51, 53,
54, 55, 56, 59, 62, 64, 67, 70, 73, 75, 77, 78, 80, 84, 91, 92, 93, 95,
98, 100, 101, 102, 106, 110, 113, 114, 116
© Peter Nadin, pg: 11, 15
© Jason Mandella, pg: 27, 28
© Ricardo de Oliveira, pg: 30, 31, 32
© Guillaume Ziccarelli, pg: 44, 126
© Valerie Skakun, pg: 88, 140
© Dario Lasagni, pg: 120, 121, 122, 123
© Roman Spataro, pg: 129, 131

First Mark installation photographs courtesy
Gavin Brown's Enterprise

Second Mark installation photographs courtesy
James Fuentes Gallery

The Distance from a Lemon to Murder
installation photographs courtesy Off Paradise

*The Distance from a Lemon to Murder: A Conversation
with Peter Nadin*—courtesy *The Paris Review*

Special Thanks:

Diane L. Ackerman
Robert Becker
Gary Elwyn
Solveig Fernlund
Michel Gauthier
J Grabowski
Eznic Karakashian
Anne Kennedy
Raymond J. Learsy
Marjolaine Lévy
Anna Page Nadin
Gina Nanni
Claude Rutault

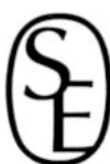

Silvana Editoriale

Chief Executive
Michele Pizzi

Editorial Director
Sergio Di Stefano

Art Director
Giacomo Merli

Editorial Coordinator
Maria Chiara Tulli

Copy Editing
Cristina Pradella

Production Coordinator
Antonio Micelli

Editorial Assistant
Giulia Mercanti

Photo Editor
Silvia Sala

Press Office
Alessandra Olivari, press@silvanaeditoriale.it

ISBN 978-88-366-5685-1

Available through ARTBOOK | D.A.P.
155 Sixth Avenue, 2nd Floor,
New York, N.Y. 10013
Tel: (212) 627-1999
Fax: (212) 627-9484

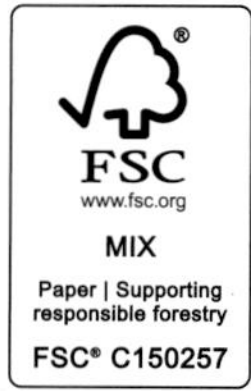

Silvana Editoriale S.p.A.
via dei Lavoratori, 78
20092 Cinisello Balsamo, Milano
tel. 02 453 951 01
www.silvanaeditoriale.it

Reproductions, printing and binding
in Italy
Printed by Tipo Stampa S.r.l., Moncalieri, Torino
in June 2024